Superstitions of the ~~~~~~~~~~

& islands of Scotland

John Gregorson Campbell

Alpha Editions

This edition published in 2019

ISBN : 9789353861759

Design and Setting By
Alpha Editions
email - alphaedis@gmail.com

Superstitions

of the

Highlands & Islands of Scotland

Collected entirely from Oral Sources

By

John Gregorson Campbell
Minister of Tiree

Glasgow

James MacLehose and Sons

Publishers to the University

1900

GLASGOW : PRINTED AT THE UNIVERSITY PRESS
BY ROBERT MACLEHOSE AND CO.

EDITOR'S NOTE.

THIS volume is the result of many years' labour by the late Rev. JOHN GREGORSON CAMPBELL, while minister of Tiree during the years 1861— to 1891.

Much of the material was already collected before Mr. J. F. Campbell of Islay published his *Popular Tales of the West Highlands* in 1860, and readers of Lord Archibald Campbell's volumes on *Waifs and Strays of Celtic Tradition* are already acquainted with the valuable work contributed to that series by the Rev. J. Gregorson Campbell.

It is hoped that this volume on the *Superstitions of the Scottish Highlands*, full as it is of racy stories, may throw fresh light on an extremely interesting subject.

The MS. of a corresponding work by the same author on *Witchcraft and Second-Sight in the West Highlands*, is in the editor's hands, and in the event of the present work meeting with the reception which the editor thinks it deserves, the volume on Witchcraft will be published next year.

Mrs. Wallace, Hynish, Tiree, the author's sister, has kindly read the proofs.

August, 1900.

PREFACE.

THE object aimed at in the following pages is to put before the reader a statement, as complete and accurate as the writer can attain to, of the Superstitions and Antiquities of the Scottish Highlands and Islands. In other words, the writer has endeavoured to gather full materials relating to that subject, and to arrange them in a form that may prove of some scientific value.

In pursuit of this object, it has been deemed advisable to derive information solely from oral sources. Books have been purposely avoided as authorities, and a rule has been laid down, and strictly adhered to, not to accept any statement in print regarding a Highland belief, unless also found current among the people. In the few books there are, having any reference to Gaelic lore, the statements have been so frequently found at variance with popular beliefs that this rule has been a necessity. There are a few honourable exceptions, but in general what is to be found in print on this subject is not trustworthy.

A want of acquaintance with the Gaelic language or with Highland feelings and modes of thought, is usually the cause of error. The writers think in English, and are not careful to eliminate from their statements thoughts derived from English or classical literature, or to keep from confusing with Celtic beliefs ideas derived from foreign sources, and from analogous creeds existing elsewhere. This gives an unconscious tinge to their statements, and (what is more to be regretted) sometimes makes them fill up with extraneous and foreign elements what seems to them gaps or blanks in beliefs they but imperfectly understand.

The writer's information has been derived from widely separated districts in the North, West, and Central Highlands, and from the Islands. Naturally, the bulk of the information was obtained in Tiree, where the writer had most opportunity of making inquiries, but information from this or any other source has not been accepted without comparison with the same beliefs in other districts. The writer has not been able personally to visit all parts of the Highlands, but his informants have spent their lives in districts far apart. The reader will fall into a mistake who supposes that the whole information is within the belief, or even knowledge, of any one individual, or of any one district.

The beliefs of one district do not differ essentially from those of another. In one or two cases several versions of a tale are given to show to some extent the nature of the variations of popular tradition.

The writer has thankfully to acknowledge, and he cannot but remember with pleasure, the readiness and courtesy, and in very many cases the great intelligence with which his inquiries have been answered. Some of his informants have shown a quickness and retentiveness of memory which he could not but envy, and an appreciation of, and an acquaintance with ancient lore that seemed to him to indicate in those who were strangers to the world of letters powers of mind of a high order.

The objection to books and print as authorities has also been extended to written correspondence. No doubt much that is additional and interesting could be obtained through these channels, but if the account given is to serve any purpose higher than that of mere amusement, strict accuracy is of such importance that all these sources of possible error have been avoided; they cannot be sifted by cross-examination and further inquiry so readily or thoroughly as information obtained by word of mouth. The whole has thus passed through the writer's own hands directly from what he has found current among the people. Care has been taken that no statement be made conveying an idea different in the slightest from what has been heard. A popular Gaelic saying can be quoted as applicable to the case: "If it be a lie as told by me, it was a lie as told to me" (*Ma's breug bh'uam e, is breug dhomh e*). It is as free to another as it has been to the writer, to draw his inferences from the statements given, and it is thought no genuine tale or oral tradition will be found to contradict the statements made in the following pages.

In the translations given of Gaelic, the object aimed at has been to give the corresponding English expression, that is, one conveying the same meaning to the English reader that the Gaelic expression conveys to the Gaelic reader. Accuracy has been looked to on this point rather than grace of diction. Where there is anything striking in the Gaelic idiom the literal meaning is also given. In poetry there is consequently a baldness, to which the original is a stranger; but this, it may be urged, is a fault inherent in all translations, however carefully executed. The transference of ideas from one language to another weakens the force and beauty of an expression ; what is racy and witty, or musical and expressive in one, becomes tame and insipid in another. This trite observation is made to deprecate unfavourable opinions being formed of the genius and force of the Gaelic language from the translations given.

CONTENTS

CHAPTER I

The Fairies

CHAPTER II

Tales Illustrative of Fairy Superstition

CHAPTER III

Tutelary Beings

CHAPTER IV

The Urisk, The Blue Men, and The Mermaid

CHAPTER V

The Water-Horse

CHAPTER VI

Superstitions about Animals

CHAPTER VII

Miscellaneous Superstitions

CHAPTER VIII

Augury

CHAPTER IX

Premonitions and Divination

CHAPTER X

Dreams and Prophecies

CHAPTER XI

Imprecations, Spells, and the Black Art

CHAPTER XII

The Devil

CHAPTER I.

THE FAIRIES.[1]

In any account of Gaelic superstition and popular belief, the first and most prominent place is to be assigned to the Fairy or Elfin people, or, as they are called both in Irish and Scottish Gaelic, the *sìth* people, that is, 'the people of peace,' the 'still folk,' or 'silently-moving' people. The antiquity of the belief is shown by its being found among all branches of the Celtic and Teutonic families, and in countries which have not, within historical times, had any communication with each other. If it be not entirely of Celtic origin, there can be no doubt that among the Celtic races it acquired an importance and influence accorded to it nowhere else. Of all the beings, with which fear or fancy peopled the supernatural, the Fairies were the most intimately associated with men's daily life. In the present day, when popular poetical

[1] The words Elfin and Fairy are, in these pages, used indifferently as equivalents of the Gaelic names, sìth (or shi) people, etc.

A

ideas are extinguished in the universal call for " facts "
and by " cold material laws," it is hard to understand
how firm a hold a belief like this had upon men in
a more primitive state of society, and how unwillingly
it is surrendered.

Throughout the greater part of the Highlands of
Scotland the Fairies have become things of the past.
A common belief is that they existed once, though
they are not now seen.   There are others to whom
the elves have still a real existence, and who are
careful to take precautions against them.   The changes,
which the Highlands are undergoing, have made the
traces of the belief fainter in some districts than in
others, and in some there remains but a confused
jumbling of all the superstitions.   It would be difficult
to find a person who knows the whole Fairy creed,
but the tales of one district are never contradictory
of those of another.   They are rather to be taken as
supplemental of each other, and it is by comparison
and such supplementing that the following statement has
been drawn out.   It is thought that it will not be found
at variance with any genuine Highland Fairy Tale.

The Fairies, according to the Scoto-Celtic belief, are
a race of beings, the counterparts of mankind in person,
occupations, and pleasures, but unsubstantial and un-
real, ordinarily invisible, noiseless in their motions,
and having their dwellings underground, in hills and
green mounds of rock or earth.   They are addicted to

visiting the haunts of men, sometimes to give assistance, but more frequently to take away the benefit
of their goods and labours, and sometimes even their
persons.   They may be present in any company,
though mortals do not see them.   Their interference
is never productive of good in the end, and may
prove destructive.   Men cannot therefore be sufficiently
on their guard against them.

NAMES GIVEN TO FAIRIES.

The names by which these dwellers underground
are known are mostly derivative from the word *sìth*
(pronounced *shee*).   As a substantive (in which sense
it is ordinarily used) *sìth* means 'peace,' and, as an
adjective, is applied solely to objects of the supernatural world, particularly to the Fairies and whatever
belongs to them.   Sound is a natural adjunct of the
motions of men, and its entire absence is unearthly,
unnatural, not human.   The name *sìth* without doubt
refers to the 'peace' or silence of Fairy motion, as
contrasted with the stir and noise accompanying the
movements and actions of men.   The German 'still
folk' is a name of corresponding import.   The Fairies
come and go with noiseless steps, and their thefts or
abductions are done silently and unawares to men.
The wayfarer resting beside a stream, on raising his
eyes, sees the Fairy woman, unheard in her approach,
standing on the opposite bank.   Men know the Fairies

have visited their houses only by the mysterious disappearance of the substance of their goods, or the sudden and unaccountable death of any of the inmates or of the cattle. Sometimes the elves are seen entering the house, gliding silently round the room, and going out again as noiselessly as they entered. When driven away they do not go off with tramp and noise, and sounds of walking such as men make, or melt into thin air, as spirits do, but fly away noiselessly like birds or hunted deer. They seem to glide or float along rather than to walk. Hence the name *sìthche* and its synonyms are often applied contemptuously to a person who sneaks about or makes his approach without warning. Sometimes indeed the elves make a rustling noise like that of a gust of wind, or a silk gown, or a sword drawn sharply through the air, and their coming and going has been even indicated by frightful and unearthly shrieks, a pattering as of a flock of sheep, or the louder trampling of a troop of horses. Generally, however, their presence is indicated at most by the cloud of dust raised by the eddy wind, or by some other curious natural phenomenon, by the illumination of their dwellings, the sound of their musical instruments, songs, or speech.

For the same reason *sìth* is applied not merely to what is Fairy, but to whatever is Fairy-like, unearthly, not of this world. Of this laxer use of the term the following may be given as illustrations :

Breac shìth, ' Elfin pox,' hives, are spots that appear on the skin in certain diseases, as hooping-cough, and indicate a highly malignant stage of the malady. They are not ascribed to the Fairies, but are called *sìth*, because they appear and again disappear as it were 'silently,' without obvious cause, and more mysteriously than other symptoms. Cows, said to have been found on the shores of Loscantire in Harris, Scorrybrec in Skye, and on the Island of Bernera, were called *cro sìth*, ' fairy cows,' simply because they were of no mortal breed, but of a kind believed to live under the sea on *meillich*, seaweed. Animals in the shape of cats, but in reality witches or demons, were called *cait shìth*, ' Elfin cats,' and the Water Horse, which has no connection whatever with the elves, is sometimes called *each sìth*, unearthly horse. The cuckoo is an *eun sìth*, a ' Fairy bird,' because, as is said, its winter dwelling is underground.

A banner in the possession of the family of Macleod, of Macleod of Skye, is called 'Macleod's Fairy Banner' (*Bratach shìth MhicLèoid*), on account of the supernatural powers ascribed to it. When unfurled, victory in war (*buaidh chogaidh*) attends it, and it relieves its followers from imminent danger.[1] Every pregnant woman who sees it is taken in premature labour (a misfortune which happened, it is said, to the English wife of a former

---

[1] These virtues it is to have only thrice, and it has been already unfurled twice. Many of the common people wanted it brought out at the time of the potato failure.

chief in consequence of her irrepressible curiosity to see the banner), and every cow casts her calf (*cha bhi bean no bo nach tilg a laogh*). Others, however, say the name is owing to the magic banner having been got from an Elfin sweetheart. .

A light, seen among the Hebrides, a sort of St. Elmo's light or Will-of-the-wisp, is called *teine sìth*, 'Fairy light,' though no one ever blamed the Fairies as the cause of it. In a semi-satirical song, of much merit for its spirit and ease of diction, composed in Tiree to the owner of a crazy skiff that had gone to the Ross of Mull for peats and staid too long, the bard, in a spirited description of the owner's adventures and seamanship, says :—

> " Onward past Greenock,
>   Like the deer of the cold high hills,
> Breasting the rugged ground
>   With the hunter in pursuit ;
> She *sailed with Fairy motion*,[1]
>   Bounding smoothly in her pride,
> Cleaving the green waves,
>   And passing to windward of the rest." [2]

[1] Fairy motion, *i.e.* not rising and falling on the waves, but gliding smoothly along.

[2] " Seachad air Grianaig,
>   Mar fhiadh nam beann fuara,
> Direadh ri uchd garbhlaich,
>   'S an sealgair ga ruagadh,
> Ise is siubhal, sith aice,
>   Sìnteagan uallach,
> Sgoltadh nan tonn uaine
>   'S a fuaradh air chàch."
>   Long aig Callum MacShlomain.

This latitude in the use of the word has led some writers on the subject to confound with the Fairies beings having as little connection with them as with mankind. A similar laxness occurs in the use of the English word Fairy. It is made to include kelpies, mermaids, and other supernatural beings, having no connection with the true Fairy, or Elfin race.

The following are the names by which the ' Folk ' are known in Gaelic. It is observable that every one of the names, when applied to mortals, is contemptuous and disparaging.

Sithche (pronounced *sheeche*) is the generic and commonest term. It is a noun of common gender, and its plural is *sithchean* (sheechun). In Graham's *Highlands of Perthshire*, a work more than once quoted by Sir Walter Scott, but unreliable as an authority, this word is written *shi'ich.*

Sireach, plur. *sirich*, also *sibhrich*, is a provincial term; *an siriche du,* ' the black elf,' *i.e.* the veriest elf.

Sithbheire (pronounced *sheevere*), a masculine noun, is mostly applied to changelings, or the elf substituted for children and animals taken by the Fairies. Applied to men it is very contemptuous.

Siochaire is still more so. Few expressions of scorn are more commonly applied to men than *siochaire grannda,* " ugly slink."

Duine sith (plur. *daoine sith*), ' a man of peace, a noiselessly moving person, a fairy, an elf ' ; fem. *Bean shìth* (gen. *mna sìth*, plur. *mnathan sìth*, gen. plur. with the article *nam ban shìth*), ' a woman of peace, an Elle woman,' are names that include the whole Fairy race. *Bean shìth* has become naturalized in English under the form *Banshi.* The term was introduced from Ireland, but there appears no reason to suppose the Irish belief different from that of the Scottish Highlands. Any seeming difference has arisen since the introduction of the Banshi to the literary world, and from the too free exercise of imagination by book-writers on an imperfectly understood tradition.

The *leannan sìth*, 'fairy sweetheart, familiar spirit,' might be of either sex. The use of this word by the translators of the Bible into Gaelic is made a great handle of by the common people, to prove from Scripture that Fairies actually exist. The Hebrew word so translated is rendered 'pythons' by the Vulgate, and 'consulters of the spirits of the dead ' by modern scholars. Those said to have familiar spirits were probably a class of magicians, who pretended to be media of communication with the spirit world, their 'familiar' making himself known by sounds muttered from the ground through the instrumentality, as the Hebrew name denotes, of a skin bottle.

Brughadair, ' a person from a brugh, or fairy dwelling,' applied to men, means one who does a stupid or senseless action.

Other names are *sluagh*, ' folk, a multitude '; *sluagh*

eutrom, 'light folk'; and *daoine beaga*, 'little men,' from the number and small size ascribed to the elves.

Daoine Còire, 'honest folk,' had its origin in a desire to give no unnecessary offence. The 'folk' might be listening, and were pleased when people spoke well of them, and angry when spoken of slightingly. In this respect they are very jealous. A wise man will not unnecessarily expose himself to their attacks, for, 'Better is a hen's amity than its enmity' (*S'fhearr sìth ciree na h-aimhreit*). The same feeling made the Irish Celt call them *daoine matha*, 'good people,' and the lowland Scot 'gude neighbours.'

THE SIZE OF FAIRIES.

The difference in size ascribed to the race, though one of the most remarkable features in the superstition, and lying on its surface, has been taken little notice of by writers. At one time the elves are small enough to creep through key-holes, and a single potato is as much as one of them can carry; at another they resemble mankind, with whom they form alliances, and to whom they hire themselves as servants; while some are even said to be above the size of mortals, gigantic hags, in whose lap mortal women are mere infants. In the Highlands the names *sithche* and *daoine sìth* are given to all these different sizes alike, little men, elfin youth, elfin dame, and elfin hag, all of whom are not mythical beings of different classes or kinds,

but one and the same race, having the same
characteristics and dress, living on the same food,
staying in the same dwellings, associated in the same
actions, and kept away by the same means.   The
easiest solution of the anomaly is that the fairies had
the power of making themselves large or small at
pleasure.   There is no popular tale, however, which
represents them as exercising such a power, nor is it
conformable to the rest of their characteristics that it
should be ascribed to them.   The true belief is
that the Fairies are a small race, the men 'about four
feet or so' in height, and the women in many cases
not taller than a little girl (*cnapach caileig*).   Being
called 'little,' the exaggeration, which popular imagination loves, has diminished them till they appear as elves
of different kinds.   There is hardly a limit to the
popular exaggeration of personal peculiarities.   Og,
King of Bashan, was a big man, and the Rabbis
made his head tower to the regions of perpetual
snow, while his feet were parched in the deserts of
Arabia.   Finmac Coul was reputed strong, at least
he thrashed the devil, and made him howl.   A weaver
in Perthshire, known as 'the weaver with the nose'
(*figheadair na eròine*), had a big nose, at least he carried
his loom in it.   Similarly the 'little men' came down
to the 'size of half an ell,' and even the height of
a quart bottle.

The same peculiarity exists in the Teutonic belief.

At times the elf is a dwarfish being that enters through key-holes and window-slits; at other times a great tall man. In different localities the Fairies are known as Alfs, Huldra-Folk, Duergar, Trolls, Hill Folk, Little Folk, Still Folk, Pixies, etc. A difference of size, as well as of name, has led to these being described as separate beings, but they have all so much in common with the Celtic Fairies that we must conclude they were originally the same.

FAIRY DWELLINGS.

The Gaelic, as might be expected, abounds in words denoting the diversified features of the scenery in a mountainous country. To this the English language itself bears witness, having adopted so many Gaelic words of the kind, as strath, glen, corrie, ben, knock, dun, etc. From this copiousness it arises that the round green eminences, which were said to be the residences of the Fairies, are known in Gaelic by several names which have no synonym in English.

Sìthein (pron. shĭ-en) is the name of any place in which the Fairies take up their residence. It is known from the surrounding scenery by the peculiarly green appearance and rounded form. Sometimes in these respects it is very striking, being of so nearly conical a form, and covered with such rich verdure, that a second look is required to satisfy the observers it is not artificial. Its external appearance has led to its being also known by various other names.

Tolman is a small green knoll, or hummock, of earth ; *bac*, a bank of sand or earth ; *cnoc*, knock, Scot. ' a knowe,' and its diminutive *cnocan*, a little knowe ; *dùn*, a rocky mound or heap, such, for instance, as the Castle rock of Edinburgh or Dumbarton, though often neither so steep nor so large ; *òthan*, a green elevation in wet ground ; and *tigh*, a provincial term of much the same import as tolman. Even lofty hills have been represented as tenanted by Fairies, and the highest point of a hill, having the rounded form, characteristic of Fairy dwellings is called its shí-en (*sìthein na beinne*). Rocks may be tenanted by the elves, but not caves. The dwellings of the race are below the outside or superficies of the earth, and tales representing the contrary may be looked upon with suspicion as modern.

There is one genuine popular story in which the Fairy dwelling is in the middle of a green plain, without any elevation to mark its site beyond a horse-skull, the eye-sockets of which were used as the Fairy chimney.

These dwellings were tenanted sometimes by a single family only, more frequently by a whole community. The elves were said to change their residences as men do, and, when they saw proper themselves, to remove to distant parts of the country and more

desirable haunts. To them, on their arrival in their
new home, are ascribed the words :

"Though good the haven we have left,
Better be the haven we have found."[1]

The Fairy hillock might be passed by the strangers
without suspicion of its being tenanted, and cattle
were pastured on it unmolested by the "good people."
There is, however, a common story in the Western
Isles that a person was tethering his horse or cow
for the night on a green *tolman* when a head appeared
out of the ground, and told him to tether the beast
somewhere else, as he let rain into "their" house,
and had nearly driven the tether-pin into the ear of
one of the inmates. Another, who was in the habit
of pouring out dirty water at the door, was told by
the Fairies to pour it elsewhere, as he was spoiling
their furniture. He shifted the door to the back of
the house, and prospered ever after. The Fairies
were very grateful to any one who kept the shï-en
clean, and swept away cow or horse-droppings falling
on it. Finding a farmer careful of the roof of their
dwelling, keeping it clean, and not breaking the
sward with tether-pin or spade, they showed their
thankfulness by driving his horses and cattle to the
sheltered side of the mound when the night proved
stormy. Many believe the Fairies themselves swept

[1] "Ged is math an cala dh' fhàg sinn,
Gum bu fearr an cala fhuair sinn."

the hillock every night, so that in the morning its surface was spotless.

Brugh (brŭ) denotes the Fairy dwelling viewed as it were from the inside—the interiors—but is often used interchangeably with *sìthein*. It is probably the same word as burgh, borough, or bro', and its reference is to the *number* of inmates in the Fairy dwelling.[1]

FAIRY DRESSES.

The Fairies, both Celtic and Teutonic, are dressed in green. In Skye, however, though Fairy women, as elsewhere, are always dressed in that colour, the men wear clothes of any colour like their human neighbours. They are frequently called *daoine beaga ruadh*, "little red men," from their clothes having the appearance of being dyed with the lichen called *crotal*, a common colour of men's clothes, in the North Hebrides. The coats of Fairy women are shaggy, or ruffled (*caiteineach*), and their caps curiously fitted or wrinkled. The men are said, but not commonly, to have *blue* bonnets, and in the song to the murdered Elfin lover, the Elf is said to have a hat bearing "a smell of honied apples." This is perhaps the only Highland instance of a hat, which is a prominent object

---

[1] Few villages in the Highlands of Scotland are without a *shi-en* in their neighbourhood, and often a number are found close to each other. Strontian, well known to geologists from the mineral which bears its name, is *Sròn an t-sìthein*, "the nose of the Fairy hillock."

in the Teutonic superstition, being ascribed to the
Fairies.

THE DEFECTS OF FAIRIES.

Generally some personal defect is ascribed to them,
by which they become known to be of no mortal race.
In Mull and the neighbourhood they are said to have
only one nostril, the other being imperforate (*an leth
choinnlein aca druid-te*). The Elfin smith who made
Finmac Coul's sword, "the son of Lun that never
asked a second stroke" (*Mac an Luin, nach d'fhàg
riamh fuigheal bheum*), had but one gloomy eye in his
forehead. The *Bean shìth* was detected by her extraordinary voracity (a cow at a meal), a frightful front
tooth, the entire want of a nostril, a web foot, praeternaturally long breasts, etc. She is also said to be
unable to suckle her own children, and hence the Fairy
desire to steal nursing women.

THEIR OCCUPATIONS.

The Fairies, as has been already said, are counterparts of mankind. There are children and old
people among them ; they practise all kinds of trades
and handicrafts ; they possess cattle, dogs, arms ; they
require food, clothing, sleep ; they are liable to disease,
and can be killed. So entire is the resemblance that
they have even been betrayed into intoxication. People
entering their brughs, have found the inmates engaged

in similar occupations to mankind, the women spinning, weaving, grinding meal, baking, cooking, churning, etc., and the men sleeping, dancing, and making merry, or sitting round a fire in the middle of the floor (as a Perthshire informant described it) "like tinkers." Sometimes the inmates were absent on foraging expeditions or pleasure excursions. The women sing at their work, a common practice in former times with Highland women, and use distaff, spindle, handmills, and such like primitive implements. The men have smithies, in which they make the Fairy arrows and other weapons. Some Fairy families or communities are poorer than others, and borrow meal and other articles of domestic use from each other and from their neighbours of mankind.

FESTIVITIES.

There are stated seasons of festivity which are observed with much splendour in the larger dwellings. The brugh is illumined, the tables glitter with gold and silver vessels, and the door is thrown open to all comers. Any of the human race entering on these occasions are hospitably and heartily welcomed ; food and drink are offered them, and their health is pledged. Everything in the dwelling seems magnificent beyond description, and mortals are so enraptured they forget everything but the enjoyment of the moment. Joining in the festivities, they lose all thought as to the passage of time. The food is the most sumptuous, the clothing the most gorgeous ever seen, the music the sweetest ever heard, the dance the sprightliest ever trod. The whole dwelling is lustrous with magic splendour.

All this magnificence, however, and enjoyment are nothing but semblance and illusion of the senses. Mankind, with all their cares, and toils, and sorrows, have an infinitely more desirable lot, and the man is greatly to be pitied whom the Elves get power over, so that he exchanges his human lot and labour for their society or pleasures. Wise people recommend that, in the circumstances, a man should not utter a word till he comes out again, nor, on any account, taste Fairy food or drink. If he abstains he is very likely before long dismissed, but if he indulges he straightway loses the will and the power ever to return to the society of men. He becomes insensible to the passage of time, and may stay, without knowing it, for years, and even ages, in the brugh. Many, who thus forgot themselves, are among the Fairies to this day. Should they ever again return to the open air, and their enchantment be broken, the Fairy grandeur and pleasure prove an empty show, worthless, and fraught with danger. The food becomes disgusting refuse, and the pleasures a shocking waste of time.

The Elves are great adepts in music and dancing, and a great part of their time seems to be spent in the practice of these accomplishments. The changeling has often been detected by his fondness for them. Though in appearance an ill-conditioned and helpless brat, he has been known, when he thought himself unobserved, to play the pipes with surpassing skill, and dance with superhuman activity. Elfin music is more melodious than human skill and instruments can produce, and there are many songs and tunes which are said to have been originally learned from the Fairies. The only musical instrument of the Elves is the bagpipes, and some of the most celebrated pipers in Scotland are said to have learned their music from them.

FAIRY RAIDS.

The Gaelic belief recognizes no Fairyland or realm different from the earth's surface on which men live and move. The dwellings are underground, but it is on the natural face of the earth the Fairies find their sustenance, pasture their cattle, and on which they forage and roam.

The seasons on which their festivities are held are the last night of every quarter (*h-uile latha ceann ràidhe*), particularly the nights before Beltane, the first of summer, and Hallowmas, the first of winter. On these nights, on Fridays, and on the last night of the year, they are given to leaving home, and taking away whomsoever of the human race they find helpless, or unguarded or unwary. They may be encountered

any time, but on these stated occasions men are to
be particularly on their guard against them.

On Fridays they obtrusively enter houses, and have
even the impudence, it is said, to lift the lid off the
pot to see what the family have on the fire for
dinner. Any Fairy story, told on this day, should be
prefixed by saying, ' a blessing attend their departing
and travelling! this day is Friday and they will not
hear us' (*Beannachd nan siubhal 's nan isneachd! 'se
'n diugh Di-haoine 's cha chluinn iad sinn*). This
prevents Fairy ill-will coming upon the narrator for
anything he may chance to say. No one should call
the day by its proper name of Friday (*Di-haoine*),
but ' the day of yonder town' (*latha bhatl' ud thall*).
The Fairies do not like to hear the day mentioned,
and if anyone is so unlucky as to use the proper name,
their wrath is directed elsewhere by the bystander
adding ' on the cattle of yonder town' (*air cro a bhail'
ud thall*), or ' on the farm of So-and-so,' mentioning
anyone he may have a dislike to. The fear of Fairy
wrath also prevented the sharpening of knives on this
day.

They are said to come always from the west. They
are admitted into houses, however well guarded otherwise, by the little hand-made cake, the last of the
baking (*bonnach beag boise*), called the *Fallaid* bannock,
unless there has been a hole put through it with the
finger, or a piece is broken off it, or a live coal is

put on the top of it ;[1] by the water in which men's feet have been washed ; by the fire, unless it be properly ' raked ' (*smàladh*), *i.e.* covered up to keep it alive for the night ; or by the band of the spinning wheel, if left stretched on the wheel.

The reason assigned for taking water into the house at night was that the Fairies would suck the sleeper's blood if they found no water in to quench their thirst. The water in which feet were washed, unless thrown out, or a burning peat were put in it, let them in, and was used by them to plash about in (*gan loireadh fhéin ann*) all night. Unless the band was taken off the spinning wheel, particularly on the Saturday evenings, they came after the inmates of the house had retired to rest and used the wheel. Sounds of busy work were heard, but in the morning no work was found done, and possibly the wheel was disarranged.[2]

On the last night of the year they are kept out by decorating the house with holly ; and the last handful of corn reaped should be dressed up as a Harvest Maiden (*Maighdean Bhuan*), and hung up in the farmer's house to aid in keeping them out till next harvest.

---

[1] *Bonnach beag boise, gun bhloigh gun bhearn, Eirich 's big sinne a stigh, i.e.* Little cake, without gap or fissure, rise and let us in, is the Elfin call.

[2] In the north of Ireland the band was taken off the spinning wheel to prevent the Fairies spoiling the linen.

WHEN SEEN.

There seems to be no definite rule as to the circumstances under which the Fairies are to be seen. A person whose eye has been touched with Fairy water can see them whenever they are present; the seer, possessed of second sight, often saw them when others did not; and on nights on which the *shĭ-en* is open the chance passer-by sees them rejoicing in their underground dwellings. A favourite time for their encounters with men seems to be the dusk and wild stormy nights of mist and driving rain, when the streams are swollen and 'the roar of the torrent is heard on the hill.' They are also apt to appear when spoken of and when a desire is expressed for their assistance; when proper precautions are omitted and those whose weakness and helplessness call for watchfulness and care, are neglected; when their power is contemned and when a sordid and churlish spirit is entertained. Often, without fault or effort, in places the most unexpected, mortals have been startled by their appearance, cries, or music.

FOOD.

Fairy food consists principally of things intended for human food, of which the Elves take the *toradh*, *i.e.* the substance, fruit, or benefit, leaving the semblance or appearance to men themselves. In this manner they

take cows, sheep, goats, meal, sowens, the produce of
the land, etc.   Cattle falling over rocks are particularly
liable to being taken by them, and milk spilt in
coming from the dairy is theirs by right.   They have,
of food peculiar to themselves and not acquired from
men, the root of silver weed (*brisgein*), the stalks of
heather (*cuiseagan an fhraoich*), the milk of the red
deer hinds and of goats, weeds gathered in the fields,
and barleymeal.   The *brisgein* is a root plentifully
turned up by the plough in spring, and ranked in olden
times as the 'seventh bread.'   Its inferior quality
and its being found underground, are probably the
cause of its being assigned to the Fairies.   It is a
question whether the stalks of heather are the tops or
the stems of the plant.   Neither contain much sap or
nourishment.   The Banshi Fairy, or Elle woman, has
been seen by hunters milking the hinds, just as women
milk cows.

Those who partake of Fairy food are as hungry after
their repast as before it.   In appearance it is most
sumptuous and inviting, but on grace being said turns
out to be horse-dung.   Some, in their haste to partake
of the gorgeous viands, were only disenchanted when
'returning thanks.'

GIFTS BESTOWED BY FAIRIES.

The Fairies can bestow almost any gift upon their
favourites—great skill in music and in work of all kinds

—give them cows and even children stolen for the purpose from others, leave them good fortune, keep cattle from wandering into their crops at night, assist them in spring and harvest work, etc. Sometimes their marvellous skill is communicated to mortals, sometimes they come in person to assist. If a smith, wright, or other tradesman catches them working with the tools of his trade (a thing they are addicted to doing) he can compel them to bestow on him the *Ceaird Chomuinn,* or association craft, that is to come to his assistance whenever he wants them. Work left near their hillocks over night has been found finished in the morning, and they have been forced by men, entering their dwellings for the purpose, to tell the cure for diseases defying human skill.

In every instance, however, the benefit of the gift goes ultimately to the Fairies themselves, or (as it is put in the Gaelic expression) 'the fruit of it goes into their own bodies' (*Theid an toradh nan cuirp fhéin*). Their gifts have evil influence connected with them, and, however inviting at first, are productive of bad luck in the end. No wise man will desire either their company or their kindness. When they come to a house to assist at any work, the sooner they are got rid of the better. If they are hired as servants their wages at first appear trifling, but will ultimately ruin their employer. It is unfortunate even to encounter any of the race, but to consort with them is disastrous in the extreme.

LOANS.

'The giving and taking of loans,' according to the proverb, 'always prevailed in the world' (*Bha toirt is gabhail an iasad dol riamh feadh an t-saoghail*), and the custom is one to which the 'good neighbours' are no strangers.

They are universally represented as borrowing meal, from each other and from men. In the latter case when they returned a loan, as they always honestly did, the return was in *barleymeal*, two measures for one of oatmeal ; and this, on being kept in a place by itself, proved inexhaustible, provided the bottom of the vessel in which it was stored was never made to appear, no question was asked, and no blessing was pronounced over it. It would then neither vanish nor become horse-dung !

When a loan is returned to them, they accept only the fair equivalent of what they have lent, neither less nor more. If more is offered they take offence, and never give an opportunity for the same insult again.

We hear also of their borrowing a kettle or cauldron, and, under the power of a rhyme uttered by the lender at the time of giving it, sending it back before morning.

EDDY WIND.

When 'the folk' leave home in companies, they travel in eddies of wind. In this climate these eddies

are among the most curious of natural phenomena.
On calm summer days they go past, whirling about
straws and dust, and as not another breath of air is
moving at the time their cause is sufficiently puzzling.
In Gaelic the eddy is known as ' the people's puff of
wind' (*oiteag sluaigh*), and its motion 'travelling on
tall grass stems' (*falbh air chuiseagan treòrach*). By
throwing one's left (or *toisgeul*) shoe at it, the Fairies
are made to drop whatever they may be taking away—
men, women, children, or animals. The same result is
attained by throwing one's bonnet, saying, 'this is
yours, that's mine' (*Is leatsa so, is leamsa sin*), or a
naked knife, or earth from a mole-hill.

In these eddies, people going on a journey at night
have been 'lifted,' and spent the night careering through
the skies. On returning to the earth, though they
came to the house last left, they were too stupefied to
recognize either the house or its inmates. Others,
through Fairy despite, have wandered about all night
on foot, failing to reach their intended destination
though quite near it, and perhaps in the morning finding themselves on the top of a distant hill, or in some
inaccessible place to which they could never have made
their way alone. Even in daylight some were carried
in the Elfin eddy from one island to another, in great
terror lest they should fall into the sea.

RAIN AND SUNSHINE, WIND AND RAIN.

When there is rain with sunshine, the 'little people,'
according to a popular rhyme, are at their meat,

" Rain and sun,
Little people at their meat."

When wind and rain come from opposite directions
(which may for an instant be possible in a sudden shift
of wind), by throwing some horse-dung against the
wind, the Fairies are brought down in a shower !

FAIRY ARROWS, ETC.

Natural objects of a curious appearance, or bearing a
fanciful resemblance to articles used by men, are also
associated with the Fairies. The reedmace plant is
called ' the distaff of the Fairy women ' (*cuigeal nam
ban shìth*), the foxglove the ' thimble of the Fairy old
women ' (*miaran nan cailleacha sìth*), though more
commonly 'the thimble of dead old women ' (*m. nan
cailleacha marbh*). A substance, found on the shores of
the Hebrides, like a stone, red (*ruadh*), and half dark
(*lith dhorcha*), holed, is called ' Elf's blood ' (*fuil
siochaire*).[1]

The Fairy arrow (*Saighead shìth*) owes its name to
a similar fancy. It is known also as ' Fairy flint' (*spor
shìth*), and consists of a triangular piece of flint, bear-

[1] Similarly, in Dorsetshire fossil belemnites are called colepexies' fingers,
and in Northumberland a fungous excrescence, growing about the roots of
old trees, is called Fairy butter. So in Ireland, the round towers are
ascribed to them.

ing the appearance of an arrow head. It probably
originally formed part of the rude armoury of the
savages of the stone period. Popular imagination,
struck by its curious form, and ignorant of its origin,
ascribed it to the Fairies. It was said to be frequently
shot at the hunter, to whom the Elves have a special
aversion, because he kills the hinds, on the milk of
which they live. They could not throw it themselves,
but compelled some mortal (*duine saoghailte*) who was
being carried about in their company to throw it for
them. If the person aimed at was a friend, the
thrower managed to miss his aim, and the Fairy arrow
proved innocuous. It was found lying beside the
object of Fairy wrath, and was kept as a valuable pre-
servation in future against similar dangers, and for
rubbing to wounds (*suathadh ri creuchdun*). The man
or beast struck by it became paralyzed, and to all
appearance died shortly after. In reality they were
taken away by the elves, and only their appearance
remained. Its point being blunt was an indication
that it had done harm.

The Fairy spade (*caibe sìth*) is a smooth, slippery,
black stone, in shape 'like the sole of a shoe.' It
was put in water, given to sick people and cattle.

CATTLE.

Everywhere, in the Highlands, the red-deer are
associated with the Fairies, and in some districts, as

Lochaber and Mull, are said to be their only cattle. This association is sufficiently accounted for by the Fairy-like appearance and habits of the deer. In its native haunts, in remote and misty corries, where solitude has her most undisturbed abode, its beauty and grace of form, combined with its dislike to the presence of man, and even of the animals man has tamed, amply entitle it to the name of *sìth.* Timid and easily startled by every appearance and noise, it is said to be unmoved by the presence of the Fairies. Popular belief also says that no deer is found dead with age, and that its horns, which it sheds every year, are not found, because hid by the Fairies. In their transformations it was peculiar for the Fairy women to assume the shape of the red-deer, and in that guise they were often encountered by the hunter. The elves have a particular dislike to those who kill the hinds, and, on finding them in lonely places, delight in throwing elf-bolts at them. When a dead deer is carried home at night the Fairies lay their weight on the bearer's back, till he feels as if he had a house for a burden. On a penknife, however, being stuck in the deer it becomes very light. There are occasional allusions to the Fairy women having herds of deer. The Carlin Wife of the Spotted Hill (*Cailleach Beinne Bhric horò*), who, according to a popular rhyme, was 'large and broad and tall,' had a herd which she would not allow to descend to the beach, and which 'loved the water-cresses by the fountain high in the hills better than the black weeds of the shore.' The old women of Ben-y-Ghloe, in Perthshire, and of Clibrich, in Sutherlandshire,[1] seem to have been *sìth* women of the same sort. 'I never,' said an old man (he was upwards of eighty years of age) in the Island of Mull, questioned some years ago on the subject, 'heard of the Fairies having cows, but I always heard that deer were their cattle.'

In other parts of the Highlands, as in Skye, though the Fairies are said to keep company with the deer, they have cows like those of men. When one of them appears among a herd of cattle the whole fold of them grows frantic, and follows lowing wildly. The strange animal disappears by entering a rock or knoll, and the others, unless intercepted, follow and are never more seen. The Fairy cow is dun (*odhar*) and 'hummel,' or hornless. In Skye, however, Fairy cattle are said to be speckled and red (*crodh breac ruadh*), and to be able to cross the sea. It is not on every place that they graze. There were not above ten such spots in all Skye. The field of Annat (*achadh na h-annaid*), in the Braes of Portree, is one. When the cattle came home at night from pasture, the following were the words used by the Fairy woman, standing on Dun Gerra-sheddar (*Dùn*

---

[1] Campbell's *West Highland Tales*, ii. 46.

Ghearra-seadar), near Portree, as she counted her charge :

> " Crooked one, dun one,
> Little wing grizzled,
> Black cow, white cow,
> Little bull black-head,
> My milch kine have come home,
> O dear ! that the herdsman would come ! "

HORSES.

In the Highland creed the Fairies but rarely have horses. In Perthshire they have been seen on a market day riding about on white horses ; in Tiree two Fairy ladies were met riding on what seemed to be horses, but in reality were ragweeds ; and in Skye the elves have galloped the farm horses at full speed and in dangerous places, sitting with their faces to the tails.

When horses neigh at night it is because they are ridden by the Fairies, and pressed too hard. The neigh is one of distress, and if the hearer exclaims aloud, " Your saddle and pillion be upon you " (*Do shrathair 's do phillein ort*) the Fairies tumble to the ground.

DOGS.

The Fairy dog (*cu sìth*) is as large as a two-year-old stirk, a dark green colour, with ears of deep green. It is of a lighter colour towards the feet.

In some cases it has a long tail rolled up in a coil
on its back, but others have the tail flat and plaited
like the straw rug of a pack-saddle. Bran, the famous
dog that Finmac Coul had, was of Elfin breed, and
from the description given of it by popular tradition,
decidedly parti-coloured :

> " Bran had yellow feet,
>   Its two sides black and belly white ;
>   Green was the back of the hunting hound,
>   Its two pointed ears blood-red."

Bran had a venomous shoe (*Bròg nimhe*), with which
it killed whatever living creature it struck, and when
at full speed, and ' like its father ' (*dol ri athair*),
was seen as three dogs, intercepting the deer at three
passes.

The Fairy hound was kept tied as a watch dog in
the brugh, but at times accompanied the women on
their expeditions or roamed about alone, making its
lairs in clefts of the rocks. Its motion was silent and
gliding, and its bark a rude clamour (*blaodh*). It went
in a straight line, and its bay has been last heard, by
those who listened for it, far out at sea. Its immense
footmarks, as large as the spread of the human hand,
have been found next day traced in the mud, in the
snow, or on the sands. Others say it makes a noise
like a horse galloping, and its bay is like that of
another dog, only louder. There is a considerable
interval between each bark, and at the third (it only

barks thrice) the terror-struck hearer is overtaken and destroyed, unless he has by that time reached a place of safety.

Ordinary dogs have a mortal aversion to the Fairies, and give chase whenever the elves are sighted. On coming back, the hair is found to be scraped off their bodies, all except the ears, and they die soon after.

CATS.

Elfin cats (*cait shìth*) are explained to be of a wild, not a domesticated, breed, to be as large as dogs, of a black colour, with a white spot on the breast, and to have arched backs and erect bristles (*crotach agus mùr-lach*). Many maintain these wild cats have no connection with the Fairies, but are witches in disguise.

FAIRY THEFT.

The elves have got a worse name for stealing than they deserve. So far as taking things without the knowledge or consent of the owners is concerned, the accusation is well-founded ; they neither ask nor obtain leave, but there are important respects in which their depredations differ from the pilferings committed among men by jail-birds and other dishonest people.

The Fairies do not take their booty away bodily ; they only take what is called in Gaelic its *toradh*, *i.e.* its substance, virtue, fruit, or benefit. The outward appearance is left, but the reality is gone. Thus, when a cow is elf-taken, it appears to its owner only as suddenly smitten by some strange disease (*chaidh am beathach ud a ghonadh*). In reality the cow is gone, and only its semblance remains, animated it may be by an Elf, who receives all the attentions paid to the sick cow, but gives nothing in return. The seeming cow lies on its side, and cannot be made to rise. It consumes the provender laid before it, but does not yield milk or grow fat. In some cases it gives plenty of milk, but milk that yields no butter. If taken up a hill, and rolled down the incline, it disappears altogether. If it dies, its flesh ought not to be eaten—it is not beef, but a stock of alder wood, an aged Elf, or some trashy substitute. Similarly when the *toradh* of land is taken, there remains the appearance of a · crop, but a crop without benefit to man or beast—the ears are unfilled, the grain is without weight, the fodder without nourishment.

A still more important point of difference is, that the Fairies only take away what men deserve to lose. When mortals make a secret of (*cleth*), or grumble (*ceasad*) over, what they have, the Fairies get the benefit, and the owner is a poor man, in the midst of his abundance. When (to use an illustration the writer has more than once heard) a farmer speaks disparagingly of his crop, and, though it be heavy, tries to conceal his good fortune, the Fairies take away the benefit of his increase. The advantage goes away mysteriously 'in pins and needles' (*na phrìneachan 's na shnàdun*), 'in alum and madder' (*na alm 's na mhadair*), as the saying is, and the farmer gains nothing from his crop. Particularly articles of food, the possession of which men denied with oaths (*air a thiomnadh*), became Fairy property.

The elves are also blamed for lifting with them articles mislaid. These are generally restored as mysteriously and unaccountably as they were taken away. Thus, a woman blamed the elves for taking her thimble. It was placed beside her, and when looked for could not be found. Some time after she was sitting alone on the hillside and found the thimble in her lap. This confirmed her belief in its being the Fairies that took it away. In a like mysterious manner a person's bonnet might be whipped off his head, or the pot for supper be lifted off the fire, and left by invisible hands on the middle of the floor.

The accusation of taking milk is unjust. It is brought against the elves only in books, and never in the popular creed. The Fairies take cows, sheep, goats, horses, and it may be the substance or benefit (*toradh*) of butter and cheese, but not milk.

Many devices were employed to thwart Fairy inroads. A burning ember (*eibhleag*) was put into 'sowens' (*cabhruich*), one of the weakest and most unsubstantial articles of human food and very liable to Fairy attack. It was left there till the dish was ready for boiling, *i.e.* about three days after. A sieve should not be allowed out of the house after dark, and no meal unless it be sprinkled with salt. Otherwise, the Fairies may, by means of them, take the substance out of the whole farm produce. For the same reason a hole should be put with the finger in the little cake (*bonnach beag's toll ann*), made with the remnant of the meal after a baking, and when given to children, as it usually is, a piece should be broken off it. A nail driven into a cow, killed by falling over a precipice, was supposed by the more superstitious to keep the elves away.

One of the most curious thefts ascribed to them was that of querns,[1] or handmills (*Bra, Brathuinn*). To keep them away these handy and useful implements should be turned *deiseal, i.e.* with the right hand turn, as sunwise. What is curious in the belief is, that the handmill is said to have been originally

---

[1] The use of some kind of mill, generally a hand mill, is as universal as the growth of grain, and the necessity for reducing the solid grain into the more palatable form of meal no doubt led to its early invention. The Gaelic *meil* (or *beil*), to grind, the English *mill*, the Latin *mola*, and the Greek μυλη, show that it was known to the Aryan tribes at a period long anterior to history. The handmill mentioned in Scripture, worked by two women, seems the same with that still to be found in obscure corners in the West Highlands.

An instrument so useful to man in the less advanced stages of his civilization could not fail to be looked upon with much respect and good feeling. In the Hebrides it was rubbed every Saturday evening with a wisp of straw 'for payment' of its benevolent labours (*sop ga shuathadh ris a bhrà ga pàigheadh*). Meal ground in it is coarser than ordinary meal, and is known as *gairbhein*.

got from the Fairies themselves. Its sounds have
often been heard by the belated peasant, as it was
being worked inside some grassy knoll, and songs,
sung by the Fairy women employed at it, have been
learned.

STEALING WOMEN AND CHILDREN.

Most frequently it was women, not yet risen from
childbed, and their babes that the Fairies abducted.
On every occasion of a birth, therefore, the utmost
anxiety prevailed to guard the mother and child from
their attacks. It is said that the Fairy women are
unable to suckle their own children, and hence their
desire to secure a human wet-nurse. This, however,
does not explain why they want the children, nor
indeed is it universally a part of the creed.

The first care was not to leave a woman alone
during her confinement. A house full of women
gathered and watched for three days, in some places
for eight. Various additional precautions against the
Fairies were taken in various localities. A row of
iron nails were driven into the front board of the
bed ; the smoothing iron or a reaping hook was placed
under it and in the window ; an old shoe was put
in the fire ; the door posts were sprinkled with *maistir*,
urine kept for washing purposes—a liquid extremely
offensive to the Fairies ; the Bible was opened, and
the breath blown across it in the face of the woman

in childbed; mystic words of threads were placed about the bed; and, when leaving at the end of the three days, the midwife left a little cake of oatmeal with a hole in it in the front of the bed. The father's shirt wrapped round the new-born babe was esteemed a preservative, and if the marriage gown was thrown over the wife she could be recovered if, notwithstanding, or from neglect of these precautions, she were taken away. The name of the Deity solemnly pronounced over the child in baptism was an additional protection. If the Fairies were seen, water in which an ember was extinguished, or the burning peats themselves, thrown at them, drove them away. Even quick wit and readiness of reply in the mother has sent them off.[1]

It is not to be supposed that these precautions were universally known or practised. In that case such a thing as an elf-struck child would be unknown. The gathering of women and the placing of iron about the bed seem to have been common, but the burning of old shoes was confined to the Western Isles. If it existed elsewhere, its memory has been forgotten. That it is an old part of the creed is evident from the dislike of

---

[1] Other charms used on the occasion were the taking of the woman to be delivered several times across the byre-drain (*inne*), the opening of every lock in the house, and ceremonies by means of

" A grey hank of flax and a cockscomb,
Two things against the commandments."

These practices seem to have been known only to the very superstitious, and to have been local. The first belonged to Ross-shire, the second to the north-west mainland of Argyllshire, and the last to Tiree.

the Fairies to strong smells, being also part of the
Teutonic creed. The blowing of the breath across
the Bible existed in Sunart, part of the west of
Inverness-shire.

CHANGELINGS.

When they succeeded in their felonious attempts,
the elves left instead of the mother, and bearing her
semblance, a stock of wood (*stoc maide*), and in place of
the infant an old mannikin of their own race. The
child grew up a peevish misshapen brat, ever crying
and complaining. It was known, however, to be a
changeling by the skilful in such matters, from the
large quantities of water it drank—a tubful before
morning, if left beside it—its large teeth, its inordinate
appetite, its fondness for music and its powers of dancing, its unnatural precocity, or from some unguarded
remark as to its own age. It is to the aged elf, left in
the place of child or beast, that the name *sithbheire*
(pron. *sheevere*) is properly given, and as may well be
supposed, to say of one who has an ancient manner
or look, 'he is but a sithbheire,' or 'he is only
one that came from a brugh,' is an expression of
considerable contempt. When a person does a senseless action, it is said of him, that he has been 'taken
out of himself' (*air a thoirt as*), that is, taken away
by the Fairies.

The changeling was converted into the stock of a

tree by saying a powerful rhyme over him, or by sticking him with a knife. He could be driven away by running at him with a red-hot ploughshare; by getting between him and the bed and threatening him with a drawn sword; by leaving him out on the hillside, and paying no attention to his shrieking and screaming; by putting him sitting on a gridiron, or in a creel, with a fire below; by sprinkling him well out of the *maistir* tub; or by dropping him into the river. There can be no doubt these modes of treatment would rid a house of any disagreeable visitor, at least of the human race.

The story of the changeling, who was detected by means of egg-shells, seems in some form or other to be as widespread as the superstition itself. Empty egg-shells are ranged round the hearth, and the changeling, when he finds the house quiet and thinks himself unobserved, gets up from bed and examines them. Finding them empty, he is heard to remark sententiously, as he peers into each, "this is but a wind-bag (*chaneil a' so ach balg fàs*); I am so many hundred years old, and I never saw the like of this."

DEFORMITIES.

Many of the deformities in children are attributed to the Fairies. When a child is incautiously left alone by its mother, for however short a time, the Fairies may come and give its little legs such a twist as will leave it hopelessly lame ever after. To give them their due, however, they sometimes took care of children whom they found forgotten, and even of grown up people sleeping incautiously in dangerous places.

NURSES.

The elves have children of their own, and require the services of midwives like the human race. ' Howdies,' as they are called, taken in the way of their profession to the Fairy dwelling, found on coming out that the time they had stayed was incredibly longer or shorter than they imagined, and none of them was ever the better ultimately of her adventure.

THE MEN OF PEACE.

The Gaelic *sìthche*, like the English elf, has two ideas, almost amounting to two meanings, attached to it. In the plural, *sìthchean*, it conveys the idea of a diminutive race, travelling in eddy winds, lifting men from the ground, stealing, and entering houses in companies; while in the singular, *sìthche*, the idea conveyed is that of one who approaches mankind in dimensions. The ' man and woman of peace' hire themselves to the human race for a day's work or a term of service, and contract marriages with it. The elfin youth (*Gille sìth*) has enormous strength, that of a dozen men it is said, and the elfin women (or Banshis) are remarkably handsome. The aged of the race were generally

the reverse, in point of beauty, especially those of them
,substituted for Fairy-abducted children and animals.

Mortals should have nothing to do with any of the
race. No good comes out of the unnatural connection.
However enchanting. at first, the end is disaster and
death. When, therefore, the *sìthche* is first met, it is
recommended by the prudent to pass by without notic-
ing ; or, if obliged or incautious enough to speak, and
pressed to make an appointment, to give fair words,
saying, ' If I promise that, I will fulfil it ' (*ma gheallas
mi sin, co-gheallaidh mi e*), still sufficiently near houses
to attract the attention of the dogs. They immediately
give chase, and the Fairy flies away.

The *Gille sìth* (or Elfin youth) is very solicitous
about his offspring when his mortal mistress bears him
children, and the love that women have to him as
their lover or familiar spirit (*leannan sìth*) is unnaturally passionate. The Elfin mistress is not always
so secure of the affections of her human lover. He
may get tired of her and leave her. On meeting
her first he is put under spells to keep appointments
with her in future every night. If he dares for one
night to neglect his appointment, she gives him such
a sound thrashing the first time she gets hold of him
that he never neglects it again. She disappears at
the cock-crowing. While he remains faithful to her,
she assists him at his trade as farmer, shepherd, etc.,
makes him presents of clothes, tells him when he is

to die, and even when he is to leave her and get married. She gives *Sian* a magic belt or other charm, to protect him in danger. If offended, however, her lover is in danger of his life. The children of these alliances are said to be the *urisks*.

Those who have taken Elfin women for wives have found a sad termination to their mesalliance. The defect or peculiarity of the fair enchantress, which her lover at first had treated as of no consequence, proves his ruin. Her voracity thins his herds, he gets tired of her or angry with her, and in an unguarded moment reproaches her with her origin. She disappears, taking with her the children and the fortune she brought him. The gorgeous palace, fit for the entertainment of kings, vanishes, and he finds himself again in his old black dilapidated hut, with a pool of rain-drippings from the roof in the middle of the floor.

THE BEAN NIGHE, OR WASHING WOMAN.

At times the Fairy woman (*Bean shìth*) is seen in lonely places, beside a pool or stream, washing the linen of those soon to die, and folding and beating it with her hands on a stone in the middle of the water. She is then known as the *Bean-nighe*, or washing woman ; and her being seen is a sure sign that death is near.

In Mull and Tiree she is said to have praeternaturally long breasts, which are in the way as she stoops at her washing. She throws them over her shoulders, and they hang down her back. Whoever sees her must not turn away, but steal up behind and endeavour to approach her unawares. When he is near enough he is to catch one of her breasts, and, putting it to his mouth, call herself to witness that she is his first nursing or foster-mother (*muime cìche*). She answers that he has need of that being the case, and will then communicate whatever knowledge he desires. If she says the shirt she is washing is that of an enemy he allows the washing to go on, and that man's death follows ; if it be that of her captor or any of his friends, she is put a stop to.

In Skye the Bean-nighe is said to be squat in figure (*tiughiosal*), or not unlike a 'small pitiful child' (*paisde beag brònach*). If a person caught her she told all that would befall him in after life. She answered all his questions, but he must answer hers. Men did not like to tell what she said. Women dying in child-bed were looked upon as dying prematurely, and it was believed that unless all the clothes left by them were washed they would have to wash them themselves till the natural period of their death. It was women 'dreeing this weird' who were the washing women. If the person hearing them at work beating their clothes (*slacartaich*) caught them before being observed, he could not be heard by them; but if they saw him first, he lost the power of his limbs (*lùgh*).

In the highlands of Perthshire the washing woman is represented as small and round, and dressed in pretty green. She spreads by moonlight the linen winding sheets of those soon to die, and is caught by getting .between her and the stream.

She can also be caught and mastered and made to communicate her information at the point of the sword. Oscar, son of the poet Ossian, met her on his way to the Cairbre's feast, at which the dispute arose which led to his death. She was encountered by Hugh of the Little Head on the evening before his last .battle, and left him as her parting gift (*fàgail*), that he should become the frightful apparition he did after death, the most celebrated in the West Highlands.

SONG.

The song of the Fairy woman foreboded great calamity, and men did not like to hear it. Scott calls it

"The fatal Banshi's boding scream,"

but it was not a scream, only a wailing murmur (*torman mulaid*) of unearthly sweetness and melancholy.

GLAISTIG.

The Banshi is sometimes confounded with the Glais-tig, the apparition of a woman, acting as tutelary guardian of the site to which she is attached. Many people use Banshi and Glaistig as convertible terms, and the confusion thence arising extends largely to books. The true Glaistig is a woman of human race, who has been put under enchantments, and to whom a Fairy nature has been given. She wears a *green* dress, like Fairy women, but her face is wan and grey, whence her name Glaistig, from *glas*, grey. She differs also in haunting castles and the folds of the cattle, and confining herself to servant's work.

ELFIN QUEEN.

The Banshi is, without doubt, the original of the Queen of Elfland, mentioned in ballads of the South of Scotland. The Elfin Queen met Thomas of Ercildoune by the Eildon tree, and took him to her enchanted realm, where he was kept for seven years. She gave him the power of foretelling the future, 'the tongue that never lied.' At first she was the most beautiful woman he had ever seen, but when he next looked—

> " The hair that hung upon her head,
>   The half was black, the half was grey,
> And all the rich clothing was away
>   That he before saw in that stead ;
> Her eyes seemed out that were so grey,
>   And all her body like the lead."

In Gaelic tales seven years is a common period of detention among the Fairies, the *leannan sìth* communicates to her lover the knowledge of future events, and in the end is looked upon by him with aversion. There is no mention, however, of Fairyland, or of an Elfin King or Queen, and but rarely of Fairies riding. True Thomas, who is as well known in Highland lore as he is in the Lowlands, is said to be still among the Fairies, and to attend every market on the look-out for suitable horses. When he has made up his complement he will appear again among men, and a great battle will be fought on the Clyde.

PROTECTION AGAINST FAIRIES.

The great protection against the Elfin race (and this is perhaps the most noticeable point in the whole superstition) is *Iron*, or preferably steel (*Cruaidh*). The metal in any form—a sword, a knife, a pair of scissors, a needle, a nail, a ring, a bar, a piece of reaping-hook, a gunbarrel, a fish-hook (and tales will be given illustrative of all these)—is all-powerful. On entering a Fairy dwelling, a piece of steel, a knife, needle, or fish-hook, stuck in the door, takes from the Elves the power of closing it till the intruder comes out again. A knife stuck in a deer carried home at night keeps them from laying their weight on the animal. A knife or nail in one's pocket prevents his being 'lifted' at night. Nails in the front bench of the bed keep Elves from women 'in the straw,' and their babes, As additional safe-guards, the smoothing-iron should be put below the bed, and the reaping-hook in the window. A nail in the carcase of a bull that fell over a rock was believed to preserve its flesh from them. Playing the Jew's harp (*tromb*) kept the Elfin women at a distance from the hunter, because the tongue of the instrument is of steel. So also a shoemaker's awl in the door-post of his bothy kept a Glastig from entering.

Fire thrown into water in which the feet have been washed takes away the power of the water to admit the Fairies into the house at night ; a burning peat put in sowens to hasten their fermenting (*greasadh gortachadh*) kept the substance in them till ready to boil. Martin (*West Isl.*) says fire was carried round lying-in women, and round about children before they were christened, to keep mother and infant from the power of evil spirits. When the Fairies were seen coming in at the door burning embers thrown towards them drove them away.

Another safe-guard is *oatmeal.* When it is sprinkled on one's clothes or carried in the pocket no Fairy will venture near, and it was usual with people going on journeys after nightfall to adopt the precaution of taking some with them. In Mull and Tiree the pockets of boys going any distance after nightfall were filled with oatmeal by their anxious mothers, and old men are remembered who sprinkled themselves with it when going on a night journey. In Skye, oatmeal was not looked upon as proper Fairy food, and it was said if a person wanted to see the Fairies he should not take oatmeal with him ; if he did he would not be able to see them. When ' the folk ' take a loan of meal they do not appear to have any objections to oatmeal. The meal returned, however, was always barleymeal.

Oatmeal, taken out of the house after dark, was sprinkled with salt, and unless this was done, the Fairies might through its instrumentality take the substance out of the farmer's whole grain. To keep them from getting the benefit of meal itself, housewives, when baking oatmeal bannocks, made a little thick cake with the last of the meal, between their palms (not kneading it like the rest of the bannocks), for the youngsters to put a hole through it with the forefinger. This palm bannock (*bonnach boise*) is not to be toasted on the gridiron, but placed to the fire leaning against a stone (*leac nam bonnach*), well-known where a ' griddle ' is not available. Once the Fairies were overtaken carrying with them the benefit (*toradh*) of the farm in a large thick cake, with the handle of the quern (*sgonnan na brà*) stuck through it, and forming a pole on which it was carried. This cannot occur when the last bannock baked (*Bonnach fallaid*) is a little cake with a hole in it (*Bonnach beag 's toll ann*).[1]

---

[1] Carleton (*Tales and Stories*, p. 74) mentions an Irish belief of a kindred character connected with oatmeal. When one crossed *fair gurtha*, or hungry grass (Scot., *feur gorta*, famine grass), a spot on which the Fairies had left one of their curses, he was struck with weakness and hunger, but, "if the person afflicted but tasted as much meal or flour as would lie on the point of a penknife, he will instantaneously break the spell of the Fairies, and recover his former strength."

Maistir, or stale urine, kept for the scouring of blankets and other cloth, when sprinkled on the cattle and on the door-posts and walls of the house, kept the Fairies, and indeed every mischief, at a distance. This sprinkling was done regularly on the last evening of every quarter of the year (*h-uile latha ceann ràidhe*).

Plants of great power were the *Mòthan* (*Sagina procumbens*, trailing pearlwort) and *Achlasan Challum-chille* (*Hypericum pulcrum*, St. John's wort). The former protected its possessor from fire and the attacks of the Fairy women. The latter warded off fevers, and kept the Fairies from taking people away in their sleep. There are rhymes which must be said when these plants are pulled.

Stories representing the Bible as a protection must be of a recent date. It is not so long since a copy of the Bible was not available in the Highlands for that or any other purpose. When the Book did become accessible, it is not surprising that, as in other places, a blind unmeaning reverence should accumulate round it.

Such are the main features of the superstition of the *Sìthchean*, the still-folk, the noiseless people, as it existed, and in some degree still exists, in the Highlands, and particularly in the Islands of Scotland. There is a clear line of demarcation between it and every other Highland superstition, though the distinction has not always been observed by writers on the

D

subject. The following Fairy characteristics deserve to
be particularly noticed.

It was peculiar to the Fairy women to assume the
shape of *deer*; while witches became mice, hares, cats,
gulls, or black sheep, and the devil a he-goat or
gentleman with a horse's or pig's foot. A running
stream could not be crossed by evil spirits, ghosts, and
apparitions, but made no difference to the Fairies. If
all tales be true, they could give a dip in the passing
to those they were carrying away; and the stone, on
which the "Washing Woman" folded the shirts of the
doomed, was in the middle of water. Witches took the
milk from cows; the Fairies had cattle of their own;
and when they attacked the farmer's dairy, it was to
take away the cows themselves, *i.e.* the cow in appearance remained, but its benefit (the real cow) was gone.
The Elves have even the impertinence at times to drive
back the cow at night to pasture on the corn of the
person from whom they have stolen it. The phrenzy
with which Fairy women afflicted men was only a
wandering madness ($\phi o\iota\tau a\lambda\epsilon a$ $\mu a\nu\iota a$), which made them
roam about restlessly, without knowing what they were
doing, or leave home at night to hold appointments
with the Elfin women themselves; by druidism (*druidheachd*) men were driven from their kindred, and made
to imagine themselves undergoing marvellous adventures and changing shape. Dogs crouched, or leapt
at their master's throat, in the presence of evil spirits,

but they gave chase to the Fairies. Night alone was frequented by the powers of darkness, and they fled at the cock-crowing ; the Fairies were encountered in the day-time as well. There was no intermarriage between men and the other beings of superstition, but women were courted and taken away by Fairy men, and men courted Fairy women (or rather were courted by them), married, and took them to their houses. A well-marked characteristic is the tinge of the ludicrous that pervades the creed. The Fairy is an object of contempt as well as of fear, and, though the latter be the prevailing feeling, there is observably a desire to make the Elves contemptible and ridiculous. A person should not unnecessarily provoke the anger of those who cannot retaliate, much less of a race so ready to take offence and so sure to retaliate as the Fairies. In revenge for this species of terror, the imagination loves to depict the Elves in positions and doing actions that provoke a smile. The part of the belief which relates to the Banshi is comparatively free from this feeling, but the 'little people' and changelings come in for a full share of it. Perhaps this part of the superstition is not entirely to be explained as the recoil of the mind from the oppression of a belief in invisible beings that may be cognizant of men's affairs and only wait for an opportunity to exert an evil influence over them, but its existence is striking.

CHAPTER II.

TALES ILLUSTRATIVE OF FAIRY SUPERSTITION.

LURAN.

THIS is a tale, diffused in different forms, over the whole West Highlands. Versions of it have been heard from Skye, Ardnamurchan, Lochaber, Craignish, Mull, Tiree, differing but slightly from each other.

The Charmed Hill (*Beinn Shianta*), from its height, greenness, or pointed summit, forms a conspicuous object on the Ardnamurchan coast, at the north entrance of the Sound of Mull. On 'the shoulder' of this hill, were two hamlets, Sginid and Corryvulin, the lands attached to which, now forming part of a large sheep farm, were at one time occupied in common by three tenants, one of whom was named Luran Black (*Luran Mac-ille-dhui*). One particular season a cow of Luran's was found unaccountably dead each morning. Suspicion fell on the tenants of the Culver (*an cuilibheir*), a green knoll in Corryvulin, having the reputation of being tenanted by the Fairies. Luran resolved to watch his cattle for

a night, and ascertain the cause of his mysterious
losses. Before long he saw the Culver opening, and a
host of little people pouring out. They surrounded a
grey cow (*mart glas*) belonging to him and drove it
into the knoll. Not one busied himself in doing this
more than Luran himself; he was, according to the
Gaelic expression, 'as one and as two' (*mar a h-aon 's
mar a dhà*) in his exertions. The cow was killed and
skinned. An old Elf, a tailor sitting in the upper part
of the brugh, with a needle in the right lappel of his
coat, was forcibly caught hold of, stuffed into the cow's
hide, and sewn up. He was then taken to the door
and rolled down the slope. Festivities commenced,
and whoever might be on the floor dancing, Luran was
sure to be. He was 'as one and as two' at the dance,
as he had been at driving the cow. A number of
gorgeous cups and dishes were put on the table, and
Luran, resolving to make up for the loss of the grey
cow, watched his opportunity and made off with one
of the cups (*còrn*). The Fairies observed him and
started in pursuit. He heard one of them remark :

" Not swift would be Luran
If it were not the hardness of his bread." [1]

His pursuers were likely to overtake him, when a
friendly voice called out :

" Luran, Luran Black,
Betake thee to the black stones of the shore." [2]

[1] Cha bu luath Luran
Mar a bhi cruas arain.

[2] Lurain, Lurain Mhic-ille-dhui
Thoir ort clacha du a chladaich.

Below high water mark, no Fairy, ghost, or demon can come, and, acting on the friendly advice, Luran reached the shore, and keeping below tide mark made his way home in safety. He heard the outcries of the person who had called out to him (probably a former acquaintance who had been taken by 'the people') being belaboured by the Fairies for his ill-timed officiousness. Next morning, the grey cow was found lying dead with its feet in the air, at the foot of the Culver, and Luran said that a needle would be found in its right shoulder. On this proving to be the case, he allowed none of the flesh to be eaten, and threw it out of the house.

One of the fields, tilled in common by Luran and two neighbours, was every year, when ripe, reaped by the Fairies in one night, and the benefit of the crop disappeared. An old man was consulted, and he undertook to watch the crop. He saw the shïen of Corryvulin open, and a troop of people coming out. There was an old man at their head, who put the company in order, some to shear, some to bind the sheaves, and some to make stooks. On the word of command being given, the field was reaped in a wonderfully short time. The watcher, calling aloud, counted the reapers. The Fairies never troubled the field again.

Their persecution of Luran did not, however, cease. While on his way to Inveraray Castle, with his Fairy cup, he was lifted mysteriously with his treasure out of the boat, in which he was taking his passage, and was never seen or heard of after.

According to another Ardnamurchan version, Luran was a butler boy in Mingarry Castle. One night he entered a Fairy dwelling, and found the company within feasting and making merry. A shining cup, called *an cupa cearrarach*, was produced, and whatever liquor the person having it in his hand wished for and named, came up within it. Whenever a dainty appeared on the table, Luran was asked, " Did you ever see the like of that in Mingarry Castle ? " At last, the butler boy wished the cup to be full of water, and throwing its contents on the lights, and extinguishing them, ran away with it in his hand. The Fairies gave chase. Some one among them called out to Luran to make for the shore. He reached the friendly shelter, and made his way below high-water mark to the castle, which he entered by a stair leading to the sea. The cup remained long in Mingarry Castle, but was at last lost in a boat that sank at Mail Point (*Rutha Mhàil*).

A Tiree version of the tale says that Luran entered an open Fairy dwelling (*brugh*), where he found the inmates asleep, and a large cauldron, or copper, standing on the floor. He took up the kettle, and made off with it. When going out at the door, the cauldron struck one of the door-posts, and made a ringing noise. The Fairies, sixteen men in number, started out of sleep, and gave chase. As they pressed on Luran, one of them (probably a friend who had at one time been ' taken ') called out, " Luran, Luran, make for the black stones of the shore." He did so, and made his escape. It was then the Fairies remarked : " Luran would be swift if it were not the hardness of his bread. If Luran had warm milk and soft barley bread, not one among the sixteen of us could catch him."

According to the Lochaber story, the Fairies stole a white cow from a farmer, and every night took it back again to pasture on his corn. He chased them with his dog Luran, but they threw bread behind them, which the dog loitered to devour, so that it never over-took the white cow. The Fairies were heard saying among themselves, " Swift would be Luran if it were not the hardness of his bread. If Luran got bread singed and twice turned, it would catch the white cow." The field where this occurred is known as the Field of the White Cow (*acha na bò bàin*), above Brackletter, in Lochaber.

According to a Skye version, the Fairies came to take with them the benefit (*toradh*) of the farmer's land, but his dog Luran drove them away. One night they were overheard saying, " Swift would be Luran if it were not the hardness of his bread. If thin porridge were Luran's food, deer would not overtake Luran." Next day thin porridge, or ' crowdie,' was given to Luran, and it ate too much, and could not run at all.

The Fairies got away, laughing heartily at the success of their trick.

In Craignish, Argyllshire, Luran was a dog, old, and unable to devour quickly the bread thrown it by the Fairies. There are, no doubt, many other versions of the story current, but these are sufficient to show the want of uniformity in popular tales of this kind.

THE CUP OF THE MACLEODS OF RAASA.

In Raasa, a man, named Hugh, entered a Fairy dwelling where there was feasting going on. The Fairies welcomed him heartily, and pledged his health. "Here's to you, Hugh," "I drink to you, Hugh" (*cleoch ort, Eoghain*), was to be heard on every side. He was offered drink in a fine glittering cup. When he got the cup in his hands he ran off with it. The Fairies let loose one of their dogs after him. He made his escape, and heard the Fairies calling back the dog by its name of "Farvann" (*Farbhann! Farbhann!*). The cup long remained in the possession of the Macleods of Raasa.

THE FAIRIES ON FINLAY'S SANDBANK.

The sandbank of this name (*Bac Fhionnlaidh*) on the farm of Ballevulin, in Tiree, was at one time a noted Fairy residence, but has since been blown level with the ground. It caused surprise to many that no traces of the Fairies were found in it. Its Fairy tenants were at one time in the habit of sending every evening to the house of a smith in the neighbourhood for the loan of a kettle (*iasad coire*). The smith, when giving it, always said :

> " A smith's due is coals,
> And to send cold iron out ;
> A cauldron's due is a bone,
> And to come safe back." [1]

Under the power of this rhyme the cauldron was restored safely before morning.   One evening the smith was from home, and his wife, when the Fairies came for the usual loan, never thought of saying the rhyme.   In consequence the cauldron was not returned. On finding this out the smith scolded savagely, and his wife, irritated by his reproaches, rushed away for the kettle. She found the brugh open, went in, and (as is recommended in such cases), without saying a word, snatched up the cauldron and made off with it.   When going out at the door she heard one of the Fairies calling out :

> " Thou dumb sharp one, thou dumb sharp,
> That came from the land of the dead,
> And drove the cauldron from the brugh—
> Undo the Knot, and lose the Rough." [2]

She succeeded in getting home before the Rough, the

[1] " Dlighe gobhainn gual
Is iarrunn fuar a chuir amach
'S dlighe coire cnàimh
'Se thighinn slàn gu tigh."

[2] " A Gheur bhalbh ud, 's a Gheur bhalbh,
Thàinig oirnn a tìr na marbh,
Dh' fhuadaich an coire o'n bhrugh,—
Fuasgail an dul is leig an Garbh."

Fairy dog, overtook her, and the Fairies never again came for the loan of the kettle.

This story is given, in a slightly different form, by Mr. Campbell, in his *Tales of the West Highlands* (Vol. ii., p. 44), and the scene is laid in Sanntrai, an island near Barra. The above version was heard in Tiree by the writer, several years before he saw Mr. Campbell's book. There is no reason to suppose the story belongs originally either to Tiree or Barra. It is but an illustration of the tendency of popular tales to localize themselves where they are told.

PENNYGOWN FAIRIES.

A green mound, near the village of Pennygown (*Peigh'nn-a-ghobhann*), in the Parish of Salen, Mull, was at one time occupied by a benevolent company of Fairies. People had only to leave at night on the hillock the materials for any work they wanted done, as wool to be spun, thread for weaving, etc., telling what was wanted, and before morning the work was finished. One night a wag left the wood of a fishing-net buoy, a short, thick piece of wood, with a request to have it made into a ship's mast. The Fairies were heard toiling all night, and singing, " Short life and ill-luck attend the man who asked us to make a long ship's big mast from the wood of a fishing-net buoy." [1]

---

[1] Dìomaich is mi-bhuaidh air an fhear a dh'iarr oirnn crann mòr luinge fada dheanadh de mhaide bhola liòn.

In the morning the work was not done, and these Fairies never after did anything for any one.

BEN LOMOND FAIRIES.

A company of Fairies lived near the Green Loch (*Lochan Uaine*), on Ben Lomond. Whatever was left overnight near the loch—cloth, wool, or thread—was dyed by them of any desired colour before morning. A specimen of the desired colour had to be left at the same time. A person left a quantity of undyed thread, and a piece of black and white twisted thread along with it, to show that he wanted part of the hank black and part white. The Fairies thought the pattern was to be followed, and the work done at one and the same dyeing. Not being able to do this, they never dyed any more.

CALLUM CLARK AND HIS SORE LEG.

Some six generations ago there lived at Port Vista (*Port Bhissta*), in Tiree, a dark, fierce man, known as Big Malcolm Clark (*Callum mòr mac-a-Chleirich*). He was a very strong man, and in his brutal violence produced the death of several people. Tradition also says of him that he killed a water-horse, and fought a Banshi with a horse-rib at the long hollow, covered in winter with water, called the *Léig*. In this encounter his own little finger was broken. When sharpening knives, old women in Tiree said, " Friday in Clark's

town " (*Di-haoine am baile mhic-a-Chleirich*), with the
object of making him and his the objects of Fairy
wrath.   One evening, as he was driving a tether-pin
into a hillock, a head was popped up out of the ground,
and told him to take some other place for securing his
beast, as he was letting the rain into 'their' dwelling.
Some time after this he had a painfully sore leg (*bha i
gu dòruinneach doirbh*).   He went to the shï-en, where
the head had appeared, and, finding it open, entered in
search of a cure for his leg.   The Fairies told him to
put 'earth on the earth' (*Cuir an talamh air an talamh*).
He applied every kind of earth he could think of to
the leg, but without effect.   At the end of three months
he went again to the hillock, and when entering put
steel (*cruaidh*) in the door.   He was told to go out,
but he would not, nor would he withdraw the steel till
told the proper remedy.   At last he was told to apply
the red clay of a small loch in the neighbourhood
(*criadh ruadh Lochan ni'h fhonhairle*).   He did so, and
the leg was cured.

THE YOUNG MAN IN THE FAIRY KNOLL.

Two young men, coming home after nightfall on
Hallowe'en, each with a jar of whisky on his back,
heard music by the roadside, and, seeing a dwelling
open and illuminated, and dancing and merriment
going on within, entered.   One of them joined the
dancers, without as much as waiting to lay down the

burden he was carrying. The other, suspecting the place and company, stuck a needle in the door as he entered, and got away when he liked. That day twelvemonths he came back for his companion, and found him still dancing with the jar of whisky on his back. Though more than half-dead with fatigue, the enchanted dancer begged to be allowed to finish the reel. When brought to the open-air he was only skin and bone.

This tale is localized in the Ferintosh district, and at the Slope of Big Stones (*Leathad nan Clacha mòra*) in Harris. In Argyllshire people say it happened in the north. In the Ferintosh story only one of the young men entered the brugh, and the door immediately closed. The other lay under suspicion of having murdered his companion, but, by advice of an old man, went to the same place on the same night the following year, and by putting steel in the door of the Fairy dwelling, which he found open, recovered his companion. In the Harris story, the young men were a bridegroom and his brother-in-law, bringing home whisky for the marriage.

Two young men in Iona were coming in the evening from fishing on the rocks. On their way, when passing, they found the shì-en of that island open, and entered. One of them joined the dancers, without waiting to lay down the string of fish he had in his hand. The other stuck a fish-hook in the door, and when he wished made his escape. He came back for his companion that day twelvemonths, and found him still dancing with the string of fish in his hand. On taking him to the open air the fish dropped from the string, rotten.

Donald, who at one time carried on foot the mails from Tobermory, in Mull, to Grass Point Ferry (*Ru-an-fhiarain*), where the mail service crosses to the mainland, was a good deal given to drink, and consequently to loitering by the way. He once lay down to have a quiet sleep near a Fairy-haunted rock above Drimfin. He saw the rock open, and a flood of light pouring out at the door. A little man came to him and said in English, "Come in to the ball, Donald," but Donald fled, and never stopped till he reached the houses at Tobermory, two miles off. He said he heard the whizz and rustling of the Fairies after him the whole way. The incident caused a good deal of talk in the neighbourhood, and Donald and his fright were made the subject of some doggerel verse, in which the Fairy invitation is thus given :

> " Rise, rise, rise, Donald,
>   Rise, Donald, was the call,
>   Rise up now, Donald,
>   Come in, Donald, to the ball."

It is well known that Highland Fairies, who speak English, are the most dangerous of any.

A young man was sent for the loan of a sieve, and,

mistaking his way, entered a brugh, which was that evening open. He found there two women grinding at a handmill, two women baking, and a mixed party dancing on the floor. He was invited to sit down, " Farquhar MacNeill, be seated " (*Fhearchair 'ie Neill, bi 'd shuidhe*). He thought he would first have a reel with the dancers. He forgot all about the sieve, and lost all desire to leave the company he was in. One night he accompanied the band among whom he had fallen on one of its expeditions, and after careering through the skies, stuck in the roof of a house. Looking down the chimney (*fàr-leus*), he saw a woman dandling a child, and, struck with the sight, exclaimed, " God bless you " (*Dia gu d'bheannachadh*). Whenever he pronounced the Holy Name he was disenchanted, and tumbled down the chimney ! On coming to himself he went in search of his relatives. No one could tell him anything about them. At last he saw, thatching a house, an old man, so grey and thin he took him for a patch of mist resting on the house-top. He went and made inquiries of him. The old man knew nothing of the parties asked for, but said perhaps his father did. Amazed, the young man asked him if his father was alive, and on being told he was, and where to find him, entered the house. He there found a very venerable man sitting in a chair by the fire, twisting a straw-rope for the thatching of the house (*snìomh sìomain*). This man also, on being questioned, said he knew nothing of the people, but perhaps his father did. The father referred to was lying in bed, a little shrunken man, and he in like manner referred to his father. This remote ancestor, being too weak to stand, was found in a purse (*sporran*) suspended at the end of the bed. On being taken out and questioned, the wizened creature said, " I did not know the people myself, but I often heard my father speaking of them." On hearing this the young man crumbled in pieces, and fell down a bundle of bones (*cual chnàmh*).

The incident of the very aged people forms part of some versions of the story, " How the Great Description (a man's name) was put to Death " (*Mar a chaidh an Tuairisgeul mòr a chur gu bàs*). Another form is that a stranger came to a house, and at the door found an old man crying, because his father had thrashed him. He went in, and asking the father why he had thrashed his aged son, was told it was because the grandfather had been there the day before, and the fellow had not the manners to put his hand in his bonnet to him !

BLACK WILLIAM THE PIPER.

William M'Kenzie was weaver to the Laird of Barcaldine. He and a friend were going home with two gallons of whisky in jars strapped on their backs. They saw a hillock open and illuminated, and entered. William's companion stuck a knife in the door when

E

entering. They found inside an old man playing the bagpipes, and a company of dancers on the floor. William danced one reel, and then another, till his companion got tired waiting, and left. When, after several days, M'Kenzie did not turn up, the other was accused of having murdered him, and was advised, if his story was true, to get spades and dig into the hillock for his missing friend. A year's delay was given, and when the hillock was entered M'Kenzie was found still dancing on the floor. After this adventure he became the chief weaver in the district ; he did more work in a shorter time than any other. At the first throw of the shuttle he said, " I and another one are here " (*mise 's fear eile so !*). He also began to make pipes, but though a better weaver and piper than he had been before, he never prospered. He became known as " Black William of the Pipes " (*Uilleam du na pìoba*).

It is said in Sutherlandshire that a weaver, getting a shuttle from the Fairies, can go through three times as much work as another man. (Cf. Tale of M'Crimmon, p. 139.)

THE HARRIS WOMAN AND HER BAKING.

A woman in Harris was passing *Creag Mhanuis*, a rock having on its face the appearance of a door, which she saw opening, and a woman dressed in green standing before it, who called to her to come in to see a sick person. The woman was very unwilling to go, but was

compelled, and went in without taking any precaution.
She found herself among a large company, for whom
she was immediately to begin baking bread, and was
told that when the quantity of meal, not very large,
given her was entirely used, she would be allowed to
go away. She began to bake, and made all possible
haste to finish the work, but the more she strove the
less appearance there was of the labour being finished,
and her courage failed when day after day passed,
leaving her where she began. At last, after a long
time, the whole company left for the outer world,
leaving her, as she thought, alone. When the last
tramp of their footsteps could no longer be heard, she
was startled by hearing a groan. On looking through
an opening which she found in the side of the dwelling,
she saw a bed-ridden old man, who, on seeing her head
in the opening, said, " What sent you here ? " " I did
not come by my own will," she replied. " I was made
to come to attend to a sick person." He then asked
what work was given her to do. She told him, and
how the baking was never likely to be finished. He
said she must begin again, and that she was not to
put the dusting meal (*an fhallaid*) at any time back
among the baking. She did as he told her, when she
found her stock of meal soon exhausted, and she got
out and away before the others returned, much to their
discomfiture.

A woman in Skye was taken to see a sick person in

a *dùn*, and after attending to her patient, she saw a
number of women in green dresses coming in and
getting a loan of meal. They took the meal from a
skin bag (*balgan*), which seemed as if it would never be
exhausted. The woman asked to be sent home, and
was promised to be allowed to go, on baking the meal
left in the bag, and spinning a tuft of wool on a distaff
handed to her. She baked away, but could not ex-
haust the meal bag; and spun, but seemed never nearer
the end of her task. A woman came in, and advised
her to "put the remnant of the meal she baked into
the little bag, and to spin the tuft upon the distaff as
the sheep bites the hillock "[1]—*i.e.*, to draw the wool in
small tufts, like sheep bites, from the distaff. On doing
this, the task was soon finished, the Fairies saying, " A
blessing rest on you, but a curse on the mouth that
taught you." [2] On coming out, the woman found she
had been in the *dùn* for seven years.

LIFTED BY THE FAIRIES.

Black Donald of the Multitude (*Dòmhnull du an
t-sluaigh*), as he was ever afterwards known, was
ploughing on the farm of Baile-pheutrais, in the island
of Tiree, when a heavy shower came on from the west.
In these days it required at least two persons to work

[1] Cuir an fhallaid anns' a bhalgan, agus snìomh an toban mara chriomas
a chaora an tom.

[2] Beannachd dhuit-sa ach mollachd do bheul t' ionnsachaidh.

a plough, one to hold it, and one to lead the horses. Donald's companion took shelter to the lee of the team. When the shower passed, Donald himself was nowhere to be found, nor was he seen again till evening. He then came from an easterly direction, with his coat on his arm. He said the Fairies had taken him in an Eddy wind to the islands to the north—Coll, Skye, etc. In proof of this, he told that a person (naming him) was dead in Coll, and people would be across next day for whiskey for the funeral to Kennovay, a village on the other side of Bally-pheutrais, where smuggling was carried on at the time. This turned out to be the case. Donald said he had done no harm while away, except that the Fairies had made him throw an arrow at, and kill, a speckled cow in Skye. When crossing the sea he was in great terror lest he should fall.

Nial Scrob (Neil the Scrub), a native of Uist, was on certain days lifted by the Fairies and taken to Tiree, and other islands of the Hebrides, at least so he said himself. Once he came to Saälun, a village near the north-east end of Tiree, and at the fourth house in the village was made to throw the Fairy arrow. There is an old saying—

> " Shut the north window,
>   And quickly close the window to the south ;
> And shut the window facing west,
>   Evil never came from the east." [1]

[1] " Dùin an uinneaga tuath,
        'S gu luath an uinneaga deas ;
     'S dùin uinneag na h-àirde 'n iar,
        Cha d'thainig ole riamh o'n àirde 'n ear."

And the west window was this night left open. The
arrow came through the open window, and struck on
the shoulder a handsome, strong, healthy woman of
the name of M'Lean, who sat singing cheerfully at her
work. Her hand fell powerless by her side, and before
morning she was dead. Neil afterwards told that he
was the party whom the Fairies had compelled to do
the mischief. In this, and similar stories, it must
be understood that, according to popular belief, the
woman was taken away by the Fairies, and may still
be among them; only her semblance remained and
was buried.

About twenty years ago a cooper, employed on
board a ship, was landed at Martin's Isle (*Eilein
Mhàrtiunn*), near Coigeach, in Ross-shire, to cut
brooms. He traversed the islet, and then somehow
fell asleep. He felt as if something were pushing
him, and, on awakening, found himself in the island
of Rona, ten miles off. He cut the brooms, and a
shower of rain coming on, again fell asleep. On
awaking he found himself back in Martin's Isle.
He could only, it is argued, have been transported
back and forward by the Fairies.

A seer gifted with the second sight (*taibhseis*), resident
at Bousd, in the east end of Coll, was frequently lifted
by Fairies, that staid in a hillock in his neighbourhood. On one occasion they took him to the sea-girt
rock, called *Eileirig*, and after diverting themselves

with him for an hour or two took him home again. So he said himself.

A man who went to fish on Saturday afternoon at a rock in Kinnavara hill (*Beinn Chinn-a-Bharra*), the extreme *west* point of Tiree, did not make his appearance at home until six o'clock the following morning. He said that after leaving the rock the evening before, he remembered nothing but passing a number of beaches. The white beaches of Tiree, from the surrounding land being a dead level, are at night the most noticeable features in the scenery. On coming to his senses, he found himself on the top of the Dùn at Caolis in the extreme *east* end of the island, twelve miles from his starting point.

A few years ago, a man in Lismore, travelling at night with a web of cloth on his shoulder, lost his way, walked on all night without knowing where he was going, and in the morning was found among rocks, where he could never have made his way alone. He could give no account of himself, and his wanderings were universally ascribed to the Fairies.

Red Donald of the Fairies (*Dòmhnull ruadh nan sìthehean*), as he was called (and the name stuck to him all his life), used when a boy to see the Fairies. Being herd at the Spital (*an Spideal*) above Dalnacardoch in Perthshire, he was taken by them to his father's house at Ardlàraich in Rannoch, a distance of a dozen miles, through the night. In the morning he was found sitting at the fireside, and as the door was barred, he must have been let in by the chimney.

An old man in Achabeg, Morvern, went one night on a gossiping visit (*céilidh*) to a neighbour's house. It was winter time, and a river near the place was in flood, which, in the case of a mountain torrent, means that it was impassable. The old man did not return home that night, and next morning was found near the shī-en of *Luran na leaghadh* in Sasory, some distance across the river. He could give no account of how he got there, only that when on his way home a storm came about him, and on coming to himself he was where they had found him.

When Dr. M'Laurin was tenant of Invererragan, near Connal Ferry in Benderloch, at the end of last century, " *Calum Clever*," who derived his name from his skill in singing tunes and expedition in travelling (gifts given him by the Fairies), stayed with him whole nights. The doctor sent him to Fort William with a letter, telling him to procure the assistance of "his own people" and be back with an immediate answer. Calum asked as much time as one game at shinty (*aon taghal air a bhall*) would take, and was back in the evening before the game was finished. He never could have travelled the distance without Fairy aid.

FAIRIES COMING TO HOUSES.

Ewen, son of Allister Og, was shepherd in the Dell of Banks (*Coira Bhaeaidh*), at the south end of Loch Ericht (*Loch Eireachd*), and stayed alone in a bothy far away from other houses. In the evenings he put the porridge for his supper out to cool on the top of the double wall (*anainn*) of the hut. On successive evenings he found it pitted and pecked all round on the margin, as if by little birds or heavy rain-drops. He watched, and saw little people coming and pecking at his porridge. He made little dishes and spoons of wood, and left them beside his own dish. The Fairies, understanding his meaning, took to using these, and let the big dish alone. At last they became quite familiar with Ewen, entered the hut, and stayed whole evenings with him. One evening a woman came with them. There was no dish for her, and she sat on the other side of the house, saying never a word, but grinning and making faces at the shepherd whenever he looked her way. Ewen at last asked her, "Are you always like that, my lively maid?"[1] Owing to the absurdity of the question, or Ewen's failure to understand that the grinning was a hint for food, the Fairies never came again.

The Elves came to a house at night, and finding it

[1] Am bi thu mar sin daonnan, a bhuineagag ?

closed, called upon 'Feet-water' (*uisge nan cas*) *i.e.*, water in which the feet had been washed, to come and open the door. The water answered from somewhere near, that it could not, as it had been poured out. They called on the Band of the Spinning Wheel to open the door, but it answered it could not, as it had been thrown off the wheel. They called upon Little Cake, but it could not move, as there was a hole through it and a live coal on the top of it. They called upon the 'raking' coal (*smàladh an teine*), but the fire had been secured in a proper manner, to keep it alive all night. This is a tale not localized anywhere, but universally known.

A man observed a band of people dressed in green coming toward the house, and recognising them to be Fairies, ran in great terror, shut and barred the door, and hid himself below the bed. The Fairies, however, came through the keyhole, and danced on the floor, singing. The song extended to several verses, to the effect that no kind of house could keep out the Fairies, not a turf house (*tigh phloc*), nor a stone house (*tigh cloiche*), etc.

The Fairies staying in Dunruilg came to assist a farmer in the vicinity in weaving and preparing cloth, and, after finishing the work in a wonderfully short space of time, called for more work. To get rid of his officious assistants, the farmer called outside the

door that Dunvuilg was on fire.[1]   The Fairies immediately rushed out in great haste, and never came back.
Of this story several versions are given in the *Tales
of the West Highlands* (ii. 52-4).   In some form or
other it is extensively known, and in every locality the
scene is laid in its own neighbourhood.   In Mull the
Fairy residence is said to have been the bold headland
in the south-west of the island known as *Tun Bhuirg*.
Some say the Elves were brought to the house by two
old women, who were tired spinning, and incautiously
said they wished all the people in Tòn Bhuirg were
there to assist.   According to others, the Elves were
in the habit of coming to Tàpull House in the Ross
of Mull, and their excessive zeal made them very
unwelcome.   In Skye the event is said to have occurred
at Dùn Bhuirbh.   There are two places of the name,
one in Lyndale, and one in *Beinn-an-ùine*, near *Druim-
uighe*, above Portree.   The rhyme they had when they
came to Tapull is known as " The rhyme of the good-
man of Tapull's servants " (*Rann gillean fir Thàbuill.*)

> " Let me comb, card, tease, spin,
> Get a weaving loom quick,
> Water for fulling on the fire,
> Work, work, work."[2]

---

[1] The man in Flodigarry got rid of his Fairy assistants by telling them
to bale out the sea.

[2] Cìream, càrdam, tlàmam, cuigealam,
Beairt fhighe gu luath,
'S bùrn luadh air teine,
Obair, obair, obair.

The cry they raised when going away, in the Skye version, runs :

> " Dunsuirv on fire,
> Without dog or man,
> My balls of thread
> And my bags of meal."[1]

A man, on the farm of Kennovay in Tiree, saw the Fairies about twelve o'clock at night enter the house, glide round the room, and go out again. They said and did nothing.

THE LOWLAND FAIRIES.

The ' people ' had several dwellings near the village of Largs[2] (*Na Leargun Gallta*, the slopes-near-the-sea of the strangers), on the coast of Ayrshire (see Introduction to Campbell's *Tales of the West Highlands*).

Knock Hill was full of *elves*, and the site of the old Tron Tree, now the centre of the village, was a favourite haunt. A sow, belonging to the man who cut down the Tron Tree, was found dead in the byre next morning. A hawker, with a basket of crockery, was met near the Noddle Burn by a Fairy woman. She asked him for a bowl she pointed out in his

---

[1] Dùn-Bhuirbh ri theine
Gun chù, gun duine,
Mo chearslagan snàth
'S mo phoeanan mine.

[2] The natives preserve the true name of the place when they call it " The Lairgs."

basket, but he refused to give it. On coming to the top of a brae near the village, his basket tumbled, and all his dishes ran on edge to the foot of the incline. None were broken but the one which had been refused to the Fairy. It was found in fragments. The same day, however, the hawker found a treasure that made up for his loss. That, said the person from whom the story was heard, was the custom of the Fairies ; they never took anything without making up for it some other way.

On market-days they went about stealing here and there a little of the wool or yarn exposed for sale. A present of shoes and stockings made them give great assistance at out-door work. A man was taken by them to a pump near the Haylee Toll, where he danced all night with them. A headless man was one of the company.

They often came to people's houses at night, and were heard washing their children. If they found no water in the house, they washed them in *kit*, or sowen water. They were fond of spinning and weaving, and, if chid or thwarted, cut the weaver's webs at night. They one night dropped a child's cap, a very pretty article, in a weaver's house, to which they had come to get the child washed. They, however, took it away the following night.

In another instance, a band of four was heard crossing over the bedclothes, two women going first and laughing, and two men following and expressing their wonder if the women were far before them.

A man cut a slip from an ash-tree growing near a Fairy dwelling. On his way home in the evening he stumbled and fell. He heard the Fairies give a laugh at his mishap. Through the night he was hoisted away, and could tell nothing of what happened till in the morning he found himself in the byre, astride on a cow, and holding on by its horns.

These are genuine popular tales of the South of Scotland, which the writer fell in with in Largs. He heard them from a servant girl, a native of the place. They are quoted as illustrations of the vitality of the creed. They are not stories of the Highlands, but are quite analogous. The student of such mythologies will recognize in them a semblance to the Fairy tales of the North of Ireland.

FAIRIES STEALING WOMEN AND CHILDREN.

The *machair* (or links) adjoining the hill of Kenna-varra, the extreme south-west point of Tiree, is after sunset one of the most solitary and weird places conceivable. The hill on its northern side, facing the Skerryvore lighthouse, twelve miles off, consists of precipices, descending sheer down for upwards of a hundred feet, with frightful chasms, where countless sea-birds make their nests, and at the base of which the Atlantic rolls with an incessant noise, which be-

comes deafening in bad weather. The hill juts into
the sea, and the coast, from each side of its inner end,
trends away in beaches, which, like all the beaches in
the island, have, after nightfall, from their whiteness and
loneliness, a strange and ghostly look. On the land-
ward side, the level country stretches in a low dark
line towards the horizon ; little is to be seen and the
stillness is unbroken, save by the sound of the surf
rolling on the beach and thundering in the chasms of
the hill. It is not, therefore, wonderful that these links
should be haunted by the Fairies, or the timid wayfarer
there meet the big black Elfin dog prowling among
the sand-banks, hear its unearthly baying in the stormy
night-wind, and in the uncertain light and the squatter-
ing of wildfowl, hear in wintry pools the Banshi washing
the garments of those soon to die.

Some seventy or eighty years ago the herdsman
who had charge of the cattle on this pasture, went to
a marriage in the neighbouring village of Balephuill
(mud-town), leaving his mother and a young child
alone in the house. The night was wild and stormy ;
there was heavy rain, and every pool and stream was
more than ordinarily swollen. His mother sat waiting
his return, and two women, whom she knew to be
Fairies, came to steal the child. They stood between
the outer and inner doors and were so tall their heads
appeared above the partition beam. One was taller
than the other. They were accompanied by a dog,

and stood one on each side, having a hold of an ear and scratching it. Some say there was a crowd of 'little people' behind to assist in taking the child away. For security the woman placed it between herself and the fire, but her precautions were not quite successful. From that night the child was slightly fatuous, 'a half idiot' (*leth oinseach*). The old woman, it is said, had the second sight.

A shepherd, living with his wife in a bothy far away among the hills of Mull, had an addition to his family. He was obliged to go for assistance to the nearest houses, and his wife asked him, before leaving her and her babe alone, to place the table beside the bed, and a portion of the various kinds of food in the house on it, and also to put the smoothing-iron below the front of the bed and the reaping-hook (*buanaiche*) in the window. Soon after he had left the wife heard a suppressed muttering on the floor and a voice urging some one to go up and steal the child. The other answered that butter from the cow that ate the pearl-wort (*mòthan*) was on the table, that iron was below the bed, and the ' reaper' in the window, how could he get the child away? As the reward of his wife's providence and good sense the shepherd found herself and child safe on his return.

A man in Morvern, known by the nickname of the ' Marquis ' (*a mor'aire*), left a band of women watching his wife and infant child. On returning at night, he

found the fire gone out, and the women fast asleep.
By the time he had rekindled the fire he saw a Banshi
entering and making for the bed where his wife and
child were. He took a faggot from the fire and threw
it at her. A flame gleamed about his eyes and he saw
the Fairy woman no more. His wife declared that she
felt at the time like one in a nightmare (*trom-a-lidhe*);
she heard voices calling upon her to go out, and felt an
irresistible inclination to obey.

A woman from Rahoy (*Ra-thuaith*) on Loch Sunart-
side was taken with her babe to Ben Iadain (*Beinn
Iadain*), a lofty hill in the parish of Morvern, rising to
a height of above 2000 feet, and at one time of great
note as an abode of the Fairies. Her husband had
laid himself down for a few minutes' rest in the front of
the bed, and fallen asleep. When he awoke his wife
and child were gone. They were taken, the woman
afterwards told, to the 'Black Door' (*a chòmhla dhu*),
as the spot forming the Fairy entrance into the interior
of the mountain is called. On entering, they found
a large company of men, women, and children. A fair-
haired boy among them came and warned the woman
not to eat any food the Fairies might offer, but to
hide it in her clothes. He said they had got his own
mother to eat this food, and in consequence he could
not now get her away. Finding the food offered her
was slighted, the head Fairy sent off a party to bring
a certain man's cow. They came back saying they

F

could not touch the cow as its right knee was resting on the plant *bruchorcan* (dirk grass). They were sent for another cow, but they came back saying they could not touch it either, as the dairymaid, after milking it, had struck it with the shackle or cow-spancel (*burach*). That same night the woman appeared to her husband in his dreams, telling him where she was, and that by going for her and taking the black silk handkerchief she wore on her marriage day, with three knots tied upon it, he might recover her. He tied the knots, took the handkerchief and a friend with him, entered the hill at the Black Door, and recovered his wife and child. The white-headed boy accompanied them for some distance from the Black Door, but returned to the hill, and is there still in all probability.

Another wife was taken from the neighbourhood of Castle *Lionnaig*, near Loch Aline (*Loch Àluinn*, the pretty loch), in the same parish, to the same hill. She was placed in the lap of a gigantic hag, who told her it was useless to attempt escaping ; her arms would close round her

> "As the ivy to the rock,
> And as the honeysuckle to the tree ;
> As the flesh round the bone,
> And as the bone round the marrow." [1]

[1] " Mar an eidheann ris a chreig
    'S mar an iadh-shlat ris an fhiodh,
    Mar an fheòil mun chnàimh
    'S mar an cnàimh mun smior."

The woman answered that she wished it was an armful of dirt the Fairy held. In saying so, she made use of a very coarse, unseemly word, and, as no such language is tolerated among the Fairies, the big woman called to take the vile wretch away, and leave her in the hollow in which she had been found, (*an lag san d' fhuaradh i*) which was done.

A man in Balemartin, on the south side of Tiree (*air an leige deas*), whose wife had died in childbed, was sitting one night soon after with a bunch of keys in his hands. He saw his wife passing and repassing him several times. The following night she came to him in his dreams, and reproached him for not having thrown the bunch of keys at her, or between her and the door, to keep the Fairies from taking her back with them. He asked her to come another night, but she said she could not, as the company she was with was removing that night to another brugh far away.

Another, somewhere on the mainland of Argyllshire, suspecting his wife had been stolen by Fairies, hauled her by the legs from bed, through the fire, and out at the door. She there became a log of wood, and serves as the threshold of a barn in the place to this day.

A woman, taken by the Fairies, was seen by a man, who looked in at the door of a brugh, spinning and singing at her work.

A wife, taken in childbed, came to her husband in his sleep, and told him that, by drawing a furrow thrice round a certain hillock sunwise (*deiseal*) with the plough, he might recover her. He consulted his neighbours, and in the end it was deemed as well not to attend to a dream of one's sleep (*bruadar cadail*). He consequently did not draw the furrow, and never recovered his wife.

A child was taken by the Fairies from Killichrenan (*Cill-a-Chreunain*), near Loch Awe, to the shï-en in Nant Wood (*Coill' an Eannd*). It was got back by the father drawing a furrow round the hillock with the plough. He had not gone far when he heard a cry behind him, and on looking back found his child lying in the furrow.

A trampling as of a troop of horses came round a house, in which a woman lay in childbed, and she and the child were taken away. At the end of seven years her sister came upon an open Fairy hillock, and thoughtlessly entered. She saw there her lost sister, with a child in her arms, and was warned by her, in the lullaby song to the child, to slip away out again.

> " Little sister, little loving sister,
> Rememberest thou the night of the horses ?
> Seven years since I was taken,
> And one like me was never seen.
>   Ialai horro, horro,
>   Ialai horro hï." [1]

[1] " A phiuthrag, 's a phiuthrag chaidreach,
 An cuimhne leat oidhche nan capull ?
 Seachd bliadhn' on thugadh as mi,
 'S bean mo choltais riamh cha-n fhacas,
  Ialai horro, horro,
  Ialai horro hì,"

READY WIT REPULSES THE FAIRIES.

A Fairy woman came to take away a child, and said to its mother, "Grey is your child." " Grey is the grass, and it grows," was the ready answer. " Heavy is your child," said the Banshi. " Heavy is each fruitful thing," the mother replied. " Light is your child," said the Banshi. " Light is each happy worldly one," said the mother, bursting into singing and saying—

> " Grey is the foliage, grey the flowers,
> And grey the axe that has a handle,
> And nought comes through the earth,
> But has some greyness in its nature." [1]

On finding herself outwitted the Banshi left.

A boy, a mere child, was left alone for a few minutes, in the islet of Soa, near Tiree. The mother was making kelp there at the time, and in her absence the Fairies came and gave the child's legs such a twist that it was lame (*liùgach*) ever after.

---

[1] " Is glas do leanamh." " Is glas am fiar 's fàsaidh e." " Is trom do leanamh." " Is trom gach torrach." " Is eutrom do leanamh." " Is eutrom gach saoghaltach sona."

> " Is glas an duilleach 's glas am feur,
> 'S glas an tuadh am bheil a chas,
> 'S chaneil ni thig roimh thalamh,
> Nach eil gnè ghlaise na aoraibh.''

The first two lines of this quatrain occur also in a song on the deceit, fulness of women, by a young man, whose first love had forsaken him. She " killed him with a stony stare," and merely asked, " whence comes the sallow stripling?" (*Co ar tha'n corra-ghille glas ?* ")

KINDNESS TO A NEGLECTED CHILD.

The Elves sometimes took care of neglected children. The herd who tendered the Baile-phuill cattle on Heynist Hill sat down one day on a green eminence (*cnoc*) in the hill, which had the reputation of being tenanted by the Fairies. His son, a young child, was along with him. He fell asleep, and when he awoke the child was away. He roused himself, and vowed aloud, that unless his boy was restored he would not leave a stone or clod of the hillock together. A voice from underground answered that the child was safe at home with its mother, and they (the 'people') had taken it lest it should come to harm with the cold.

THE BRIDEGROOM'S BURIAL.

A young woman in Islay was promised in marriage to a rich neighbour, and the marriage day was fixed. She had a sweetheart who, on hearing this, said to a brother older than himself that if he had means to keep a wedding feast he would run away with the bride. His brother promised him all he had, being thirty-five gallons of whisky. On getting this, the young man took the bride away, and gave a nuptial feast himself that lasted a month. At the end of that time, when he was taking a walk with his wife, an eddy wind was seen coming. As it passed the young man was seized with sickness, which in a short time ended in his death.

Before his death his wife said to him, " If the dead have feeling, I ordain that you be not a night absent from your bed." [1]   The night after the funeral he came back, to the consternation of his wife.   He told her not to be alarmed, that he was still sound and healthy (*slàn fallain*), that he had only been taken in the eddy by the Lady of the Green Island (*Baintighearna 'n Eilein Uaiue*), and that by throwing a dirk at the eddy wind, when next she encountered it, she would get him back again.   The wife threw a dirk at the next eddy wind she saw, and her husband dropped at her feet. He told he had been with the light people (*sluagh eutrom*), and in the tomb in which they supposed him buried would be found only a log of alder wood (*maide fearna*).   His wife's relatives were sent for, and they came, thinking the young widow had lost her wits through grief.   The grave was opened, and an alder stick found in the coffin instead of the body proved the husband's account of his disappearance.

THE CROWING OF THE BLACK COCK.

A woman in Islay (the story was heard in Tiree) was taken by the Fairies, leaving an infant who was baptised by the name of Julia (*Sìle*).   To appearance the mother died and was buried.   Every night, however, she came back, and was heard singing to her child.   Her husband watched one night and caught

---

[1] Ma tha tùr aig marbh, nach bi thu oidhche dhìth do leabaidh.

her. She told that by going to a hillock, which she named, on a certain night he might recover her. He went, taking with him, according to her instructions, a black cock born in the busy time of year (*coileach du màrt*)[1] and a piece of steel (*cruaidh*). He found the door of the brugh open, put steel in one of the posts, entered, having the cock in his arms, and hid himself in a corner. Towards morning the cock crew. The head or principal Fairy caused a search to be made, and ' Big Martin without clemency or mercy ' (*Martuinn Mòr gun iochd gun tròcair*) was found in the brugh. On withdrawing the steel he was allowed to go home, and his wife along with him.

THROWING THE ARROW.

A weaver at the Bridge of Awe (*Drochaid Atha*) was left a widower with three or four children. He laboured at his trade all day, and when the evening came, being a hard-working, industrious man, did odd jobs about the house to maintain his helpless family. One clear moonlight, when thatching his house with fern (*ranach*), he heard the rushing sound of a high wind, and a multitude of little people settled on the housetop and on the ground, like a flock of black starlings. He was told he must go along with them to

[1] My informant could not say whether this was seed-time (*màrt cur an t-sìl*) or harvest (*màrt buain*) probably the former (cf. Campbell's *West Highland Tales*, ii., p. 98).

Glen Cannel in Mull, where they were going for a woman. He refused to go unless he got whatever was foraged on the expedition to himself. On arriving at Glen Cannel, the arrow was given him to throw. Pretending to aim at the woman he threw it through the window and killed a pet lamb. The animal at once came out through the window, but he was told this would not do, he must throw again. He did so, and the woman was taken away and a log of alder-wood (*stoc fearna*) was left in her place. The weaver claimed his agreement, and the Fairies left the woman with him at the Bridge of Awe, saying they would never again make the same paction with any man. She lived happily with him and he had three children by her. A beggar came the way and staid with him that night. The whole evening the beggar stared at the wife in a manner that made his host at last ask him what he meant. He said he had at one time been a farmer in Glen Cannel in Mull, comfortable and well-to-do, but his wife having died, he had since fallen into poverty, till he was now a beggar, and that the weaver's wife could be no other than the wife he had lost. Explanations were entered into, and the beggar got his choice of the wife or the children. He chose the former,[1] and again became prosperous in the world.

[1] It may interest the reader that the man (a shrewd enough person in ordinary life) from whom this story was heard, adduced it as proof of the existence of Fairies, of which he said there could be no doubt; he had heard the story from his father, who knew the weaver.

THE WOMAN STOLEN FROM FRANCE.

" MacCallum of the Humming Noise" (*Mac Challum a Chrònain*), who resided in Glen Etive subsequent to the '45, was the last to observe the habits of the Fairies and ancient hunters. He ate three days' allowance of food before setting out on his hunting expeditions, and when he got hungry merely tightened his belt another hole. The Indians of Labrador are said to do the same at the present day. These hunters can go for nine days without food, merely tightening their belts as they get thin. In MacCallum's time, a woman was for seven years observed among the deer of Ben Cruachan, as swift of foot and action as the herd with which she consorted. A gathering was made to catch her. The herd was surrounded by men and dogs, and on her being caught, she was taken to Balinoe, where MacCallum resided. There were rings on her fingers, from which it was ascertained that she came from France. Inquiries were made, and she was sent home by a ship from Greenock. She had been taken away in childbed doubtless by the Fairies. This story was believed by the person from whom it was heard. He had heard it from good authority, he said.

CHANGELINGS.

A young lad was sent for the loan of a corn sieve to a neighbour's house. He was a changeling, and in the house to which he went there was another like himself. He found no one in but his fellow-elf. A woman, in a closet close by, overheard the conversation of the two. The first asked for the sieve, and the other replied, " Ask it in an honest way (that is, in Fairy language) seeing I am alone."[1] The first then said (and his words have as much sense in English as in Gaelic):

> " The muggle maggle
> Wants the loan of the black luggle laggle,
> To take the maggle from the grain."[2]

The words are a ludicrous imitation of the sound made by the fan in winnowing corn, and several versions of them exist.

A child, in Skye, ate such a quantity of food, people suspected it could not be 'canny.' A man of skill was sent for, and on his saying a rhyme over it, the changeling became an old man.

A changeling in Hianish (some say Sanndaig), Tiree, was driven away by a man of skill who came, and, standing in the door, said:

> " Red pig, red pig,
> Red one-eared pig,
> That Fin killed with the son of Luin,
> And took on his back to Druim-derg."[3]

---

[1] Iarr air choìr e, 's gun agam ach mi fhìn.

[2] Dh'iarr a mhugaill a mhagaill
Iased an du-lugaill lagaill
Thoirt a mhagaill as an t-siòl.

[3] " Muc dhearg, muc dhearg,
Muc leth-chluasach dhearg,
Mharbh Fionn le Mac-a-Luin,
'S a thug e air a mhuin gu Druim-dearg.'

Drim-derg, or the Red Ridge, is a common in the neighbourhood of Hianish. Fin's sword, 'the son of Luin,' was of such superior metal that it cut through six feet of whatever substance was struck by it, and an inch beyond. Its peculiar virtue was " never to leave a remnant from its blow." When the changeling heard the bare mention of it, with the aversion of his race to steel, he jumped, like a fish out of the water (*thug e iasg-leum as*), rushed out of the house and was never seen again. The real child was found outside the house.

A woman was told by her neighbours that her child, which was not thriving, was a changeling, and that she ought to throw it in the river. The imp, frightened by the counsel, advised the contrary in an expression, which is now proverbial, " Whether it be fat or lean, every man should rear a calf for himself" (*Air dha bhi reamhar na caol, is mairg nach beathaicheadh laogh dha fhéin*).

TAKING AWAY COWS AND SHEEP.

A farmer had two good cows that were seized one spring with some unaccountable malady. They ate any amount of food given them, but neither grew fat nor yielded milk. They lay on their sides and could not be made to rise. An old man in the neighbourhood advised that they should be hauled up the hill, and rolled down its steepest and longest incline. The brutes, he said, were not the farmer's cows at all, but two old men (*bodaich*) the Fairies had substituted for them. The farmer acted on this advice, and at the bottom of the descent, down which the cows were sent rolling, nothing was found, neither cow nor man, either dead or alive.

There are old people still living in Iona who remember a man driving a nail into a bull that had fallen over a rock, to keep away the Fairies.

A man in Ruaig, Tiree, possessed of the second sight, saw a wether sheep (*molt*) belonging to himself whirled through the sky, and was so satisfied the Fairies had taken it in their eddy wind, that he did not, when the animal was killed, eat any of its mutton.

DWELLINGS.

An old man kept a green hillock, near his house, on which he frequently reclined in summer, very clean, sweeping away any filth or cow or horse droppings he might find on it. One evening, as he sat on the hillock, a little man, a stranger to him, came and thanked him for his care of the hillock, and added, that if at any time the village cattle should leave their enclosure during the night, he and his friends would show their gratitude by keeping them from the old man's crops. The village in these days was in common, ridge about, and the Fairy promise, being tested, was found good.

Of hills having the reputation of being tenanted by Fairies may be mentioned Schiehallion (*Sith-chaillionn*), in Perthshire, and Ben-y-ghloe (*Beinn a Ghlotha*); and in Argyllshire, *Sìthein na Rapaich*, 'the Fairy dwelling of tempestuous weather,' in Morven and Dunniquoich (*Dùn Cuaich*, the Bowl-shaped hill) Dùn-deacainn and Shien-sloy (*sìthein sluaigh*, the multitude's residence), near Inverary. The three latter hills are in sight of each other, and the preference of the Fairies for the last is mentioned in a popular rhyme:

> Dùn-deacainn is Dùn-cuaich
> Sìthein sluaigh is Airde-slios;
> Nam faighinnsa mo roghainn de 'n triùir
> B'e mo rùn a bhi san t-slios.

At the head of Glen-Erochty (*Gleann-Eireochd-aidh*, the Shapely glen), in Athol, in Perthshire, there is a mound known as *Càrn na Sleabhach*, which at one time was of much repute as a Fairy haunt. Alasdair Challum, a poor harmless person, who went about the country making divinations for his entertainers by means of a small four-sided spinning top (*dòduman*), was asked by a widow where her late husband now was. Allistir spun round his teetotum and, examining it attentively, said, "He is a baggage horse to the Fairies in Slevach Cairn, with a twisted willow withe in his mouth." [1]

---

[1] Tha e na each bagais aig na sìthchean an càrn na Sleabhach, agus gad seillich na bhialthaobh.

Alasdair used to say the men of the present day were very small compared to their ancestors, and to prophecy with his teetotum, they

A native of the Island of Coll went to pull some wild-briar plants (*fearra-dhris*). He tried to pull one growing in the face of a rock. The first tug he gave he heard some one calling to him from the inside of the rock, and he ran away without ever looking behind. To this day he says no one need try to persuade him there are no Fairies, for he heard them himself.

A shepherd at Lochaweside, coming home with a wedder sheep on his back, saw an open cave in the face of a rock where he had never noticed a cave before. He laid down his burden, and stepping over to the entrance of the cave, stuck his knife into a fissure of the rock forming a side of the entrance. He then leisurely looked in, and saw the cave full of guns and arms and chests studied with brass nails, but no appearance of tenants. Happening to turn his head for a moment to look at the sheep, and seeing it about to move off, he allowed the knife to move from its place. On looking again at the rock, he only saw water trickling from the fissure from which the knife had been withdrawn.

A person who had a green knoll in front of his house and was in the habit of throwing out dirty water at the door, was told by the Fairies to remove the door to the other side of the house, as the water

would continue growing smaller and smaller, till at last it would take six of them to pull a wisp of hay.

was spoiling their furniture and utensils. He did this, and he and the Fairies lived on good terms ever after.

In the evening a man was tethering his horse on a grassy mound. A head appeared out of the ground, and told him to drive his tether pin somewhere else, as he was letting the rain into their house, and had nearly killed one of the inmates by driving the peg into his ear.

Beinn Feall is one of the most prominent hills in the Island of Coll. It is highly esteemed for the excellence of its pasture, and was of old much frequented by the Fairies. A fisherman going to his occupation at night saw it covered with green silk, spread out to dry, and heard all night the sound of a quern at work in the interior. On another occasion, similar sounds were heard in the same hill, and voices singing:

> "Though good the haven we left,
> Seven times better the haven we found."[1]

A man who avoided tethering horse or cow on a Fairy hillock near his house, or in any way breaking the green sward that covered it, was rewarded by the Fairies driving his horse and cow to the lee of the hillock in stormy nights.

FAIRY ASSISTANCE.

A man in Flodigarry, an islet near Skye, expressed a wish his corn were reaped, though it should be by

[1] "Ged bu mhath an cala dh'fhàg sinn,
Seachd fearr an cala fhuais sinn."

Fairy assistance. The Fairies came and reaped the field in two nights. They were seen at work, seven score and fifteen, or other large number. After reaping the field they called for more work, and the man set them to empty the sea.

One of the chiefs of Dowart was hurried with his harvest, and likely to lose his crop for want of shearers. He sent word through all Mull for assistance. A little old man came and offered himself. He asked as wages only the full of a straw-rope he had with him of corn when the work was over. M'Lean formed no high opinion of the little man, but as the work was urgent and the remuneration trifling, he engaged his services. He placed him along with another old man and an old woman on a ridge by themselves, and told them never to heed though they should be behind the rest, to take matters easy and not fatigue themselves. The little man, however, soon made his assistants leave the way, and set them to make sheaf-bands. He finished shearing that ridge before the rest of the shearers were half-way with theirs, and no fault could be found with the manner in which the work was done. M'Lean would not part with the little reaper till the end of harvest. Fuller payment was offered for his excellent services, but he refused to take more than had been bargained for. He began putting the corn in the rope, and put in all that was in the field, then all that was in the stackyard, and finally all that was in the barn. He

G

said this would do just now, tightened the rope, and lifted the burden on his back. He was setting off with it, when M'Lean, in despair, cried out, "Tuesday I ploughed, Tuesday I sowed, Tuesday I reaped ; Thou who did'st ordain the three Tuesdays, suffer not all that is in the rope to leave me." "The hand of your father and grandfather be upon you!" said the little man, "it is well that you spoke."[1]

Another version of the tale was current in Morvern. A servant, engaged in spring by a man who lived at *Aodienn Mòr* ('Big Face') in Liddesdale, when told to begin ploughing, merely thrust a walking-stick into the ground, and, holding it to his nose, said the earth was not yet ready (*cha robh an talamh air dàir fathast*). This went on till the neighbours were more than half-finished with their spring work. His master then peremptorily ordered the work to be done. By next morning the whole Big Face was ploughed, sown, and harrowed. The shearing of the crop was done in the same mysterious and expeditious manner. The servant had the Association-craft, which secured the assistance of the Fairies. When getting his wages he was like to take away the whole crop, and was got rid of as in the previous version.

An old man in Còrnaig, Tiree, went to sow his croft,

[1] "Màrt a threabh mi, màrt a chuir mi, màrt a bhuain mi; Fhir a dh'òrduich na trì màirt, na leig na bheil san ròp' uamsa." "Làmh t'athar 's do sheanar ort, bha feum agad labhairt."

or piece of land. He was scarce of seed oats, but putting the little he had in a circular dish made of plaited straw, called *plàdar,* suspended from his shoulder by a strap (*iris*), commenced operations. His son followed, harrowing the seed. The old man went on sowing long after the son expected the seed corn was exhausted. He made some remark expressive of his wonder, and the old man said, " Evil befall you, why did you speak ? I might have finished the field if you had held your tongue, but now I cannot go further," and he stopped. The piece sown would properly take four times as much seed as had been used.

A man in the Ross of Mull, about to sow his land, filled a sheet with seed oats, and commenced. He went on sowing, but the sheet remained full. At last a neighbour took notice of the strange phenomenon, and said, " The face of your evil and iniquity be upon you, is the sheet never to be empty ? " When this was said a little brown bird leapt out of the sheet, and the supply of corn ceased. The bird was called *Torc Sona, i.e.* ' Happy Hog,' and when any of the man's descendants fall in with any luck they are asked if the *Torc Sona* still follows the family.

A man in the Braes of Portree, in Skye, with a large but weak family, had his spring and harvest work done by the Fairies. No one could tell how it was done, but somehow it was finished as soon as that of any of

his neighbours.   All his family, however, grew up
' peculiar in their minds.'

THE BATTLE OF TRAI-GRUINARD.

On 5th August, 1598, one of the bloodiest battles
in the annals of clan feuds was fought at the head of
Loch Gruinard, in Islay, between Sir Lachlan Mor
M'Lean, of Dowart, and Sir James Macdonald, of Islay,
for possession of lands forfeited by the latter's uncle,
of which the former had received a grant.   Of the
M'Leans, Sir Lachlan and 80 of his near kinsmen and
200 clansmen were killed ; and of the Macdonalds,
30 were killed, and 60 wounded.[1]   According to
tradition, a trifling looking little man came to Sir
Lachlan, and offered his services for the battle.   The
chief, who was himself of giant frame and strength,
answered contemptuously, he did not care which side
the little man might be on.   The Elf then offered himself to Macdonald, who said he would be glad of the
assistance of a hundred like him.   All day Sir Lachlan,
who was clothed from head to foot in armour of steel,
was followed by the little man, and on his once lifting
the vizor of his helmet an arrow struck him in the forehead at the division of the hair, and came out at the
back of his head.   It proved to be one of those arrows
known as Elf-bolts.   Macdonald was sorry for the
death of his rival, and after the battle made enquiry as

[1] Gregory's *West Highlands and Islands*, p. 285.

to who had killed him. " It was I " said the little man,
" who killed your enemy ; and unless I had done so he
would have killed you." " What is your name ? "
asked Macdonald. "I am called" he said, "*Du-sìth*"
(*i.e.* Black Elf),[1] " and you were better to have me with
you than against you."

DUINE SITH, MAN OF PEACE.

A wright in the island of Mull, on his way home in
the evening from work, got enveloped in a mist.   He
heard some one coming towards him whistling.   He
entered into talk with the stranger, and was told,
a legacy would be left him, and would continue in the
line of his direct descendants to the third generation.
His grandson is unmarried, and well advanced in years;
to the credit of the whistler's prophecy.

Davie, a south country ploughman, or grieve, was
brought to Tiree, about the beginning of the present
century, by the then Chamberlain or ' Baillie ' of the

---

[1] Tradition is pretty uniform that Sir Lachlan was killed by the arrow of
a little man, and the above is probably only a superstitious version of the
real circumstances.   The story of powerful warriors, however, struck in the
forehead by the arrows of little men, like the stories of Tell and the apple,
and Alfred and the cakes, is told of too many persons to be above the
suspicion of being a popular myth.

The natives of one of the villages in Tiree are known by the nickname of
"Clann Du-shith" and "Sìthbheirean."   The assertion that Du-sìth was
the ancient name of Duncan is incorrect, as one of those from whom the
village nickname was derived was called Donnchadh mòr mac Dhu-shìth.
The little man, who killed Lachunn Mor is also known as *an t-ochdarann
bodaich*, the eighth part measure of a carle.

Island.   Ploughing one day on Crossapol farm, he saw
before him in the furrow a very little man.   Not
understanding that the diminutive creature was a Fairy,
Davie cried out in broken Gaelic, " What little man are
you ?   Get out of that."

A former gardener in Tìr Mhine (Meal Land) in
Glenorchy, a good deal given to drinking, was crossing
Loch Awe one night in a boat alone.   He saw a little
man sitting in the stern of the boat, and spoke to him
several times but received no answer.   He at last
struck at the little man, and himself tumbled overboard.
Now, asked the old woman, who told this story, what
could the little man be, but a *brughadair* (*i.e.* one that
came from the Fairy dwelling, an Elf) ?   To the reader
the case will appear one of simple hallucination
produced by ardent spirits, but it is of interest as
shewing the interpretation put upon it under a belief
in the Fairies.

BEAN SHITH, ELLE WOMAN, OR WOMAN OF PEACE.

While supper was being prepared in a farmer's
house in Morvern, a very little woman, a stranger to
the inmates, entered.   She was invited to share the
supper with the family, but would take none of the
food of which the meal consisted, or of any other the
inmates had to offer.   She said her people lived on
the tops of heather, and in the loch called *Lochan
Fasta Litheag.*   There does not seem to be any loch

of the name in Morvern. The name is difficult to translate, but indicates a lakelet covered with weeds or green scum. The little woman left the house as she came, and fear kept every one from following her, or questioning her further.

A woman at Kinloch Teagus (*Ceann Loch Téacais*), in the same parish, was sitting on a summer day in front of the house, preparing green dye, by boiling heather tops and alum together. This preparation is called *ailmeid*. A young woman, whom she had never seen before, came to her, and asked for something to eat. The stranger was dressed in green, and wore a cap bearing the appearance of the king's hood of a sheep (*currachd an righ caorach*). The housewife said the family were at the shielings with the cattle, and there was no food in the house; there was not even a drink of milk. The visitor then asked to be allowed to make brose of the dye, and received permission to do what she liked with it. She was asked where she stayed, and she said, "in this same neighbourhood." She drank off the compost, rushed away, throwing three somersaults, and disappeared.

A young man, named Callum, when crossing the rugged hills of *Ard-meadhonach* (Middle Height), in Mull, fell in with some St. John's wort (*Achlusan Challumchille*), a plant of magic powers, if found when neither sought nor wanted. He took some of it with him. He had *dùcun* (small swellings below the toes) on his feet, and on coming to a stream sat down and bathed them in the water. Looking up, he saw an ugly little woman, having no nostrils, on the other side of the stream, with her feet resting against his own. She asked him for the plant he had in his hand, but he refused to give it. She asked him to make snuff of it then and give her some. He answered, " What could she want with snuff, when she had no nostril to put it in?" He left her and went further on. As he did not come home that night his friends and neighbours next day went in search of him through the hills. He was found by his father asleep on the side of a *cnoc*, a small hillock, and when awakened, he thought, from the position of the sun, he had only slept a few minutes. He had, in fact, slept for twenty-four hours. His dog lay sleeping in the hollow between his two shoulders, and had 'neither hair nor fur' on. It is supposed it had lost the hair in chasing away the Fairies, and protecting its master.

In what seems to be only another version of this story, a herd-boy was sitting in the evening by a stream bathing his feet. A beautiful woman appeared on the other side of the stream, and asked him to pull a plant she pointed out, and make snuff of it for her. He refused, asking what need had she of snuff, when she had no nostrils? She asked him to cross the stream, but he again refused. When he went home his step-mother gave him his food and milk as usual.

He gave the whole of it to his dog, and the dog died from the effects.

A herdsman at Baile-phuill, in the west end of Tiree, fell asleep on *Cnoc Ghrianal,* at the eastern base of Heynish Hill, on a fine summer afternoon. He was awakened by a violent slap on the ear. On rubbing his eyes, and looking up, he saw a woman, the most beautiful he had ever seen, in a green dress, with a brooch fastening it at the neck, walking away from him. She went westward and he followed her for some distance, but she vanished, he could not tell how.

A person in Mull reported that he saw several Fairy women together washing at a stream. He went near enough to see that they had only one nostril each.

The places in Tiree where *cailleacha sìth* (Fairy hags) were seen were at streams and pools of water on *Druim-buidhe* (the Yellow Back), the links of Ken-navara, and the bend of the hill (*lùbadh na beinne*) at Baile-phendrais. They have long since disappeared, the islanders having become too busy to attend to them.

A Skyeman was told by one of these weird women never to put the burning end of a peat outside when making up the fire for the night.

DONALD THRASHED BY THE FAIRY WOMAN.

A man in Mull, watching in the harvest field at night, saw a woman standing in the middle of a stream that ran past the field. He ran after her, and seemed sometimes to be close upon her, and again to be as far from her as ever. Losing temper he swore himself to the devil that he would follow till he caught her. When he said the words the object of his pursuit allowed herself to be overtaken, and showed her true character by giving him a sound thrashing. Every night after he had to meet her. He was like to fall into a decline through fear of her, and becoming thoroughly tired of the affair, he consulted an old woman of the neighbourhood, who advised him to take with him to the place of appointment the ploughshare and his brother John. This would keep the Fairy woman from coming near him. The Fairy, however, said to him in a mumbling voice, "You have taken the plough-share with you to-night, Donald, and big, pock-marked, dirty John your brother," and catching him she administered a severer thrashing than ever. He went again to the old woman, and this time she made for his protection a thread, which he was to wear about his neck. He put it on, and, instead of going to the place of meeting, remained at the fireside. The Fairy came, and, taking him out of the house, gave him a still severer thrashing. Upon this, the wise woman said she would make a chain to protect him against all the powers of darkness, though they came. He put this chain about his neck, and remained by the fireside. He heard a voice calling down the chimney, " I cannot come near you to-night, Donald, when the pretty smooth-white is about your neck."

IONA BANSHI.

A man in Iona, thinking daylight was come, rose and went to a rock to fish. After catching some fish, he observed he had been misled by the clearness of the moonlight, and set off home. On the way, as the night was so fine, he sat down to rest himself on a hillock. He fell asleep, and was awakened by the pulling of the fishing rod, which he had in his hand. He found the rod was being pulled in one direction and the fish in another. He secured both, and was making off, when he heard sounds behind him as of a woman weeping. On his turning round to her, she said, "Ask news, and you will get news." He answered, "I put God between us." When he said this, she caught him and thrashed him soundly. Every night after he was compelled to meet her, and on her repeating the same words and his giving the same answer, was similarly drubbed. To escape from her persecutions he went to the Lowlands. When engaged there cutting drains, he saw a raven on the bank above him. This proved to be his tormentor, and he was compelled to meet her again at night, and, as usual, she thrashed him. He resolved to go to America. On the eve of his departure, his Fairy mistress met him and said, "You are going away to escape from me. If you see a hooded crow when you land, I am that crow." On landing in America he saw a crow sitting on a tree, and knew it to be his old enemy. In the end the Fairy dame killed him.

TIREE BANSHI.

At the time of the American War of Independence, a native of Tiree, similarly afflicted and wishing to escape from his Fairy love, enlisted and was drafted off to the States. On landing he thanked God he was now where the hag could not reach him. Soon after, however, she met him. "You have given thanks," she said, "for getting rid of me, but it is as easy for me to make my appearance here as in your own country." She then told him what fortunes were to befall him, that he would survive the war and return home, and that she would not then trouble him any more. "You will marry there and settle. You will have two daughters, one of whom will marry and settle in Croy-Gortan (*Cruaidh-ghortain*, stone-field), the other will marry and remain in your own house. The one away will ask you to stay with herself, as her sister will not be kind to you. Your death will occur when you are crossing the *Leige*" (a winter stream falling into Loch Vasipol). All this in due course happened.

About four generations ago, a native of Cornaig in Tiree was out shooting on the Reef plain, and returning home in the evening, at the streamlet, which falls into

Balefetrish Bay, near Kennovay, was met by a Fairy dame. He did not at first observe anything in her appearance different from other women, but, on her putting over her head and kissing him, he saw she had but one nostril. On reaching home he was unable to articulate one word. By the advice of an old man he composed, in his mind, a love song to the Fairy. On doing this, his speech came back.

MACPHIE'S BLACK DOG.

[This tale was taken down in Gaelic from the dictation of Donald Cameron, Ruaig, Tiree, in 1863, and is here given in his words as closely as a translation will allow. It is a very good specimen of a class of tales found in the Highlands, and illustrates many remarkable traits of the belief regarding the Fairy women, their enmity to the hunter, their beauty and powers of enchanting men at first, their changing their shape to that of deer, and the aversion dogs have to them ; also the size and character of the Fairy hound.]

Mac-vic-Allan of Arasaig, lord of Moidart, went out hunting in his own forest when young and unmarried. He saw a royal stag before him, as beautiful an animal as he had ever seen. He levelled his gun at it, and it became a woman as beautiful as he had ever seen at all. He lowered his gun, and it became a royal stag as before. Every time he raised the gun to his eye, the figure was that of a woman, and every time he let it down to the ground, it was a royal stag. Upon this he raised the gun to his eye and walked up till he was close to the woman's breast. He then sprang and caught her in his arms. "You will not be separated from me at all," he said, "I will never marry any but you." "Do not do that, Mac-vic-Allan," she said, "you have no business with me, I will not suit you. There will never be a day, while you have me with you, but you will need to kill a cow for me." "You will get that," said the lord of Moidart, "though you should ask two a day."

But Mac-vic-Allan's herd began to grow thin. He tried to send her away, but he could not. He then went to an old man, who lived in the townland, and was his counsellor. He said he would be a broken man, and he did not know what plan to take to get rid of her. The honest old man told him, that unless Macphie of Colonsay could send her away, there was not another living who could. A letter was instantly sent off to Macphie. He answered the letter, and came to Arasaig.

"What business is this you have with me," said Macphie, "Mac-vic-Allan?"

Mac-vic-Allan told him how the woman had come upon him, and how he could not send her away.

"Go you," said Macphie, "and kill a cow for her to-day as usual; send her dinner to the room as usual ; and give me my dinner on the other side of the room."

Mac-vic-Allan did as he was asked. She commenced her dinner, and Macphie commenced his. When Macphie got his dinner past, he looked over at her.

" What is your news, Elle-maid ? " said he.
" What is that to you, Brian Brugh," said she.
" I saw you, Elle-maid," said he,
" When you consorted with the Fingalians,
  When you went with Dermid o Duvne
  And accompanied him from covert to covert."
" I saw you, Brian Brugh," she said,
  When you rode on an old black horse,
  The lover of the slim Fairy woman,
  Ever chasing her from brugh to brugh."

" Dogs and men after the wretch," cried Macphie, " long have I known her."

Every dog and man in Arasaig was called and sent after her. She fled away out to the point of Arasaig, and they did not get a second sight of her.

Upon this Macphie went home to his own Colonsay. One day he was out hunting, and night came on before he got home. He saw a light and made straight for it. He saw a number of men sitting in there, and an old grey-headed man in the midst. The old man spoke and said, " Macphie, come forward." Macphie went forward, and what should come in his way but a bitch, as beautiful an animal as he had ever seen, and a litter of pups with it. He saw one pup in particular, black in colour, and he had never seen a pup so black or so beautiful as it.

" This dog will be my own," said Macphie.

"No," said the man, "you will get your choice of the pups, but you will not get that one."

" I will not take one," said Macphie, " but this one."

" Since you are resolved to have it," said the old man, "it will not do you but one day's service, and it will do that well. Come back on such a night and you will get it."

Macphie reached the place on the night he promised to come. They gave him the dog, " and take care of it well," said the old man, " for it will never do service for you but the one day."

The Black Dog began to turn out so handsome a whelp that no one ever saw a dog so large or so beautiful as it. When Macphie went out hunting he called the Black Dog, and the Black Dog came to the door and then turned back and lay where it was before. The gentlemen who visited at Macphie's house used to tell him to kill the Black Dog, it was not worth its food. Macphie would tell them to let the dog alone, that the Black Dog's day would come yet.

At one time a number of gentlemen came across from Islay to visit Macphie and ask him to go with them to Jura to hunt. At that time Jura was a desert, without anyone staying on it, and without its equal anywhere as hunting ground for deer and roe. There was a place there where those who went for sport used to stay, called the Big Cave. A boat was made ready to cross the sound that same day. Macphie rose to go, and the sixteen young gentlemen along with him. Each of them called the Black Dog, and it reached the door, then turned and lay down where it was before. "Shoot it," cried the young gentlemen. "No," said he, "the Black Dog's day is not come yet." They reached the shore, but the wind rose and they did not get across that day.

Next day they made ready to go ; the Black Dog was called and reached the door, but returned where it was before. "Kill it," said the gentlemen, "and don't be feeding it any longer." "I will not kill it," said Macphie, "the Black Dog's day will come yet." They failed to get across this day also from the violence of the weather and returned. "The dog has foreknowledge," said the gentlemen. "It has foreknowledge," said Macphie, "that its own day will come yet."

On the third day the weather was beautiful. They took their way to the harbour, and did not say a syllable this day to the Black Dog. They launched the boat to go away. One of the gentlemen looked and said the Black Dog was coming, and he never saw a creature like it, because of its fierce look. It sprang, and was the first creature in the boat. "The Black Dog's day is drawing near us," said Macphie.

They took with them meat, and provisions, and

H

bedclothes, and went ashore in Jura. They passed
that night in the Big Cave, and next day went to hunt
the deer. Late in the evening they came home. They
prepared supper. They had a fine fire in the cave
and light. There was a big hole in the very roof
of the cave through which a man could pass. When
they had taken their supper the young gentlemen lay
down, Macphie rose, and stood warming the back of
his legs to the fire. Each of the young men said he
wished his own sweetheart was there that night.
" Well," said Macphie, " I prefer that my wife should
be in her own house ; it is enough for me to be here
myself to-night."

Macphie gave a look from him and saw sixteen
women entering the door of the cave. The light went
out and there was no light except what the fire
gave. The women went over to where the gentlemen
were. Macphie could see nothing from the darkness
that came over the cave. He was not hearing a sound
from the men. The women stood up and one of them
looked at Macphie. She stood opposite to him as
though she were going to attack him. The Black Dog
rose and put on a fierce bristling look and made a
spring at her. The women took to the door, and the
Black Dog followed them to the mouth of the cave.
When they went away the Black Dog returned and
lay at Macphie's feet.

In a little while Macphie heard a horrid noise

overhead in the top of the cave, so that he thought
the cave would fall in about his head. He looked up
and saw a man's hand coming down through the hole,
and making as if to catch himself and take him out
through the hole in the roof of the cave. The Black
Dog gave one spring, and between the shoulder and
the elbow caught the Hand, and lay upon it with all its
might. Now began the play between the Hand and
the Black Dog. Before the Black Dog let go its hold,
it chewed the arm through till it fell on the floor.
The Thing that was on the top of the cave went away,
and Macphie thought the cave would fall in about his
head. The Black Dog rushed out after the Thing that
was outside. This was not the time when Macphie
felt himself most at ease, when the Black Dog left him.
When the day dawned, behold the Black Dog had returned. It lay down at Macphie's feet, and in a few
minutes was dead.

When the light of day appeared Macphie looked,
and he had not a single man alive of those who were
with him in the cave. He took with him the Hand,
and went to the shore to the boat. He went on board
and went home to Colonsay, unaccompanied by dog or
man. He took the Hand up with him that men might
see the horror he had met with, the night he was in
the cave. No man in Islay or Colonsay ever at all saw
such a hand, nor did they imagine that such existed.

There only remained to send a boat to Jura and

take home the bodies that were in the cave. That was the end of the Black Dog's day.

A short tale, similar to the first part of the above legend, is given in Campbell's *Tales of the West Highlands* (ii. 52). A fairy changeling in Gaolin Castle, Kerrera, is detected by a visitor from Ireland as the Fairy sweetheart of a countryman—*Brian Mac Braodh.* On being detected the Elle woman ran into the sea from the point since called *Rutha na Sirich.* The name *Brian Brugh* of the one tale and *Brian Mac Braodh* of the other renders it probable the two tales had originally more in common.

The expression, "The Black Dog's day will come yet" (*Thig latha choindui fhathast*), has passed into a proverb to denote that a time will yet come when one now despised will prove of service. The English proverb, "Every dog has its day," means that everyone has his own time of enjoyment.

The Macphies or MacDuffies were Lairds of Colonsay till the middle of the 17th century. In 1623 the celebrated Colkitto was delated for the murder of umquhill Malcolm Macphie of Colonsay; and one of the race lies buried in Iona, with the inscription on his tomb

HIC JACET MALCOLUMBUS MACDUFFIE DE COLONSAY.

If the same Malcolm is referred to in both cases,

these traces of his fame, slight though they be, create some presumption that he may be the person round whom romance has gathered the incidents of the above tale. In 1615 Malcolm Macphie joined Sir James Macdonald of Dunyveg, in Islay, in the last and unsuccessful attempt made by the once powerful Clandonald of Islay and Cantyre to retain their possessions from the Campbells. He was one of the principal leaders of the rebels and a remarkable man. The family was one of the oldest and most esteemed in the West Highlands.

The following are other versions of the tale in circulation. They are of interest when compared with each other in showing the growth and character of a popular tale.

Macphie of Colonsay was kept captive by a mermaid in a cave by the shore. She supplied him with whatever he needed or desired, but he was not happy, and took advantage of her absence to make his escape. She missed him on her return and went in pursuit. He had with him a large black dog, which he had kept in spite of everyone's remonstrances. When the mermaid overtook him he threw it into the water and it fought the mermaid. The end of the battle was that the dog killed the mermaid and the mermaid killed the dog.

This version is the one which supplied the ground work of Leyden's beautiful ballad " The Mermaid."

Considerable changes must have been made by him upon the legend as it came to his hand. The dog, which in all the versions is the principal character, is left out; Macphie's name is changed to Macphail; a magic ring (a thing unknown in Highland lore) is introduced, etc. Leyden fell in with the version, of which he made use, in his travels in the Highlands in 1801.

Macphie of Colonsay was in an island hunting, and in the course of his ramblings came to a hut, which he entered. He found no one in, and threw himself on a bed for a little rest. He was accompanied by a dog as large as a year old calf. A dark object (*dùthra*) came to the door and the dog attacked it. The Thing made a hideous screaming. When Macphie saw the dog's hair beginning to smoke, he made his escape to the boat that had come with him to the island. Before long the dog came rushing after him, like a mad beast, with a green flame issuing from its jaws. Macphie had prepared himself for this .by loading his double-barrelled gun[1] with two crooked sixpences. He fired the two shots at the dog, as it rushed to attack him, and killed it. The Banshi, it had fought with, was left cruelly mauled, and she crawled or dragged herself to the shore, throwing rocks and stones out of

---

[1] It is often observable in popular tales that articles of modern use are ascribed to those who lived before their invention. Anachronisms are not heeded in popular lore.

her way. Her track is still known as the Carlin's
Furrow (*Sgrìob na Caillich*). The boat left the shore
before she reached it. She tried to bring it back by
throwing a ball of thread after it, but without success.
This was in Islay.

Macphie of Colonsay, when he went hunting, was
met in a particular glen by a man who accompanied
him during the rest of the excursion. His companion
had a brindled bitch (*galla riabhach*), to which Macphie
took a fancy. He asked the man to sell it. " I will
not," said the man, " sell it to you or any one else, but
as you have rested your eye upon it, I will give it to
you for a while. It will have two pups, one like itself
and one black. The brindled one you can keep, but
the black one must be returned along with its mother.
You will meet me at this same spot on such a day."
Macphie took the brindled bitch home, and in due
time the animal had two pups, both very pretty.
When the time came, Macphie went back, according to
promise, to the place appointed, but instead of taking
the black pup, took the brindled one. The man said
to him, " You have not brought the Black Dog ; it
would have been better for you if you had ; but keep
it. It will give you but one night's service ; you
will not gain much by the Black Dog." After this the
Black Dog began to wither ; it grew large and tall but
lank and lean. The servants thrashed and kicked it
about, as if it never was likely to come to any good.

Macphie himself seemed to have an unaccountable regard for it, and was very angry when he saw it abused. Two gentlemen came to see him, with the intention of taking him with them to hunt in some neighbouring islet. On the morning of their intended expedition they rose early, and were getting the guns ready, when the Black Dog rose and whined and fawned upon Macphie. On reaching the boat the Black Dog was the first to spring on board. The night became stormy, and the party were not able to get home that night. They passed the night in a cave. A noise as of walking was heard overhead, and a Hand appeared through the roof as if to grasp one of Macphie's friends. All the dogs fled into the corners of the cave. Macphie himself had a Jew's harp (which is said to be the holiest kind of musical instrument), and when he played fast upon it the Hand drew back; when he played slow the Hand came nearer. At last he was almost exhausted. He called upon the Black Dog, and the Black Dog rose. " My Black Dog," said Macphie, " if you cannot do it now, I am undone." The Dog attacked the Hand, and made it disappear. It then rushed out and gave chase. It came back, spotted and speckled, with its hair stripped off. When the hunters got home on the following night the Dog . disappeared.

Macphie from Colonsay was cast ashore at Ormsaig, in the district of Brolas in Mull, clinging to a log of

wood. He stayed for some time at Ormsaig, and was in
the habit of going to the hill with his gun. A Fairy
woman met him there, and from her he received the
present of a young dog, which she said would yet be of
service to him, but only for one day. He had seventeen foster brothers, and, on his return home, they
came and asked him to go with them to shoot cor-
morants at the Paps of Jura. The Dog, which had by
this time grown very large, and had never before given
any indication of being useful, this day ·eagerly accompanied the hunters. Macphie's wife had often urged
him to kill the dog, but he had insisted on keeping it.
When Jura was reached, a servant was left in charge of
the boats, and the company passed the night in a cave.
As they reclined round the cave, each expressed a
wish, that his sweetheart were there. Macphie, who
was standing by the fire, said he had no such wish, it
was better for his mistress to be at home. Before
long, seventeen women in green dresses entered the
cave, and went over to the beds of heather where
Macphie's foster brothers were, and Macphie heard the
crackling sound of breaking bones. The seventeen
women then came up, as if to attack himself. Afraid
of their number, he called to the Black Dog, "if
you assist me not now, I am a lost man." The dog
attacked the women, drove them out of the cave, and
went off in pursuit. Macphie fled to the boat, and
he and the servant left in charge quitted the shore

with all haste. When they were well out to sea, the
servant said there was a fiery star coming after them.
Macphie said it was the Black Dog, and its heart had
taken fire. He made ready, and when the dog overtook them, cut off its head.

THE CARLIN OF THE SPOTTED HILL (*Cailleach Beinne Bhric*).

The Fairy wife, who owned the deer of Ben Breck,
is well known in the Highlands.

It is told of her that on one occasion, as she milked
a hind, the animal became restive and gave her a kick.
In return she struck the hind with her open palm and
expressed a wish that the arrow of Donald, the son of
John (a noted hunter in his day), might come upon it.
That very day the restive hind fell to Dò'il MacJain's
arrow.[1]

It is also told of this Elfin wife that while three
hunters were passing the night in a bothy on Ben
Breck, the Carlin wife came to the door and sought
admittance. A dog that accompanied the hunters

---

[1] This *Dò'il MacJain* is probably the *Dò'il du beag Innse-ruithe*, a
celebrated bowman and follower of Cameron of Locheil, and, as his name
denotes, a person of small stature, who, according to tradition, shot the
arrow that nailed the hand of Big Angus Macian (Aonghas Mòr Mac'ic
Eòin) of Ardnamurchan, one of the most stalwart men of his day, to his
forehead, in Coir Ospuinn, in Morvern, circ. A.D. 1596. Others say *Jain
du beag* (little black John) was the hunter whose arrow struck the hind.
Another (perhaps the same) celebrated Lochaber archer was *Jain beag a
bhuilg bhàin* (little John of the white bag) from Coiruanain.

sprang up to attack her. She retreated and asked one of the men to tie up his dog. He refused. She asked him again, and a second time he refused. She asked a third time, and he replied he had nothing to tie it with. She pulled a hair out of her head and told him to tie his dog with that, it was strong enough to hold a four-masted ship at anchor. He pretended to consent, and the hag, on trying again to enter, found the dog was not secured. She then went away, saying it was well for the hunter the dog had not been tied, and threatening to come again. It does not appear, however, that she ever came back.

She was last seen about twenty years ago in Lochaber. Age had told severely upon her. Instead of being ' broad and tall,' she had become no bigger than a teapot! She wore a little grey plaid or shawl about her shoulders.

DONALD, SON OF PATRICK.

Donald, the son of Patrick (*Dòmhnull Mac Phàruig*), or, as others say, the son of Lachlan, was a *brocair*, that is, a foxhunter or destroyer of ground vermin, in Lorn. Persons following this profession were employed by the hill farmers, and had generally long tracts of country to travel over. Their companions were their gun, a pack of terriers, and perhaps a wiry deer-hound. With these they led as lonely a life as anyone who had at all to descend to the strath and men's houses could do. Many a lonely night they watched by the fox's cairn in some remote corrie for an opportunity ' to put a hole in the red rogue's hide,' and they often passed the night in bothies and shielings far from the haunts of men. One day Donald, the son of Patrick, killed a roe, and took it to a bothy in the hills. He kindled a fire with the flint of his gun, and having cut up the roe, roasted pieces of the flesh by a large fire. As he helped himself, he threw now and then a piece to his dogs. Before long he observed, the night being moon-lit, a large dark shadow coming about the door, and then a woman snatching at the pieces of flesh he threw to the dogs. She had one tooth as big as a distaff projecting from her upper gum. The dogs prevented her entering the hut, so that she got but little of the food. She asked Donald to leash up his dogs, and on his refusing, cried out, " This is poor hospitality for the night, Donald, son of Patrick." Donald answered, " It will be no better and no worse than that." " You proved expert at raising a fire," she said. " How do you know ? " he asked. " I was," she said, " on the top of the Cruach of Rannoch (a hill far away) the first click you gave to the flint, and this is poor hospitality for the night, Donald, son of Patrick." " It will," he said, " be no better and no worse than that." In a while again she said, " This is poor hospitality for the night, Donald, son of Patrick." " Take," he said, " as you are able to win." She remained all night, and repeatedly asked him to leash up his dogs, which he refused to do. The dogs kept her at bay till she left.

Another version says that the foxhunter's name was *Iain Mac Phàruig*, that he was accompanied by sixteen dogs, that his strange visitant disappeared at the cock-crowing, and that she then told she was 'the wife of Fe-chiarain' (*Cailleach Fe-chiarain*). Some identify her with the Carlin of Ben Breck.

THE WIFE OF BEN-Y-GHLOE.

Donald and Big John (*Dòmhnull 's Iain mòr*) were out deer-hunting on the lofty mountain of Ben-y-ghloe, in Athol in Perthshire, when a heavy snowstorm came on, and they lost their way. They came to a hut in a hollow and entered. The only one in was an old woman, the like of whom they said they had never seen. Her two arms were bare, of great length, and grizzled and sallow to look at. She neither asked them to come in nor go out, and being much in need of shelter, they went in and sat at the fire. There was a look in her eye that might 'terrify a coward,' and she hummed a surly song, the words of which were unintelligible to them. They asked for meat, and she set before them a fresh salmon trout, saying, "Little you thought I would give you your dinner to-day." She also said she could do more, that it was she who clothed the hill with mist to make them come to her house. They stayed with her all night. She was very kind and hospitable. She told her name to them when leaving, that she was 'the wife of Ben-y-Ghloe.' They could not say whether she was *sìth* or *saoghalta* (Elfin or human), but they never visited her again.

FAIRY WOMEN AND DEER.

On the lands of Scalasdal in Mull, a deer was killed, which turned out afterwards to be a woman.

It is perhaps this belief in the metamorphosis of Fairy women and deer that was the origin of the tradition that Oisian's mother was a deer. In Skye it is said that after the poet's birth his mother could touch him but once with her tongue on the temple. On that corner (*air an Oisinn sin*) a tuft of fur like that of a deer grew, hence the poet's name. An informant in the centre of Argyllshire said he did not hear Oisian's mother was a deer, but he had heard the poet was nurtured by a deer. In the Northern Hebrides, a song is sometimes heard which Oisian is said to have composed to the deer.[1]

---

[1] Several versions of the song will be found in Campbell's *Leabhar na Feinne*, p. 198. According to the Skye tradition, the secret of Oisian's birth was not known till notice was taken of his never eating venison like the rest of the host. On being questioned, he said, "When everyone picks his mother's shank bone, I will pick my own mother's slender shank bone."

O'CRONICERT'S FAIRY WIFE.[1]

There was a man in Ireland, whose name was
O'Cronicert, and his dwelling place was Corr-water,
and he spent all he had on the great nobles of Ireland,
bringing them for days' entertainment and for nights'
entertainment, till he had nothing left but an old
tumble-down black house, and an old wife, and an old
lame white horse.   The thought that came into his
head was, to go to the King of Ireland for assistance,
to see what he would give.   He cut a cudgel of grey
oak in the outskirt of the wood, and sat on the back
of the old lame white horse, and set off at speed
through wood, and through moss, and through rugged
ground, till he reached the King's house.   The custom
was, that a man should be a year and a day in the
King's house before being asked the object of his
journey.   After being there a year and a day, the
King said, " O'Cronicert, it is not without a cause for
your journey you have come here."   " It is not," said
O'Cronicert, " it is for assistance I have come here.
You know it was for yourself and your great nobles I
spent my property entirely."   " You will wait," said
the King, " till I bring in the children " ; and they
were there as men called them Murdoch Mac Brian, and
Duncan Mac Brian, and Torgill Mac Brian, and Brian

---

[1] This version was originally taken down in Gaelic from the recitation of
Malcolm Sinclair, Balefuill, Tiree.   The tale was known in Ireland, and
the reputation of it still survives very extensively throughout the Highlands.

Borr Mac Cimi, and his sixteen foster brothers with every one of them.

" I will give," said Murdoch Mac Brian, " a hundred milch cows to him."

" I will give," said Duncan Mac Brian, " a hundred farrow cows to him, in case they should be in calf all in one year."

"I will give him," said Torgill Mac Brian, "a hundred brood mares."

" I will give him," said Brian Borr Mac Cimi, " a hundred sheep."

After O'Cronicert got this, he was not going away. The King told him to go away, that it was difficult to keep his herd separate from the King's own, and to take it away. He said to the King that he had one thing in view, and if he got it from the King, he would prefer it to all he had already got.

" It is certain," said the King, " it must be some bad thing or other ; you had better tell it, that I may let you away."

" It is," he said, " the lap-dog, that is out and in after the Queen, that I wish for " ; and the King gave him permission to take it with him.

He took the lap-dog, leapt on the back of the old lame white horse, and went off at speed, without one look at the herd, through wood, and through moss, and through rugged ground. After he had gone some distance through the wood, a roe-buck leapt out of the wood, and the lap-dog went after it, and in an instant they were out of sight.

Close upon the evening, he saw the lap-dog coming, and a royal stag before it, and the deer started up as a woman behind O'Cronicert, the handsomest that eye had ever seen from the beginning of the universe till the end of eternity. O'Cronicert caught her, and she asked him to let her go, and he said there would be no separation in life between them.

" Well," said she, " before I go with you, you must come under three conditions to me " ; and he promised to come under the conditions.

" The first condition is, that you will not go to ask the King of Ireland or his great nobles for a day's or a night's entertainment without telling me. The next condition is, that you will not go to a change-house without putting it in my option ; and the third thing, that you will never cast up to me that you found me an unwise animal (*beathach mi-chéillidh*) in the wood."

They reached the old tumble-down black house, and the wife he had left there was a faggot-bundle of bones in a pool of rain-drip in the middle of the floor. They cut grass in clefts and ledges of the rocks, and made a bed, and laid down.

O'Cronicert's wakening from sleep was the lowing of cattle, and the bleating of sheep, and the neighing of mares, while he himself was in a bed of gold on wheels of silver, going from end to end of the Tower of Castle

Town, the finest eye had ever seen from the beginning
of the universe till the end of eternity.

" It is no wonder," he said, " the like of this should
happen to me, when I found you an unwise animal in
the wood."

" As well as you broke that condition you will break
the rest ; rise, and drive the cattle away to pasture."

When he went out, there was no number to the
multitude of his flock, and on a day of the days after
that, while looking at the flock, he thought he would
go to ask the King of Ireland for a day and night's
entertainment. He sat on the back of the old lame
white horse, and went through wood, and moss, and
rugged ground, till he reached the King's house.

The King said to him, " Do you at all intend,
O'Cronicert, to take your flock with you ? They are
to-day so numerous that the herdsmen do not know
them from my own."

" No, I have no need of them. I have a larger stock
than yourself, and what has brought me is to ask yourself and nobles for a day and night's entertainment."

The King said to him, " We are ready, my good
fellow, to go " ; and there were there, as men called
them, Murdoch Mac Brian, and Duncan Mac Brian, and
Torgill Mac Brian, and Brian Borr Mac Cimi, and his
sixteen foster-brothers with every one of them. It
was when they were near the house O'Cronicert
remembered he had left without telling her. He told

them to make their way slowly, and he himself would go before to tell they were coming.

"You did not need, I knew very well that you went; let them come on, everything is ready."

When the King thought he had been seven days and seven nights drinking there, he said to Murdoch, his son, that it was time for them to be going. She then said to the King that it was high time for him— "You have been seven days and seven years in this place."

"If I am," said he, "I need not go back; there is not a man or living creature awaiting me."

Murdoch had a foster-brother, whose name was Keyn, the son of Loy (*Kian Mac an Luaimh*), and he fell in love with O'Cronicert's wife. He pretended to be ill and remained behind the rest. She made a drink for him and went with it to him, but instead of taking the drink he laid hold of herself. She suddenly became a filly, and gave him a kick and broke his leg. She took with her the tower of Castle Town as an armful on her shoulder and a light burden on her back, and left him in the old tumble-down black house, in a pool of rain-drip, in the middle of the floor.

In the parting O'Cronicert went to the change-house to bid the party good-bye, and it was then Murdoch Mac Brian remembered he had left his own foster-brother, Keyn, the son of Loy, behind, and said there would be no separation in life between them, and he

would go back for him. He found Keyn in the old
tumble-down black house, in the middle of the floor,
in a pool of rain-water, with his leg broken; and he
said the earth would make a nest in his sole, and the
sky a nest in his head, if he did not find a man who
would cure Keyn's leg.

The rest of the tale consists principally of *true* tales,
necessary to be told, before Keyn will consent to
stretch his leg for a salve to be applied to it.   The
King of Lochlin, or, according to others, the King of
Ireland, who is bound not to allow any one to remain
in distress, when he can relieve, tells a series of marvellous adventures that befell himself, all jointing into one
another, before Keyn stretches his foot.   The composition is of a kindred character with the *Arabian
Nights' Entertainment.*

The reader will observe that in this tale, as in that
of " Macphie's Black Dog," the Fairy wife is first encountered in the shape of a deer, that (as is alleged of
her race in other tales) she dislikes being reproached
with not being of mortal race, and calls up in one
night a palace of enchanting magnificence, in which
time passes unobserved, and in the end disappears,
leaving matters worse than at the beginning.

THE GRUAGACH BAN.

In Campbell's *West Highland Tales* (ii. 410) will be
found a tale also highly illustrative of this part of the

superstition. The hero of the tale, the Fair Long-haired One, son of the King of Ireland, encounters a woman with a narrow green kirtle (the Fairy dress), and after playing cards with her, is placed under the following spell :—" I place thee under enchantments and crosses, under the nine shackles of the roaming, wandering Fairy dame, that the most stunted and weakliest little calf take off your head, and your ears, and your livelihood, if you rest night or day, where you take your breakfast, that you will not take your dinner, and where you take your dinner, you will not take your supper, till you find out the place I am in, under the four red divisions of the world." [1]

There is also in the tale an Elfin old woman, the Carlin of the Red Stream, who is of the same class with the old wife of Ben Breck. She has a wonderful deer, which she can restore to life if she can get any of its flesh as juice to taste, and her yells split the iron hoops the prudent Fin had put round his men's heads in anticipation of her outcries.

DEER KILLED AT NIGHT.

Big Hugh, of Ardchyle (*Eòghan mòr àird-a-chaoil*), in the east of the island of Mull, a noted deer-hunter

---

[1] This rendering of the popular incantation differs somewhat from that given by Mr. Campbell himself. The Gaelic version is the best the writer has been able to fall in with. Var. *An laogh maol carrach is miosa na ainm*, " the polled-scabbed calf, that is worse than its name, take off your head," etc.

in his day, killed a deer at Torness (*Torr-an-Eas*, the eminence by the ravine), some seven miles away in Glenmore, and conveyed it home at night. He was accompanied by a man of the name of Sinclair. Sinclair asked him if the deer was heavy, and Big Hugh said he felt as if he had a house on his back. Sinclair then stuck his pen-knife in the deer, and asked again if the burden felt heavy. Big Hugh said it was now so light he could hardly believe he had a burden on his back at all. The weight had been laid on by the Fairies.

FAIRIES AND GOATS.

In Breadalbane and the Highlands of Perthshire it is said the Fairies live on goat's milk. A goat was taken home by a man in Strathfillan, in Perthshire, to be killed. In the evening a stranger, dressed in green, came to the door. He was asked to enter and rest himself. He said he could not, as he was in a hurry, and on his way to Dunbuck (a celebrated Fairy haunt near Dunbarton), an urgent message having come for him. He said that many a day that goat had kept him in milk. He then disappeared. He could be nothing but a Fairy.

FAIRIES AND COWS.

A strong-minded headstrong woman in Kianish, Tiree, had a cow, the milk of which strangely failed.

Suspecting that the cow was being milked by someone during the night, she sat up and watched. She saw a woman dressed in green coming noiselessly and milking the cow. She came behind and caught her. In explanation the Fairy woman said she had a child lying in the smallpox, and as a favour asked to be allowed to milk the cow for one month, till the child got better. This was allowed, and when the month was out, the cow's milk became as plentiful as ever.

That the Fairies took away cows at night in order to milk them, and sent them back in the morning, was a belief in Craignish, Morvern, Tiree, Lochaber, and probably in the whole Highlands. When milk lost its virtue, and yielded neither cream, nor butter, nor cheese, the work was that of witches and such like diabolical agencies. When the mischief was done by the Fairies the whole milk disappeared.

FAIRY COWS.

A strong man named Dugald Campbell was one night, about the end of last century, watching the cattle on the farm of Baile-phuill, in the west of Tiree. A little red cow came among the herd and was attacked by the other cows. It fled and they followed. Dugald also set off in pursuit. Sometimes the little red cow seemed near, sometimes far away. At last it entered the face of a rock, and one of the other cows followed and was never again seen. The whole herd would have followed had not Dugald intercepted them.

A poor person's cow, in Skye, was by some act of oppression taken from him. That night the Fairies brought him another cow, remarkable only in having green water weeds upon it. This cow throve.

Some four generations ago cows came ashore on Nisibost beach, on the farm of Loscantire (*Losg-an-tìr*), in Harris. The people got between them and the shore, with such weapons as they could get, and kept them from returning to the sea again. Even handfuls of sand thrown between the cows and the shore kept them back. These sea-cows were in all respects like ordinary highland cattle but were supposed to live under the sea on the sea-weed called *meillich*. They were called Fairy cows (*Cro sìth*), and the superiority of the Loscantire cattle was said to have originated from them. It is more probable the superiority of the stock was the origin of the Fairy cattle.

Cows of the same kind were also said to have come ashore in Bernera, in Uist, and at MacNicol's Big Rock (*Creag mhòr mhic Neacail*), on the farm of Scorrybreck, in Skye. In the latter place they were kept from returning by tossing earth between them and the sea. Earth from a burying-ground was thought to be the most effective in such cases. On the evening of the day on which the cows came ashore a voice was heard from the sea calling them

by name. From the rhyme in which this was done
we learn the cows were of different colours, one black,
another brown, brindled, red, white-faced, etc. :

> Sisgein, Brisgein,
> Meangan, Meodhran,
> Bo dhu, bo dhonn
> Bo chrom riabhach
> Sliochd na h-aona bhà maoile ruaidhe,
> Nach d' fhàg buaile riasnh na h-aonar ;
> Bo chionnan Thonn,
> È bhlàrag.

THE THIRSTY PLOUGHMAN.

A ploughman while engaged at his work heard, or
fancied he heard, a sound of churning, and said he
wished his thirst "was on the dairymaid." In a short
time after a woman appeared and offered him a drink
of buttermilk. Her green dress and sudden appearance made him refuse the offer, and she said that
next year he would not need the drink. When the
twelve months were nearly out the man died.[1]

THE FAIRY CHURNING.

A woman, near Portree, in Skye, was coming home
in the evening with her milk pails from the cattle
fold, accompanied by a dog, which went trotting along

---

[1] This version of the story is from Skye. A version from Uist is given
in Campbell's *Tales of the West Highlands*, ii. 68. It varies merely in
representing the thirsty man as a traveller, who, in consequence of refusing
from the Fairy the drink for which he had wished, was drowned at the
next ferry.

before her. Suddenly the dog was observed to run to a green hillock, fall down on its knees, and hold its ear to the ground. The woman went up to see what the matter was, and on listening heard a woman inside the hillock churning milk, and singing at her work. At the end of every verse there was a chorus or exclamation of *hŭ.* The song was learnt by the listener, and became known as the " Song of the Hillock " (*Òran a chnuic*). The writer has not been able to fall in with a copy of it. The incident occurred three generations ago.

MILK SPILT.

There was a Fairy hillock near Dowart, in Mull, close to the road which led from the cattle fold to the village. If any milk was spilt by the dairymaids on their way home with the milk pails, it was a common saying that the Fairies would get its benefit.

FAIRY MUSIC.

Two children, a brother and sister, went on a moonlight winter's night to Kennavarra Hill, to look after a snare they had set for little birds in a hollow near a stream. The ground was covered with snow, and when the two had descended into the hollow, they heard most beautiful music coming from under ground, close to where they were standing. In the extremity of terror both fled. The boy went fastest, and never looked

behind him. The girl was at first encumbered by her
father's big shoes, which she had put on for the occasion, but, throwing them off, she reached home with a
panting heart, not long after her brother. The story
was told by her when an old woman. She had never
forgot the fright the Fairy music gave her in childhood.

In the Braes of Portree there is a hillock called
"The Fairy Dwelling of the Pretty Hill" (*Sìthein
Beinne Bòidhich*). A man passing near it in the evening heard from underground the most delightful music
ever heard. He could not, however, tell the exact spot
from which the sound emanated.

Sounds of exquisite music, as if played by a piper
marching at the head of a procession, used to be heard
going underground from the Harp Hillock to the top
of the Dùn of Caolis, in the east end of Tiree. Many
tunes, of little poetical, whatever be their musical merit,
said to have been learned from the Fairies, are to be
heard. One of these, which the writer heard, seemed
to consist entirely of variations upon the word
' do-leedl'em.'

MACCRIMMON.

The MacCrimmons were pipers to Macleod, of
Macleod, and the most celebrated musicians among the
Scottish Gaël. The founder of the family is said to have
been an Italian harper from Cremona, who came with

Macleod to Dunvegan, and took the surname from his native town.   There are several versions of the story, which ascribes the excellence of the MacCrimmons in music to the Fairies.   The following two will suffice.

The first of the MacCrimmons, when a young lad, was sent to a music master to learn bagpipe playing. There was to be a competition of pipers at a wedding in the neighbourhood, and MacCrimmon asked from his master permission to attend, but was refused.   He resolved to go notwithstanding, and set off alone, taking a short cut across the hills.   On the way he fell in with a Fairy dwelling, which he entered.   He found no person in but an old woman, who spoke kindly to him, saying she knew the object of his journey, and, on his promising to go half loss and gain with her, gave him a black chanter, which, placed in his pipes, would enable him to excel his master, and every other performer. She added that she and her people were about to remove from their present dwelling, but, if he came on a certain night (naming one near at hand), they would have time to give him some lessons.   To this one night's instruction, and the magic chanter, which remained in the family as an heirloom, the MacCrimmons were indebted for their acknowledged superiority as pipers.   Their fame will last " while wind is blown into sheepskin."

'The Blind Piper' (*am Piobaire dall*) was the first of the MacCrimmons who acquired fame as a piper.

Two Banshis found him sleeping in the open air, and one of them blinded one of his eyes. The second Banshi asked that the other eye might be spared. It, however, was blinded also. The benevolent Fairy then suggested that some gift should be given that would enable the poor man to earn his living. On this the Fairy Carlin gave MacCrimmon a brindled chanter, which, placed in the bagpipes, enabled the player to outrival all pipers. When the Laird of Dungallon obtained the brindled chanter for his own piper Macintyre, the MacCrimmons never did well after. The chanter was last known to be at Callart.

Mac-an-sgialaiche, pipers at Taymouth Castle, were also said to have got their pipes from the Fairies.

FAIRY DOGS ('CU SITH').

A large black dog, passing by with a noiseless and gliding motion, was a common object of terror in the Hebrides on winter nights. The coil in the animal's tail was alone sufficiently alarming. Much of its shape depended, no doubt, on how his own hair hung over the eyes of the frightened spectator.

A man, coming across the links near Kennavara Hill in Tiree, came upon a large black dog, resting on the side of a sandbank. On observing it, he turned aside, and took another road home. Next day he recovered courage, and went to examine the spot. He found on the sand the marks of a dog's paw, as large

as the spread of his palm. He followed these huge
footmarks till he lost them on the plain. The dog had
taken no notice of him, and he felt assured, from its
size, it could be no earthly hound.

On the north shore of Tiree there is a beach of more
than a mile in length, called *Cladach a Chrògain*, well
calculated to be the scene of strange terrors. The
extensive plain (about 1500 acres in extent), of which
it forms the northern fringe, is almost a dead level, and
in instances of very high flood-tides, with north-west
gales of wind, the sea has been known to¹ overflow it,
and join the sea on the south side, three miles away,
dividing Tiree into two islands. The upper part of the
beach consists of loose round stones, a little larger than
a goose's egg, which make, when the tide is in, and
under the influence of the restless surf, a hoarse
rumbling sound, sufficiently calculated, with the ac-
companiment of strange scenery, to awaken the
imagination. An old woman, half-a-century ago,
asserted that, when a young girl, she had heard on
this beach the bark of the Fairy hound. Her father's
house was at a place called Fidden, of which no trace
now remains beyond the name of the Fidden Gate
(*Cachla nam Fidean*), given to a spot where there is no
gate. It was after night-fall, and she was playing out
about the doors, when she was suddenly startled by a
loud sound, like the baying of a dog, only much louder,
from the other end of the shore. She remembered her

father having come and taken hold of her hand, and
running with her to the house, for if the dog was heard
to bark thrice, it would overtake them. It made a
noise like a horse galloping.

At the foot of Heynish Hill, in the extreme south-
west of Tiree, there is one of those small forts to be
found in great numbers in the Hebrides (and said to
have been intended, by fires lighted upon them, to give
warning of the approach of the Danes), called Shiadar
Fort. In former days a family resided, or was out at
the summer shielings, near this fort. The byre, in
which the milch cows were kept, was some distance
from the dwelling-house, and two boys of the family
slept there to take care of the cows. One night a
voice came to the mother of the family that the two
best calves in the byre were at the point of death, and
as a proof of the warning, she would find the big
yellow cow dead at the end of the house. This proved
to be the case, and on reaching the byre the anxious
woman found her two boys nearly frightened to death.
They said they heard Fairy dogs trampling and baying
on the top of the house.

There is a natural recess in the rocks of the shore at
Baluaig in Tiree, to which tradition has given the name
of the Bed of the Fairy Dog. It is not far from
Crogan beach, already mentioned as a place where the
Fairy dog was heard, and opposite the *Gràdor*, a low-
water rock over which the sea breaks with terrible

violence in stormy weather. The loneliness and wildness of the spot might well cause it to be associated with tales of superstition.

A shepherd in Lorn came to the top of a rock, and in a nest or lair below him he saw two pups about two months old with green backs and sides. They were larger and longer than his own dogs. He got afraid and fled before the old hound made her appearance. His dogs also were afraid. So the tradition says.

DOGS CHASING FAIRIES.

Two men from Mull were engaged building a march dyke across the hills in Kintail. To be near their work, they took up their residence by themselves in a hut among the hills. One night, before retiring to rest, they heard a horrible screaming coming in the direction of the hut. They went out with sticks of firewood in their hands. Though they could see nothing, they knew something was approaching. The shrieks came nearer and nearer, and at last a large dark object passed. A little dog, 'Dun-foot' by name, which accompanied the men, gave chase. When it returned there was no hair on any part of it but on its ears, and no hair ever grew after but a sort of down.

A number of young men were out at night on the moorlands of Cornaigbeg farm in Tiree watching the cattle, to keep them from wandering into the crop lands. They went to the moss about a mile away for peats, which at the time (some sixty years ago) were plentiful in Tiree, but becoming in some way alarmed they turned back on the road. When returning they heard strange noises coming towards them, and a dog that accompanied them began to course round and round between them and the noise. At last the noise passed, with sounds like the trampling of a herd of sheep, and the dog went off in pursuit. On its return its hair was found scraped off, as if by long sharp nails, and the whole skin was left bare and white, except where here and there it was torn and bloody. It died in a short time after.

A man in Mull was sent on a journey after nightfall, and about midnight, when crossing the hills from Loch Tuath (the North Loch) and Loch Cuän (*Loch Cumhan*, the narrow loch), saw a light in the face of a hillock. He was accompanied by his dog, and before long he heard the noise of dogs fighting, mixed with sounds of lovely music. He made off as fast as he could, and, on arriving at the house to which he had been sent, was offered supper. He was unable to take any. Before bed-time his dog came with every hair on its body pulled off. It smelt its master's clothes all over, lay down at his feet, and was dead in a few minutes.

A gentleman of the name of Evan Cameron (it does not appear where) on his way home across the hills was overtaken by nightfall and lost his way. He was accompanied by a greyhound and three terriers. He

K

saw a light in a bothy or hut, used in summer, when the cattle were at pasture among the hills, but deserted during the greater part of the year. He made towards it, and on looking in at the door, saw a woman sitting by the fire, all wet, and combing her hair. She looked towards him, and said, " Will you not come after your eye, Evan ? " (*Nach d'thig thu 'n déigh do shùil, Eoghain*). " Not just now " (*Cha d'thig an dràsd*), he replied. After some further conversation he was obliged to allow his dogs to attack the strange creature. He himself held on his way, and in a few hours reached home. The greyhound found its way home, but without any hair upon its body. None of the terriers was ever heard of more.[1]

FAIRIES AND HORSES.

At Ruig, at the foot of the Storr Rock, in Skye, at the time it was occupied by small farmers (sixteen in number), all the horses on the farm, numbering as many as a hundred, were seen ridden by the Fairies, sitting with their faces to the tail, on Hallowmas night. The shore line of the farm consists of frightful precipices, and the horses, as if very madness (*an cuthach dearg*) had taken possession of them, went off at their utmost speed towards the shore. Every one thought

---

[1] This creature, haunting the pastures of the cattle, partakes more strongly of the character of the *Glaistig*, afterwards to be described, than of the Fairy women.

they would be lost, but no harm arose after all from the stampede.

Near Killin in Perthshire, a man entered a Fairy Knowe, and found inside a woman making porridge. The dish boiled so fiercely that a spark from the porridge flew and struck him in the eye. He saw the Fairies ever after with that eye. At the St. Fillan market (*Feill Fhaolain*) at Killin, he saw them in great numbers riding about the market on white horses. Meeting one, whom he recognized, he remarked, " What a number of you are here to-day." The Fairy asked which eye he saw ' the folk ' with, and on being told put it out.

A young wife had not, as was customary at that time, learned to spin and weave. She tried in every way to learn, but try as she might she made no progress, till one noon-day she wished some one would come to help her. She then saw a woman standing in the door, who said she would help her on condition that she would give her her first child when born, but if she could tell the *shi* woman's name when she came to take away the child she would be free from her promise. The young woman rashly agreed to this, and in a short time could make *clò* (cloth) better than any one around her. After some time, however, she began to be afraid her visitor would return, and she went about eagerly listening to hear

the name, when suddenly one day she saw an opening in a grassy hillock beside her, and on looking in
saw the same woman standing inside, and heard
another one calling to her.   She went home joyously
repeating the name all the way, and told her husband how she heard it.   When the *Bean shi* came
again, the mother of the child called out to her by
the name she had heard, and invited her to come in,
but she only said, " A blessing on the name, but
banning on the mouth that taught you," and she
never afterwards darkened the door.

On another day the husband was with his wife in
the fields working and looking about, when they saw
a great company of riders on white horses coming
where they were, and as they came near one of the
riders caught hold of her and took her away.   Her
husband did not know what to do.   He went wandering about looking for her, but never finding her,
till one day, to his great wonderment, he saw a
glimmer of light on the side of the hill.   He reached it,
and saw an opening.   He put a pin in the side and
went in, and saw a great company feasting and dancing,
with his lost wife in the middle of the dancers.   She
saw him also, and began to sing loudly :

> " Take no food here Ialai o horro horro,
>   Ask no drink here Ialai o horro hee."

No one took any notice of him.   He got near her,
and putting his arm around her, whisked her out of

the circle of dancers. He took her home, but she became discontented, and was never the same being as she had been before. At last it happened when they were again out together that the riders on white horses came their way. On parting with him this time she said, " If at any time he wished her to come back, he was to throw her marriage dress, which had *craobh uaine, i.e.* green tracery on the right shoulder, after her when he saw her passing in the company, and she would return home." Thinking she did not belong to this world, he did nothing, and she passed and never returned to him.

FAIRIES AND THE HANDMILL.

The invention of the handmill or quern, in the infancy of the arts, must have formed an era in the history of human progress. Whoever first found out a handy way of reducing the solid grain into meal bestowed an inestimable blessing on the human race. The instrument is still to be occasionally met with in the Hebrides, in houses not convenient to mill or market. It is usually worked by two women, like the mills in use in the East.

> " A pair of thick-set hussies
> Winding round a quern."[1]

It is a common practice with women to sing at their

[1] " Paidhir de na cailean guagach
Cuir mu'n cuairt na brathuinn-oran.''

work, as indeed they did in the Highlands in olden times at most of their labours, such as reaping, sowing, milking.

Old Archibald, for half a century servant to the ministers of Tiree, would insist to his dying day that, coming home at night with a cart from the parish mill, he heard the handmill at work inside the Red Knolls (*na Cnocana ruadha*) near the road. He could put his foot on the very spot where he heard the noise. To ask him if he was naturally troubled with singing in the ears, or show any other symptom of unbelief, was resented as an affront, and neither minister nor elder, nor a whole synod, would persuade him there were no Fairies. He had heard them himself " with his own ears."

The man who first got the loan of a quern from the Fairies never sent it home. In revenge, the elves took away all substance from his crop that year, and he derived no benefit from grain or fodder. His is the fate of many inventors. The benefit is not immediate. It seems the elves had no power but over the year's crop.

FAIRIES AND OATMEAL.

A man in Islay got a loan of oatmeal from the Fairies, and when returning it, he, out of gratitude, left at the hole, which led to the Fairy residence, and where he had been in the habit of getting and leaving such loans, more meal than he had borrowed. The

Fairies are a just race; they take no more than their exact due; they were offended by more being offered, and never after gave that man a loan of meal.

A kind-hearted woman, the wife of a well-to-do farmer in the rugged district of Kingairloch, was one day visited by a young woman, a stranger to her, who asked for, and got a loan of meal. In answer to the housewife's inquiries, the visitor said she came from the hillock above the house, on which a rowan-tree, or mountain ash, was growing. She wore an upper dress like a grey tippet. This event took place shortly before Beltane, when ploughing and other farm operations were being proceeded with. In a week after Grey Tippet came back with the meal, *but it was barley-meal,* and told the good-wife to bless this every time she took any of it. This direction was carefully attended to, and the meal never got less. One day a scatter-brain member of the family asked if that cursed barley-meal was never to be done. The next time the mistress went to the chest there was no more barley-meal.

The house of one M'Millan, at the foot of Ben Iadain in Morvern, a high hill already mentioned for its reputation as a Fairy residence, was visited by a stranger, a woman, who asked for a loan of meal. She said she stayed in that same neigbourhood, that the men were away just now in Lismore, and that the meal would be sent back on their return. This was done in due course, as promised, and M'Millan's wife was told never to allow any one but herself to bend over the chest, in which the meal was kept, and the meal would prove inexhaustible.   At last, however, when Mrs. M'Millan was ill, another opened the chest, and the meal disappeared.

Hector, son of Ferchar, in the Ross of Mull, was an easy-going, kind-hearted man, a weaver by trade, who would give away the last of his goods to any one he saw in distress.   So weak was he in this respect, that his wife did not care to trust him with anything— he was sure to give it away to the first poor man that came his way.   Having occasion to go to the summer pastures in the hill, and leave Hector alone in charge of the house, she measured out enough meal to last him for the fifteen days she expected to be away, and gave it to him in a skin bag.   When returning, she met a beggar, who said he had got a handful of meal from her husband, and Hector himself, when questioned, said he had given away sixteen such handfuls.   Yet the bag was found to be quite full.

FAIRIES AND IRON.

In Mull, a person, encountered by a *Bean shìth*, was told by her that she was kept from doing him harm by the iron he had about him.   The only iron he had was a ring round the point of his walking stick.

In the North of Ireland, an iron poker, laid across

the cradle, kept away the Fairies till the child was baptized.

The writer remembers well that, when a school-boy, great confidence was put in a knife, of which he was the envied possessor, and in a nail, which another boy had, to protect us from a Fairy (*sìthche*), which was said to have made its appearance at a spot near which the road to school passed the Hawthorn Bush between the Black Nose and the Pass of the Dead (*An Crògan Sgìthich eadar an t-Sròn du 's Bealach nam Marbh*). This was in Appin, Argyllshire.

The efficacy of iron, in warding off Fairy attacks, has already been illustrated.

NAME OF THE DEITY.

The Fairies were building a bridge across Loch Rannoch, between Camaghouran and Innis-droighinn, when a passer-by wished them God-speed. Instantly the work stopped, and was never resumed. (Cf. page 64.)

FAIRY GIFTS.

A smith, the poorest workman in his trade, from his inferior skill, only got coarse work to do, and was known as the "Smith of Ploughshares" (*Gobhainn nan Soc*). He was, besides, the ugliest man, and the rudest speaker. One day he fell asleep on a hillock, and three Fairy women, coming that way, left him each a parting gift (*fàgail*). After that he became the best workman, the best looking man, and the best speaker in the place, and became known as the "Smith of Tales" (*Gobhainn nan sgial*).

A man, out hunting, fell asleep in a dangerous place, near the brink of a precipice. When he awoke a Fairy woman was sitting at his head, singing gently.

STRUCK BY THE FAIRY ARROW SPADE.

Donald, who lived in Gortan du in Lorn, was working in a drain with a pointed spade. One evening, having left the spade standing in the drain, he was startled by something striking it with a loud knock. He found the noise was made by the blow of a smooth, polished, flint-like stone. He put this in his pocket and took it home. Some evenings after, "Callum Clever," already mentioned as frequently carried about by the Fairies, was shown the stone. He declared that it had been thrown by himself at the instigation of the Fairies, who wanted to take Donald himself. Donald of Gortan du was a cooper, and was wanted to make a barrel for a cow the elves had just killed. (Cf. page 26.)

CHAPTER III.

TUTELARY BEINGS.

I. THE GLAISTIG.

THE Glaistig was a tutelary being in the shape of a thin grey (*tana glas*) little woman, with long yellow hair reaching to her heels, dressed in green, haunting certain sites or farms, and watching in some cases over the house, in others over the cattle. She is called 'the Green Glaistig' (*a Ghlaistig uaine*) from her wan looks and dress of green, the characteristic Fairy colour. She is said to have been at first a woman of honourable position, a former mistress of the house, who had been put under enchantments and now had a Fairy nature given her. She disliked dogs, and took fools and people of weak intellect under her particular charge. She was solitary in her habits, not more than one, unless when accompanied by her own young one, being found in the same haunt. Her strength was very great, much greater than that of any Fairy, and one yell of hers was sufficient to waken the echoes of distant hills. Strong men were said to have mastered her, but ordinarily people were afraid of meeting her. She might do them a mischief and leave them a token, by which they would have cause to remember the encounter. She made herself generally useful, but in many cases was only mischievous and troublesome.

She seems in all cases to have had a special interest in the cows and the dairy, and to have resented any want of recognition of her services. A portion of milk was set apart for her every evening, in a hole for the purpose in some convenient stone, and unless this was done, something was found amiss in the dairy next morning. Others left milk for her only when leaving the summer pastures for the season.

She was seldom seen, oftenest when anything was to happen to the house she followed. She might then be seen, making her way in the evening up the slope to the castle, herding the cattle on the pastures, sunning herself on the top of a distant rock, or coming to the fold at dusk for her allowance of milk. Her cries, and the noise she made, arranging the furniture, shouting after the cattle, or at the approach of joy or sorrow, were frequently heard.

In the south Highlands, the Glaistig was represented as a little wan woman, stout and not tall, but very strong. In Skye, where most of her .duties were assigned to a male deity, the *Gruagach*, she was said to be very tall, 'a lath of a body' like a white reflection or shade.

Her name is derived from *glas*, grey, wan, or pale-green, and *stìg*, a sneaking or crouching object, probably in allusion to her invisibility, noiseless motions, or small size. In the *Highland Society's Dictionary*, she is called "a she-devil, or hag, in the shape of a goat," and the definition is accepted by M'Leod and Dewar. This, however, is a mistake. The shape of a goat, in the Highlands as elsewhere, has been assigned to the devil only, and there was nothing diabolical, or of the nature of an evil spirit, seeking the perdition of mankind, ascribed to the poor Glaistig. She occupied a middle position between the Fairies and mankind ; she was not a Fairy woman (*Bean shìth*) but one of human race, who had a Fairy nature given to her. The Fairies themselves are much nearer in character to the race of man than to that of devils. Of course all unearthly beings are to be avoided, but of all the beings, with which fear or fancy has peopled the unseen world, the Glaistig and her near relation the Brownie are among the most harmless.

The house or castle-haunting Glaistig was also known by the names of *Maighdean sheòmbair*, *i.e.* chamber-maid, *Gruagach*, young woman, lit. long-haired one, and *Gruagach sheòmbair*, 'fille de chambre,' and her attachment was not to the family but to the site or stance (*làrach*). It was always the abodes of the

affluent in which she resided, and she continued
her occupancy after a change of tenants, and even after
the building was deserted and had become a nesting
place for wild birds. In olden times there was a per-
petuity of tenure enjoyed by large tenants, and it is not
surprising that writers have fallen into the mistake of
supposing the tutelary guardian of the house to be that
of its tenants. The Glaistig had sympathy with the
tenant so far, that she broke out into loud expressions
of joy or sorrow, or made her appearance more
frequently when happiness or misfortune were to come
upon the family ; but her real attachment was to the
building or site. Indeed, none of these beings of
superstition were tutelary to the human race, or had
anything about them of the character of the Genius or
δαιμων. When the house was to be levelled, even
though the family remained on the land, and a new
house (on another site) was built, the Glaistig made a
lamentable outcry, left, and was never afterwards seen
or heard. Her usual occupation consisted in "putting
things in order" at night, sweeping the floor, drawing
chairs and tables about, and arranging the furniture.
After the household had retired to rest, she was heard
at work in apartments that were locked, and in which
no human being could be. It was then known there
would shortly be an arrival of strangers. In the morning the furniture was found in most cases untouched or
disarranged. In other cases the house was found tidied

up, and work which had been left for the Glaistig, such as washing, was found finished. She was fond of working with the spinning wheel, and, according to some, it was to prevent her coming to the house, and working with it on Sundays that old women were careful to take off the band every Saturday night. She had a similar fondness for working with tradesmen's tools, and artizans were often much annoyed at hearing her working at night, and finding in the morning their tools spoiled or mislaid. When the servants neglected their work or spoke disrespectfully of herself, or did anything to her favourites, she played pranks to punish them. She knocked down the water-stoups, disarranged the bedclothes, put dust in the meat, led the objects of her resentment a fool's chase about the house, or in the dark gave them a slap to be remembered on the side of the head. When happiness or misfortune, a marriage or a death, was to occur in the household, she was heard rejoicing or wailing long before the event occurred.

It was, however, to the being of this class, that haunted the folds of the cattle, that the name of *Glaistig* is most commonly given. Her occupation consisted in a general superintendence of the sheep, cows, and horses of the farm. When the family was at dinner, or the herdsman had fallen asleep and neglected his charge, she kept the cattle out of mischief; and, though not seen, was heard shouting after them, and driving them to their proper pastures.   In this respect, she behaved like an old and careful herdsman.   If the cows were not clean milked, she punished the dairy-maid by some unchancy prank.   At night she kept the calves from the cows (a needful and useful occupation before the days of enclosures and plentiful farm accommodation), and its substance in the milk.   In summer she accompanied the cattle to the hill pastures, and there had her portion of milk duly poured out for her in the evening in a stone near the fold.   Unless this was done the calves were found next morning with the cows, the cream not risen from the milk, a cow was found dead, or some other mischance occurred.   She was not supposed ever to enter a house, but to stay in some ravine (*eas*) near a Fairy residence.   She disliked dogs very much, and if a present of shoes or clothes were made to her, she was offended and left.   She is not generally spoken of as appearing in any shape but her own, but in some localities and tales, is said to assume the shape of a horse as 'old grey mare,' and even of a dog.

The Glaistig resembled the Fairies in being invisible, and in having a noiseless gliding motion ; in her dislike of dogs ; in affecting green in her dress ; in being addicted to meddling at night with the spinning wheel and tradesmen's tools ; in her outcries being a pre-monition of coming events ; in being kept away by steel, and in her ability to give skill in handicrafts to her favourites. The Fairies bestowed this skill on those who had the *Ceaird-Chomuinn*, or association craft, *i.e.* the assistance of the Folk. The Glaistig gave the choice of 'ingenuity without advantage' (*ealdhain gun rath*) or 'advantage without ingenuity' (*rath gun ealdhain*). Those who chose the former proved clever workmen but never prospered; and those who chose the latter turned out stupid fellows who made fortunes.

She differed in being more akin to ordinary women than the true Fairy wife (*Bean shìth*); she was stronger, and as it were more substantial; it was true woman's work which, as chamber-maid or dairy-maid, she performed. Though her 'bed' was near a Fairy dwelling, and she could command the services of the Elves, she did not engage in Fairy employments or recreations. The Fairies punished people of a discontented, grumbling disposition, by taking away the substance of their goods. The Glaistig was also offended at littleness and meanness of mind, but meanness of a different kind. Those who looked down on fools and people of weak intellect, or ill-treated them, she paid off by putting dust or soot in their meat. Akin to this was her punishment of neglect in servants.

In some parts of the Highlands the Glaistig is called *Glaisrig.* The name of her young one is *Méilleachan*, a name probably derived from its bleating or whimpering after the old one. It is also called *Isein*, a chicken, and *Gocan*, a little plug.

L.

THE GLAISTIG AT GLENDUROR.

The being which attached herself to the farm-house of Achindarroch (*Acha-nan-darach, field of oaks*) in Glenduror, Appin, Argyleshire, was variously known as the *Glaistig* and as the *Gruagach* of Glenduror. She attended to the cattle, and took particular charge of keeping the calves from the cows at night. She followed the house (not the family), and was alive not many years ago. A portion of milk was poured out for her every evening on a stone called *Clach na Glaistig* (the Glaistig stone), and once this was neglected by a new tenant, the calves were found next morning with the cows. Her face was described by those who professed to have seen her, as being like a grey stone overgrown with lichens. A servant girl, going on a dark evening to draw water from a stream flowing past the house, was asked by her fellow-servants if she was not afraid of the Glaistig. In her reply she spoke contemptuously of that being, and on her way to the stream received a slap on the cheek that twisted her head to one side. The following evening, going on the same errand, she got a slap on the other cheek that put her head right.[1]

THE GLAISTIG AT SRON-CHARMAIG.

The Glaistig attached to this house on Loch Faschan-side in Lorn was known as *Nic-ille-mhicheil*

---

[1] The same incident is related of the Sron-Charmaig Glaistig.

(*i.e.* a woman of the surname of Carmichael), and was said to have been a former mistress of the house. She lived in a ravine, called Eas-ronaich, near the mansion, and when any misfortune was about to befall the family set up a loud wailing. On sunny days she was to be seen basking on the top of *Creag Ghrianach* (the Sunny Rock), also in the neighbourhood. Before the old house was levelled, and the present mansion was built, she set up an unusually loud wailing, and then left. Fully a year before the event, she seemed greatly disturbed ; her step up and down stairs, and the noise of chairs and tables being moved about was frequently heard after people had gone to bed. At Glen-Iuchair, a man, who was in the evening convoyed across the glen by a *grey* sheep, was firmly of opinion his strange convoy could have been no other than Nic-ille-mhicheil. No real sheep could have been so attentive to him. This attachment to particular individuals was also shown in the case of a poor old woman, named *Mòr* (*i.e.* Sarah), resident on the farm. When Mor fell sick, the Glaistig used to come to the window and wail loudly.

One evening at the cattle-fold, after the cows had been milked and before the herd and dairy-maids had started home with the milk-pails, a woman, dressed in *green*, was seen coming and trying the udders of the cows, as if to see whether they had been properly milked. The herd had his dog with him, and happened

at the time to be sitting with it in his arms.　The dog
sprang from him and gave chase, and the woman fled
like a bird.　This was at a place called *Doire nan Each*,
' the Wood of the Horses,' several miles from the
mansion, and the woman was believed to be Nic-ille-
mhlcheil.

AT INVERAWE HOUSE.

This mansion-house has long been haunted by a
Glaistig known as the ' Maiden of Inverawe' (*Maighdean Inbher-atha*), who was to be heard (at least till
very recently) rustling (*srannail*) through the house.
Stoups full of water, left in the house at night, were found
in the morning upset by her, and chairs, left however
neatly arranged, were turned round.　She is said to have
been some former mistress of the house who had proved
unfaithful and had been buried alive.

AT DUNSTAFFNAGE CASTLE.

This castle (*Dùn-sta'innis*), once a seat of the kings
of Scotland, was haunted by a woman known as the
Sianag (or Elle-maid) of Dunstaffnage.　She broke
into outcries of joy or sorrow (*mulad no aighear*),
according as a happy or unfortunate event was to befall
the inmates.　A stranger, who accompanied one of the
servants to the castle and remained there that night,
had his bedclothes twice pulled off by her, and heard

her all night walking through the room and in the adjoining passages.   Her footsteps were heavy like those of a man.

IN TIREE.

A Gruagach haunted the 'Island House' (*Tigh an Eilein*, so called from being at first surrounded with water), the principal residence in the island, from time immemorial till within the present century.   She was never called Glaistig, but Gruagach and Gruagach mhara (sea-maid) by the islanders.   Tradition represents her as a little woman with long yellow hair, but a sight of her was rarely obtained.   She staid in the attics, and the doors of the rooms in which she was heard working were locked at the time.   She was heard putting the house in order when strangers were to come, however unexpected otherwise their arrival might be.   She pounded the servants when they neglected their work.

AT SLEAT, SKYE.

The Glaistig of the old Castle of Sleat (*Sléibhte*, mountain pastures), once the residence of the Lords of the Isles, was often seen at dusk standing near the *Gruagach* stone, where her allowance of milk was placed.   Her appearance was that of a young woman with long hair.

IN THE ISLAND OF COLL.

The Glaistig that haunted old Breacacha Castle, the family seat of the MacLeans of Coll, was in size 'like a lump of a lassie' (*cnapach caileig*), and had white hair like a tuft of flax (*gibeag lìn*), as long as herself. She put the house in order when strangers were to come, and guests getting up through the night were led astray by her, so that they could not find their way back to bed again. Indeed, she is even accused of maltreating strangers, while she let those she knew alone.

AT DUNOLLY CASTLE.

The Glaistig of this castle made herself very useful. The family washing had only to be left for her at night and it was done before morning. Glimpses of her were seen in the evening on her way up to the castle. During the night she tidied up the house and swept the floors. The fool (*amadan*) attached to the castle was taken under her special protection, and he often had his meat clean when others had it full of 'stour.'

AT MEARNAIG CASTLE.

This ancient ruin is on the summit of a conical rock, above a hundred feet high, close to the shore, in Glen Sanda, on the Kingerloch coast. About three or four hundred feet from it there is a beautiful and curious echo. A call of eight or nine syllables is distinctly repeated from the castle after the speaker has ceased. The only reminiscence of the castle's former tenants is the call usually given, when rousing the echo, " Are you in, maiden ?" (*Am bheil thu stigh a mhaighdean ?*) The maiden is the tutelary Glaistig that haunted all such buildings.

IN STRATHGLASS.

The Gruagach or Glaistig that haunted the house of *Mac 'ic Alasdair* (the patronymic of the chiefs of Glengarry), in Strathglass, was never seen, but was commonly heard at night putting dishes in order. She was given, like many of her sort in the old hospitable Highland days, to leading strangers astray through the house. A shepherd from Morvern came some forty years ago to the neighbourhood, and the Glaistig took a great fancy to staying with him. He suffered a great deal of annoyance from her, though no ultimate loss. If he left his jacket on the paling (*staing*) to dry, it might be away the first time he went to look for it, but the next time he might, and ultimately would, find it all safe. At times cheese disappeared for a while from the ' amry.' At night the shepherd felt the coverlet being hauled off, and heard the Glaistig giggling, with a short sort of laugh, hĭ, hĭ, hĭ.

He might leave their calves all night with the two cows he owned, the Glaistig kept them from sucking. Before being reconciled to her he tried to keep her

away by putting the New Testament above the door
and round the walls, but without effect. A party of
young men came one evening to hear the mysterious
noises. They saw and heard nothing till they were
going away. The pot was then lifted off the fire
without any visible agency and left on the floor ; while
they themselves had their eyes nearly knocked out at
the door with tough clods from the marsh (*pluic ruig-
hinn réisg*).

AT LIANACHAN.

A strong man of the name of Kennedy or MacCuaric,[1]
residing at Lianachan in Lochaber, was coming home
in the evening from setting a salmon net in the river
when a Glaistig met him on the bank of the stream.
He locked his arms round her (*ghlas e lamhun*), took
her with him to the house, and would not let her go
till she built for him a large barn of six couples (*sia
suidheachun*). This she did in one night. As her
parting gift she left a blessing and a curse to the
MacCuarics, that they should grow like rushes but
wither like ferns. This proved to be the case—the
man's family grew up tall, and straight, and handsome,
but when they attained their full strength and growth
they wasted prematurely away.

The following is a close translation of a much fuller

---

[1] Both names have the same meaning, being derived from a kind of head-
dress (*ceann-eididh*, *cuaraig*) peculiar to the clan.

and slightly different version of the legend (see volume
of Gaelic poems called *An Duanaire*, p. 123). The
Gaelic is not given as the volume is easily accessible.
It is a pity that the author of the piece, if known to
the collector, is not given.

"One night the big black lad MacCuaric was going
home from the smithy; the Glaistig met him as he was
crossing *Curr* at the ford of Croisg:

> " Hail to thee, Big Black Lad, said she,
>   Would you be the better of a rider behind?
>   Yes, and a rider before, said he ;
>   And he gave her a little big lift
>   From the bare beach,
>   And tied her before him,
>   Safely and surely,
>   On the back of the mettlesome horse,
>   With the wizard belt of Fillan ;
>   And he swore and asseverated
>   Vehemently and stubbornly,
>   He would not let her whole from his grasp,
>   Till he showed her before men.
>   Let me go, said she, and I will give
>   For loss and damage,
>   A fold full of speckled cattle,
>   White-bellied, black, white-headed,
>   Success on hill and in company
>   To yourself and your sort after you.
>   That is mine in spite of you, said he,
>   And it suffices not to set you free.
>   Let me go, and I will leave your land,
>   Where in the knoll I stayed ;
>   And I will build thee to-night,
>   On yonder field,
>   A big, strong, dike house,

A house fire will not pierce,
Water, nor arrow, nor iron,
And will keep thee dry and comfortable,
Without dread, or fear, and charmed
Against poison, caterans, and fairies.
    Fulfil your words, said he,
And from me get your leave.
    She gave a shriek with wailing,
That was heard over seven hills !
It seemed as if the Horn of Worth,
Owned by Fionn, had whistled.
Every Fairy dwelling and beetling cliff
Wakened and echoed,
And 'they' gathered round the meadow,
Waiting her orders.
    She set them to work speedily,
Calmly, orderly,
And they brought flags and stones
From the shore of Clianaig waterfall,
Reaching them from hand to hand ;
From the Knoll of Shore Islet
Were cut beams and rafters ;
And supports long,
Straight, and thick, in the Rowan wood ;
While she herself unceasing said
    One stone above two stones,
And two stones above one stone,
Fetch stake, clod, thatching pin,
Every timber in the wood
But mulberry ;
Alas for him, who gets not as he sows,
And sows not as he gets !
    And at the grey dawning
There was divot on the roof,
And smoke from it !
    He kept the coulter in the fire,
To keep him from mischance,
Since he knew the pranks

And enchantments of the Fairies.
　When the house was now finished
And she had made up each loss,
He loosened the maid
And suffered no harm.
　Going past the window in front
She stretched him her crooked palm
To bid him farewell,—
But (truly) to take him to the shïen.
The skin of her palm stuck to it (the coulter) ;
She sprang then on a grey stone
Of the Field, to pronounce his doom.
　She brought the curse of the people on him,
And the curse of the goblins,
And if we may believe as we hear,
She obtained her request.
　' Grow like rushes,
　　Wither like fern,
　　Turn grey in childhood,
　　Change in height of your strength ;
I ask not a son may not succeed.
　I am the sorrowing Glaistig
That staid in the land of the Meadow,
I built a big house on the Field,
Which caused a sore pain in my side ;
I will put out my heart's blood,
High on the peak of Finisgeig,
Which will be red for evermore.'
　And she leapt in a green flame,
Over the shoulder of the peak." [1]

IN GLENORCHY.

The Glaistig, living at the waterfall (*eas*) of Bo-
chaoil in Glenorchy, came behind a man of the name

---

[1] The last two lines suggest this to be a modern composition, and not a
popular tradition.　Supernatural beings do not go away in flames in
Highland superstition.

of Campbell, riding home in the evening to the adjoining farm-house, and jumping up behind him, urged
the horse to greater speed by crying now and then,
" Hoosh ! for a horse with two " (*Huis ! air each le
dithis*). Campbell put back his hands and caught her.
He was going to take her home, but she managed
to get away, and left as her parting gift, that no
Campbell should ever be born alive (*nach gineadh 's
nach goireadh Cairnbeulach*) above Bo-chaoil.

The water before breaking over the fall is curiously
split by an unseen pinnacle of the rock, and the Glaistig
is said to cause the appearance with her foot.

M'MILLAN OF KNAP.

The *Cnap* (that is, the Lump) is opposite Shuna
Island in Appin, and the name still remains in *Tigh
a Chnaip* (the house of the Lump), the Gaelic name of
Balachulish hotel on the road to Glencoe, well-known
to tourists. It was regarding the ownership of Knap
by the M'Millans that the oral charter ran :

> " M'Millan's right to Knap
> While wave strikes rock."[1]

A Glaistig once came behind a kilted chief of this
sept and caught him, so that he could not struggle
or escape. She asked him if he had ever been in
greater straits (*Mhic Mhaoil a Chnaip, an robh thu*

---

[1] " Coir Mhic-Mhaoilein air a Chnap,
Fhads' a bhuaileas tonn air creig."

riamh an airc is mò ?). He said he had ; she asked
when ; and he said, " Between plenty and penury "
(*Eadar féill is aimbeairt*). On this she let go her
hold. He said, " I give my word I will not be weighed
on the same scales again," [1] and stabbing her with his
dirk killed her.

THE GLAISTIG AT CRAIGNISH.

A weaver, going home in the evening with a web
(*còrn*) of cloth on his shoulder, was met by a Glaistig
at a stream. She caught hold of him and pummelled
him (*làd i e*) all night in the stream with his own
web of cloth, saying to all his remonstrances, " Weaving
weaver, you are the better of being washed " (*Figheadair fighe, 's fhearrd' thu do nigheadh*).

ON GARLIOS, MORVERN.

The lonely and rugged mountain tract, known as
the Garlios (*Garbh-shlios*, the rough country side),
extending along the coast of Morvern, from the Sound
of Mull to Kingairloch, a distance of about seven miles,
was at one time haunted by a Glaistig, whose special
employment was the herding (*buachailleachd*) of the
sheep and cattle that roamed over its desert pastures.
Tradition represents her as a small, but very strong
woman, taking refuge at night in a particular yew tree
(*craobh iuthair*), which used to be pointed out, to

[1] Bheir mise mo bhriathrun, nach d' théid mis' air na sgàlun ciadna rithis.

protect herself from wild animals that prowled over the ground. In a cave in the same locality lived a man, known as 'Yellow Dougall of the Cave' (*Dùghaill Buidhè na h-Uamh*), who supported himself and wife by taking a sheep or goat, when he required it, from the neighbouring flocks.[1] One day when about to row himself across to the opposite island of Lismore, in his coracle (*curachan*), a woman came and asked for a passage. She took the bow oar, and before long cried out, "A hearty pull, Dougall" (*Hùg orra, Dhughaill.*) "Another hearty pull then, honest woman" (*Hùgan so eil' orra, bhean chòir*), cried Dougall. Every now and then she repeated the same cry, and Dougall answered in the same way. He thought himself a good rower, and was ashamed to be beat by a woman. He never rowed so hard in his life. When the boat touched the Lismore shore, he for the first time turned round his head, and no woman was anywhere to be seen. She who was so strong and disappeared so mysteriously could only be the Glaistig.

Other accounts say that the boatman was Selvach Mac Selvach (*Sealbhach Mac Shealbhaich*), a native of Lismore, and the woman against whom he pulled for

---

[1] It was said of Dougall, that when he wanted a sheep he drove a whole flock through a particular gap in the rocks, while his wife stood in waiting to catch the animal fixed upon. Once she allowed this sheep to pass, and Dougall asked her what she meant. " How," she said, "could I take the sheep of my own godfather?" (goistidh). Dougall replied, "The man might be your godfather, but the sheep was not your godfather."

the three miles from Kingairloch to Lismore, a Glaistig that stayed in the ravine of *Alltaogain* in the latter place. Her cry was, " Pull away, Selvach " (*Hùg orra, Shealbhaich*), and his answer, " Pull away, my lass " (*Hùg orra, ghalad.*")

AT ARDNADROCHIT, MULL.

The Glaistig that followed the house of Lamont at Ardnadrochit (the height of the bridge), in Craignure parish, Mull, was commonly seen in the shape of a dog, and was said to carry a pup at the back of her head. A band came across from Lorn, the opposite mainland, to 'lift' Lamont's cattle. The Glaistig, whose charge they were, drove them up the hill out of the way to a place called *Meall na Lìre.* Here, in a dell called 'the Heroes' Hollow' (*Glaic nan Gaisgeach*), the freebooters were like to overtake her. On seeing this, she struck the cows, and converted them into grey stones, which are to be seen to this day. On coming up, the plunderers stood at these stones, and one of them, tapping with his broadsword the stone near him, said he felt sure this was the bed of the white cow (*Bo bhàn*). On his saying this, the tap of his sword split the stone in two. The Glaistig broke her heart, and was afterwards taken by Lamont and buried in a small plot of ground near the Sound of Mull, where in those days the bodies of unbaptized children were put.

ON BAUGH, TIREE.

The tenants of this farm once got the benefit of seven years' superintendence of their cattle from a Glaistig. There is a place on the farm, still called the Glaistig's Bed, where she died by falling in the gap of a dyke. She was seldom seen, but was often heard. When driving the horses to pasture, she called out, "Get along, get along, thou son of a mare! Betake thee to yonder white bank!" and when the herd-boy was at his dinner, she was heard shouting to the cattle, " Horo va ho whish! Did ever any one hear of cattle without a herdsman but these?" She prepared food for herself by dragging a bunch of eels (of which there is an over-abundance in the small lochs on the farm) through the fire-place of a kiln used for preparing corn for the hand-mill. One night, when engaged at this work along with *Goean (i.e.* a perky little fellow), her son as is supposed, some one came behind and gave her a rap on the head with a stick. She and her son fled, and as they were going away, Goean was over-heard saying to his mother, " Your old grey pate has been rapped, but see that you have the bunch of eels."

In appearance, this Glaistig is said to have been a thin sallow-looking little object, with ringletted yellow hair that reached down to her heels. She had short legs, and in person was not unlike a dwarf.

AT STRONTIAN.

An incident similar to that of the bunch of eels is told of a Glaistig that came at nights and worked in the smithy at Strontian. The smith was very much annoyed at the noises in the smithy at night, and at finding in the morning tools mislaid and the smithy in confusion. He resolved to stay up and find out the cause. He stood in the dark, behind the door, with the hammer on his shoulder ready to strike whatever should enter. The Glaistig came to the door, accompanied by her bantling, or *Isein* (*i.e.* a young chicken). The chicken thought he heard a noise, and said, "Something moving, little woman." "Hold your tongue, wretch," she said, "it is only the mice." At this point the smith struck the old one on the head with his hammer, and caught hold of the little one. On this, the *Isein* reproached his mother by saying, "Your old grey pate has got a punching ; see now if it be the mice." Before the smith let his captive go, the Glaistig left a parting gift —that the son should succeed the father as smith in the place till the third generation. This proved to be the case, and the last was smith in Strontian some forty years ago.

ON HIANISH, TIREE.

About a hundred years ago one of the tenants of this farm, which adjoins Baugh, wondering what made his cows leave the fank (or enclosure) every

M

night, resolved to watch. He built a small turf hut
near the fold to pass the night in, and sat mending his
curain (shoes or mocassins of untanned hides), when a
woman came to the door. Suspicious of her being an
earthly visitant, he stuck his awl in the door-post to
keep her out. She asked him to withdraw the awl and
let her in, but he refused. He asked her questions
which much troubled him at the time. He was afraid
of a conscription, which was then impending, and he
asked if he would have to go to the army. The
Glaistig said he would ; that though he made a hole in
the rock with his awl and hide himself in it, he would
be found out and taken away, but if he succeeded in
mounting a certain black horse before his pursuers
came, he might bid them defiance ; and he was to tell
the wife who owned the white-faced yellow cow to let
the produce of the cows home to their master. The
man was caught when jumping on the back of the
black horse to run away from the conscription, and
after service abroad, came back to tell the tale.

IN ULVA.

The Glaistig of Ardnacallich, the residence of the
Macquarries of Ulva, used to be heard crying " Ho-hò !
hò-ho ! Macquarries' cattle are in the standing corn
near the cave ! The bald girl has slept ! the bald girl
has slept ! hò-hò, ho-hò." The ' bald girl ' was no
doubt a reference to her own plentiful crop of hair.

IN IONA.

The common of this Island is called *Staonnaig*, and in former times the cattle of the east and west end people of the place came to it in summer for fourteen days alternately. In those days a Glaistig stayed in a hole of the rocks in Staonnaig, and the people, when at the summer pastures (*àiridh*) poured milk every night in a stone for her. She once entered on a very rainy day a house where there was a woman of the name of Livingstone alone and at dinner. She dried herself at the fire, holding her clothes spread out, and turning round from side to side. Her clothes took fire, and she left as her parting gift, that no fire can be kindled at dinner-time by a woman of the name of Livingstone.

IN ROSS, MULL.

A herd in this district, whenever he moved the cattle at night, heard a voice shouting after him, "Son of big black John, there is a cow behind you" (*Mhic Iain du Mhoir, tha bò ád dheighinn*). He shouted in reply, "If there is one behind there are a hundred before" (*Ma tha h-aon am dhéigh, tha ceud romham*).

Neil, who lived in *Saor-bheinn*, went to fish on the rocks. Coming home in the dusk of the evening, a voice (that of the Glaistig) followed him begging for a fish. "Give me a cuddy fish, Neil" (*Thoir dhomh cudainn, a Néil*). This occurred every evening, and if he gave a fish the Glaistig became more and more importunate, and one by one, to get rid of her solicitations, the fish were given away, the last at the door. In this way, Neil often returned empty-handed from the fishing.

Hector, son of Ferchar, lived at Hoodie-crow Hillock (*Cnoc na Feannaig*), and as was common in olden times, the door of his house was made of bunches of heather, tied together, and made more wind-tight by straw stuffed between them.   One cold frosty night he heard a scraping at the door, as if some animal were trying to pull out the straw. He rose and went out, and drove away an old white horse he found nibbling at the straw. In a while he was disturbed again by the same noise. He went out, and, taking up a big stick, chased away the old white mare. When he almost overtook her, the mare became a woman, and, laughing at Hector, said, "I have played a trick upon you, Hector, son of Ferchar."

IN CORRY-NA-HENCHOR.

The Glaistig of *Coire-na-sheanchrach*, a valley on the Mull coast, half way up the sound between that island and the mainland, met a poor fisherman of the neighbourhood every evening, when he came ashore from the fishing and always got a fish for herself.   One evening he caught nothing but lithe, and when the Glaistig came and looked at them, she said, " They are all lithe

to-night, Murdoch." Whatever offence was taken by
her in consequence she never came any more.

MAC-IAN YEAR.

This man (*Mac Iain Ghiarr*), whose name is proverbial in the West Highlands for that of a master
thief, was one of the Mac Ians of Ardnamurchan, a
persecuted race. He had a boat for going on his
thieving expeditions painted black on one side and
white on the other, so that those who saw it passing
would not recognize it on its return. Hence the proverb :

> " One side black and one side grey,
> Like Mac Ian Year's boat."

Many tales are told of his skill in thieving, and the
accomplishment is said to have been bestowed upon
him by a Glaistig.

He and his brother Ronald (his own name was
Archibald) were out hunting, and having killed a roe,
took it to a bothy and prepared it for supper. He
threw himself on a bed of heather, and Ronald sat by
the fire, roasting pieces of the roe on his dirk. A
woman entered the hut, and made an effort now and
then to snatch from him some of the roasted flesh.
Ronald threatened, unless she kept over her paw (*sall*),
he would cut it off with his knife. She appealed to
Archibald, " Ho, Archibald, will you not put a stop to
Ronald?" " I will put a stop to him, poor creature," he

said. He told Ronald to allow the poor woman, that they had plenty, and perhaps she was hungry. When leaving, the Glaistig asked him to the door, and it is supposed then bestowed upon him his wonderful gift of theft. He built a large byre when he had not a single 'hoof' to put in it, and before long it was amply stocked. He hired the Glaistig to herd for him, and she was to be heard at night on the tops of the cliffs crying "Ho hŏ, ho hŏ," to keep the cattle from wandering too near the verge. Her wages were to be a pair of brogues of untanned leather, and when she got these, like the rest of her kind, she disappeared. She seems, however, only to have returned to her former haunts, which extended all over Ardnamurchan, from the Point to Loch Sunart. When her former master died, she gave a shriek that roused the echoes of Ben Resipol (*Réiscapol*). The same night she was seen in the Coolin hills in Skye, and after that neither her shadow nor her colour (*a du no dath*) were anywhere seen.

During her period of service with Mac Ian Year, she made her appearance whenever he raised his standard, however far away she might be. Ronald's dog had a great aversion to her, and chased her whenever she came near. She was then to be heard calling out, "Ho, Archibald, will you not call off the dog?" (*Ho, Laspuig, nach caisg thu 'n cù ?*),—a common phrase in Ardnamurchan and the small isles to this day.

It is related of her, that to escape from her attentions, Mac Ian Year and his brother resolved to remove to the Outer Hebrides. They had barely kindled a fire in their new dwelling, when the Glaistig called down the chimney they had forgot the old harrow, but she had brought it, and that she was only on the top of the Coolin Hills when the first clink (*snag*) was given to the flint to kindle the fire. There was nothing for it but to return to Ardnamurchan.[1]

AT ERRAY, MULL.

At Erray (*an Eirbhe*, the outlying part of a farm[2]), near Tobermory, there was a Glaistig that paid attention principally to the barn. The herd slept in the byre, and he often heard trampling (*tartaraich*) in the adjoining barn. Whatever had been left there at night was found in the morning all in confusion, topsy-turvy (*turrach air tharrach*), one leg over the other (*cas mu seach*). All this was the Glaistig's work.

The Glaistig of Fernach on Loch Awe side conveyed persons of the name of M'Intyre across a dangerous stream in the neighbourhood. She assumed the shape of a foal.

---

[1] This story of Glaistig officiousness is an appropriation of a floating tale that had its origin long previous to Mac Ian Year's time.

[2] In olden times a wall (of turf) was commonly built to separate the crop land from the hill ground, and was known as *Gàradh bràgh'd*, or Upper Wall. The ground above the *Gàradh bràgh'd* was known as the *Eirbhe*.

II. THE GRUAGACH.

Gruagach, *i.e.* long-haired one, from *gruag*, a wig, is a common Gaelic name for a maiden, a young woman. In old tales and poems, particularly those relating to the times of Murchard Mac Brian, who was king of Ireland *circ.* A.D. 1100, the term means a chief or some person of consequence, probably a young chief. Thus, in a conversation between that king and a young woman, whose nine silk-clad brothers he had killed in battle, she says:

> " I am daughter of the heir of Dublin,
>   I would not hide it, lord of swords,
>   And to the *Gruagach* of the Isle of Birds,
>   I, in truth, bore my children." [1]

The name evidently refers to the length of the hair, which it seems to have been a custom in ancient times for men of rank and freemen to allow to grow long.

In Argyllshire, and commonly in Gaelic, the name Gruagach, applied to the tutelary being haunting farms and castles, means the same as *Glaistig*, and the idea attached to it is that of a long-haired female, well-dressed like a gentlewoman, looking after the servants, and particularly after the cattle. In parts of Skye, however, the fold-frequenting Gruagach is a tall young man, with long yellow hair, in the attire of a gentleman

---

[1] " Inghean oighre Bhaile-cliath
      Cha cheilinn a thriath nan lann,
      'S do Ghruagach Eilein nan eun,
      'S ann a rug mi féin mo chlann."

of a bygone period, having a little switch (*slatag*) in his hand, and with a white breast, as if he wore a frilled shirt. One of the writer's authorities described him as in appearance like a young man fashionably dressed in a long coat and knee breeches, with a white breast like that of a frilled shirt, and having a cane in his hand. He had even heard that the Gruagach wore a beaver hat—a head-dress which in the Highlands was at one time believed to indicate a gentleman.

This Gruagach was attentive to the herds and kept them from the rocks. He frequented certain places in the fields where the cattle were. A Gruagach was to be found in every gentleman's fold (*buaile*), and, like the Glaistig, milk had to be set apart for him every evening in a hollow in some particular stone, called the Grua-gach stone (*Clach na Gruagaich*), kept in the byres. Unless this was done no milk was got at next milking, or the cream would not rise to the surface of the milk. Some say milk was placed in the Gruagach stone only when going to and returning from the summer pastures and when passing with milk.

The Gruagach amused himself by loosing the cattle in the byre at night, and making people get out of bed several times to tie them up. The cattle loosened did not fright or gore one another, as they did when they broke loose themselves or were untied by another person. On entering the byre, the Gruagach was heard laughing and tittering in corners. Beyond this diversion he seems to have been ordinarily harmless. He sometimes walked alongside of people, but was never known to speak.

A woman was driving calves into the byre at Tota Roam in Scorrybreck. The Gruagach amused himself inside by keeping them out. The woman, in a great rage, hastily cursed him. He gave her a slap on the cheek and killed her. All that night, however, he kept the fire alive for the woman that sat up watching the body.

Dr. Johnson mentions a 'Greogaca' in Troda, an islet off the east coast of Skye. This Gruagach seems long since to have disappeared, but old people say the place is a very likely one for a being of the class to be in. At Holm, East-side, and Scorrybreck, near Portree, the stones, where the libations were poured out, may still be seen.

In Braes, the Gruagach that followed the herds was a young woman with long hair; she was also known as the Glaistig, and the rock, in which her portion of milk was poured, is in Macqueen's Big Rock (*Creagan na Glaistig an creag mhor Mhic Cuinn*).

III. BROWNIE.

The term *Brùnaidh*, signifying a supernatural being, haunting the abodes of the affluent and doing work for the servants, seems to have made its way into the Highlands only in recent times and along with south country ideas. It is generally applied only to a big,

corpulent, clumsy man, 'a fine fat fodgel wight,' and
in many districts has no other reference. Its derivation
is Teutonic and not Celtic, and Brownies are mostly
heard of in places to which, as in the south of Argyllshire, southern ideas have penetrated, or where, as in
the Orkneys and Shetland, a Teutonic race is settled.

In the islet of Càra, on the west of Cantyre, the old
house, once belonging to the Macdonalds, was haunted
by a Brownie that drank milk, made a terrific outcry
when hurt, and disliked the Campbell race. In the old
castle of Largie, on the opposite coast of Cantyre, which
belonged to the same Macdonalds, there was also a
Brownie, supposed to be the same as the Càra one.
Since the modern house was built Brownie has not been
seen or heard. In Càra he is still occasionally heard.
It is not known exactly what he is like, no one having
ever seen more than a glimpse of him. Before the
arrival of strangers he put the house in order. He
disliked anything dirty being left in the house for the
night. Dirty bed-clothes were put out by him before
morning. Dogs had to be put outside at night, as he
often killed those left in the house. He was much
addicted to giving slaps in the dark to those who soiled
the house; and there are some still alive who can
testify to receiving a slap that left their faces black.
He tumbled on the floor water-stoups left full over-night.
A man was lifted out of bed by him, and found himself 'bare naked,' on awakening, at the fire. A woman,

going late in the evening for her cows, found Brownie had been before her, and tied them securely in the barn.

In one of the castles in the centre of Argyllshire, Brownie came to the bedside of a servant woman who had retired for the night, arranged the clothes, and, pulling them above her, said : " Take your sleep, poor creature" (*dean cadal, a chreutair*).   He then went away.

In character Brownie was harmless, but he made mischief unless every place was left open at night.   He was fed with warm milk by the dairy-maid.

A native of the Shetland Isles writes me that Brownie was well known in that locality.   He worked about the barn, and at night ground with the handmill for those to whom he was attached.   He could grind a bag or two of grain in a night.   He was once rewarded for his labours by a cloak and hood left for him at the mill.   The articles were away in the morning, and Brownie never came back.   Hence the bye-word, such a man is like Brownie,

> " When he got his cloak and hood,
> He did no more good."

The same story is told of the ' Cauld Lad of Hilton,' in the valley of the Wear in England (Keightley's *Fairy Myth*, p. 296), of Brownies in the Scottish Lowlands (p. 358), and of one in Strathspey (p. 395), who said, when he went away—

> " Brownie has got a coat and cap,
> Brownie will do no more work."

It also made its way to Tiree, and was there told as follows :

GUNNA.

In olden times the tillage in Tiree was in common, the crop was raised here and there throughout the farm, and the herding was in consequence very difficult to do. In Baugh, or some farm in the west of the island (tradition is not uniform as to the locality), the cows were left in the pastures at night, and were kept from the crops by some invisible herdsman. No one ever saw him, or knew whence he came, nor, when he went away, whither he went. A *taibhseir* or seer (*i.e.* one who had the second-sight or sight of seeing ghosts) remained up to see how the cattle were kept. He saw a man without clothes after them, and taking pity upon him made him a pair of trews (*triubhas*[1]) and a pair of shoes. When the ghostly herdsman put the trews on, he said (and his name then, for the first time, became known) :

> "Trews upon Gunna,
>   Because Gunna does the herding,
>   But may Gunna never enjoy his trews,
>   If he tends cattle any more."[2]

---

[1] The trews went into the shoe, close-fitted to the legs, and was fastened with a buckle at the waist.

[2] "Triuthas air Gunna
>   'S Gunna ris a bhuachailleachd,
>   'S na na mheal Gunna 'n triuthar
>   Ma ni e tuille cuallaich."

When he said this he went away and was never more heard of.

Beings of this class seem to have had a great objection to presents of clothes. A pair of shoes made the Glaistig at Unimore leave ; a cap, coat, and breeches the Phynnodderee in the Isle of Man (Keightley, *Fairy Myth*, p. 203) ; in the Black Forest of Germany, a new coat drove away a nix, one of the little water-people, with green teeth, that came and worked with the people all day (*ibid.*, p. 261); and Brownie, as already mentioned, in several places.

THE OLD MAN OF THE BARN.

In the Highlands of Perthshire, previous to the '45, each farm or village had its own *bodachan sabhaill,* 'the little old man of the barn,' who helped to thresh the corn, made up the straw into bundles, and saw that everything was kept in order. These Brownies had the appearance of old men and were very wise. They worked always at night, and were never mischievous, but highly useful.

The *Glaisein* (lit. grey-headed man) of the Isle of Man bears a strong resemblance to them. He was very strong, frequented farms, threshed corn, and went to the sheep-folds (Campbell's *West Highland Tales*, Introd. liii.).

These house-spirits have many relations, the Nis of Scandinavia, Kobold of Germany, Niägruisar of the Faroe Islands, and it is said the English Hobgoblin. The Hinzelman that haunted Hudemuhlen Castle in Lüneberg had 'curled yellow hair,' also a characteristic of the Glaistig ; and the difference between one household tutelary being and another is only such as might be expected from differences of country and society.

The oldest member of the family is the *Lar Familiaris* of the Romans. There is a noticeable resemblance between *lar*, the Roman household deity, and *làrach* (from *làr*, the ground), the Gaelic for the stance or site of a building, to which, and not to the tenants, the Celtic household apparition attached itself. The *lares* of the Romans were the departed spirits of ancestors, which were believed to watch over their dependents. The Glaistig was held to have been a woman of honourable position, a former mistress of the house, the interests of the tenants of which she now attended to. Small waxen images of the *lares*, clothed with the skin of a dog, were placed in the hall. The Glaistig had the Fairy aversion to dogs (an aversion which was reciprocal), but many of the actions ascribed to her savour strongly of her being in some way identical with the herdsman's dogs. This would very well explain the pouring of milk for her in the evening in the hollow of a stone. The Glaistig of Ardnadrochit had the shape of a dog (see p. 175).

A satisfactory explanation of the origin of the superstition does not readily suggest itself.   In days when
men did not know what to believe in regarding the
spirit world, and were ready to believe anything, a fancy
may have arisen, that it secures the welfare of a house,
and adds to its dignity, to have a supernatural being
attached to it and looking after its interests.   It had its
origin after the tribes, among whom it is to be found,
ceased to be roving and unsettled barbarians.   In a
large establishment a being of the kind was very useful.
The master would not discredit its existence, as it
helped to frighten idle and stupid servants into attending to their work and into clean and tidy habits.
Shrewd servants would say as little against it when it
served so well to screen their own knavery or faults,
and to impose on a credulous and facile, or careless
master.   Unless it was sometimes seen or heard, or
some work was mysteriously done, the delusion, either of
master or servant, could not be long continued ; and,
when men have little else to do, there are many who
take a pleasure in imposing on their more simple-
minded fellows, and are quite ready, as much from sport
as interest, to carry on a delusion of the kind.   Besides,
when the mind is nervously anxious, engrossed with the
fear of a coming misfortune or the hope of a coming
joy, it is apt to listen to the whispers of fancy and the
confidently-told tales of others.   When it broods alone,
during the sleepless night, over the future it is not

surprising if the imagination converts the weird sounds
of night—the melancholy moaning of the wind, its
fitful gusts in the woods and round the house, the roar
of the waterfall, the sound of the surf-beaten shore, and
many noises, of which the origin is at the time unknown
and unsought—into the omens of that which makes
itself sleepless, or hears in them the song of the house-
spirit, prescient of the coming event.   It must also
be remembered that there are people who will see
and hear anything if their story is believingly listened
to, and they are themselves at the time objects of
interest.

Pennant (*Tour*, p. 330) says Brownie was stout and
blooming, had fine long flowing hair, and went about
with a switch in his hand.   He cleaned the house,
helped to churn, threshed the corn, and belaboured
those who pretended to make a jest of him.   He says
(p. 331) the *Gruagach* was in form like the Brownie,
and was worshipped by libations of milk ; and " milk-
maids still retain the custom of pouring some on
certain stones, that bear his name."   He is thought, it
is added, to be an emblem of Apollo and identical
with χρυσοκομος.

Mr. Campbell (*Tales of the West Highlands*, 1. xciii.)
supposes the Gruagach of superstition to be a Druid
fallen from his high estate, and living on milk left for
him by those whose priest he had once been.   In
another place (ii. 101) he supposes him to be a half-

tamed savage, hanging about the house, with his long hair and skin clothing.

These explanations are not satisfactory. The character, dress, and actions ascribed to the Gruagach and his congeners are incongruous to the idea of Druid, heathen deity, or savage wild or reclaimed.

CHAPTER IV.

THE URISK, THE BLUE MEN, AND THE MERMAID.

THE URISK.

THE Urisk was a large lubberly supernatural, of solitary habits and harmless character, that haunted lonely and mountainous places. Some identify him with Brownie, but he differs from the fraternity of tutelary beings in having his dwelling, not in the houses or haunts of men, but in solitudes and remote localities. There were male and female Urisks, and the race was said to be the offspring of unions between mortals and fairies, that is, of the *leannan sìth.*

The Urisk was usually seen in the evening, big and grey (*mòr glas*), sitting on the top of a rock and peering at the intruders on its solitude. The wayfarer whose path led along the mountain side, whose shattered rocks are loosely sprinkled, or along some desert moor, and who hurried for the fast approaching nightfall, saw the Urisk sitting motionless on the top of a rock and gazing at him, or slowly moving out of his way. It spoke to some people, and is even said to have thrashed them, but usually it did not meddle with the passer-by. On the contrary, it at times gave a safe convoy to those who were belated.

In the Highlands of Breadalbane the Urisk was said, in summer time, to stay in remote corries and on the highest part of certain hills. In winter time it came down to the strath, and entered certain houses at night to warm itself. It was then it did work for the farmer, grinding, thrashing, etc. Its presence was a sign of prosperity; it was said to leave comfort behind it. Like Brownie, it liked milk and good food, and a present of clothes drove it away.

An Urisk, haunting *Beinn Doohrain* (a hill beloved of the Celtic muse) on the confines of Argyllshire and Perthshire, stayed in summer time near the top of the hill, and in winter came down to the straths. A waterfall near the village of Clifton at Tyndrum, where it stayed on these occasions, is still called *Eas na h-ùruisg*, the Urisk's cascade. It was encountered by St. Fillan, who had his abode in a neighbouring strath, and banished to Rome.

The Urisk of Ben Loy (*Beinn Laoigh*, the Calf's hill), also on the confines of these counties, came down in winter from his lofty haunts to the farm of Sococh, in Glen Orchy, which lies at the base of the mountain. It entered the house at night by the chimney, and it is related that on one occasion the bar, from which the chimney chain was suspended, and on which the Urisk laid its weight in descending, being taken away, and not meeting its foot as usual, the poor supernatural got a bad fall. It was fond of staying in a cleft at Moraig water-fall, and its labours, in keeping the waters from falling too fast over the rock, might be seen by any one. A stone, on which it sat with its feet dangling over the fall, is called 'the Urisk stone' (*Clach na h-ùruisg*). It sometimes watched the herds of Sococh farm.

A man passing through Strath *Duuisg*, near Loch Sloy, at the head of Loch Lomond, on a keen frosty night, heard an Urisk on one side of the glen calling out, "Frost, frost, frost" (*reoth, reoth, reoth*). This was answered by another Urisk calling from the other side of the glen, "Kick-frost, kick-frost, kick-frost" (*ceige-reoth*, etc.). The man, on hearing this, said, "Whether I wait or not for frost, I will never while I live wait for kick-frost"; and he ran at his utmost speed till he was out of the glen.

The Urisk of the ' Yellow Water-fall ' in Glen Màili, in the south of Inverness-shire, used to come late every evening to a woman of the name of Mary, and sat watching her plying her distaff without saying a word. A man, who wished to get a sight of the Urisk, put on Mary's clothes, and sat in her place, twirling the distaff,

as best he could.   The Urisk came to the door but
would not enter.   It said :

> " I see your eye, I see your nose,
>   I see your great broad beard,
>   And though you will work the distaff,
>   I know you are a man."

Graham (*Highlands of Perthshire*, p. 19, quoted by
Sir Walter Scott in his Notes to *The Lady of the Lake*)
says the Urisk "could be gained over by kind attentions
to perform the drudgery of the farm, and it was believed
that many families in the Highlands had one of the
order attached to it."   He adds that the famous *Coire
nan ùruisgean* derives its name from the solemn stated
meetings of all the Urisks in Scotland being held there.

The Urisk, like the Brownie of England, had great
simplicity of character, and many tricks were played
upon it in consequence.   A farmer in Strathglass got it
to undergo a painful operation that it might become fat
and sleek like the farmer's own geldings.   The weather
at the time being frosty, it made a considerable outcry
for some time after.

From its haunting lonely places, other appearances
must often have been confounded with it.   In Strathfillan (commonly called simply the Straths, *Strathaibh*),
in the Highlands of Perthshire, not many years ago a
number of boys saw what was popularly said to be
an Urisk.   In the hill, when the sun was setting, something like a human being was seen sitting on the top

of a large boulder-stone, and growing bigger and bigger till they fled. There is no difficulty in connecting the appearance with the circumstance that some sheep disappeared that year unaccountably from the hill, and a quantity of grain from the barn of the farm.

In the Hebrides there is very little mention of the Urisk at all. In Tiree the only trace of it is in the name of a hollow, *Slochd an Aoirisg*, through which the public road passes near the south shore. The belief that it assisted the farmer was not common anywhere, and all over the Highlands the word ordinarily conveys no other idea than that which has been well-defined as " a being supposed to haunt lonely and sequestered places, as mountain rivers and waterfalls."

THE BLUE MEN (*Na Fir Ghorm*).

The fallen angels were driven out of Paradise in three divisions, one became the Fairies on the land, one the Blue Men in the sea, and one the Nimble Men (*Fir Chlis*), *i.e.* the Northern Streamers, or Merry Dancers, in the sky.

This explanation belongs to the North Hebrides, and was heard by the writer in Skye. In Argyllshire the Blue Men are unknown, and there is no mention of the Merry Dancers being congeners of the Fairies. The person from whom the information was got was very positive he had himself seen one of the Blue Men. A blue-coloured man, with a long grey face (*aodunn fada glas*), and floating from the waist out of the water, followed the boat in which he was for a long time, and was occasionally so near that the observer might have put his hand upon him.

The channel between Lewis and the Shant Isles (*Na h-Eileinean siant*, the charmed islands) is called ' the Stream of the Blue Men' (*Sruth nam Fear Gorm*). A ship, passing through it, came upon a blue-coloured man sleeping on the waters. He was taken on board, and being thought of mortal race, strong twine was coiled round and round him from his feet to his shoulders, till it seemed impossible for him to struggle, or move foot or arm. The ship had not gone far when two men were observed coming after it on the waters. One of them was heard to say, " Duncan will be one man," to which the other replied, " Farquhar will be two." On hearing this, the man, who had been so securely tied, sprang to his feet, broke his bonds like spider threads, jumped overboard, and made off with the two friends, who had been coming to his rescue.

The Streamers. When the Streamers (*Na Fir Chlis*, lit. the active or quickly moving men) have ' a battle royal,' as they often have, the blood of their wounded falling to the earth, and becoming congealed, forms the coloured stones called ' blood stones,' known in the Hebrides also by the name of *fuil siochaire*, Elf's blood.

THE MERMAID.

The Mermaid (*Muir-òigh, maighdean mhara*) of the Scottish Highlands was the same as in the rest of the kingdom, a sea-creature, half fish half woman, with long dishevelled hair, which she sits on the rocks by the shore to comb at night. She has been known to put off the fishy covering of her lower limbs. Any one who finds it can by hiding it detain her from ever returning to the sea again. There is a common story in the Highlands, as also in Ireland, that a person so detained her for years, married her, and had a family by her. One of the family fell in with the covering, and telling his mother of the pretty thing he had found, she recovered possession of it and escaped to the sea. She pursues ships and is dangerous. Sailors throw empty barrels overboard, and while she spends her time examining these they make their escape.

A man in Skye (*Mac-Mhannain*) caught a Mermaid and kept her for a year. She gave him much curious information. When parting he asked her what virtue or evil there was in egg-water (*i.e.* water in which eggs had been boiled). She said, " If I tell you that, you will have a tale to tell," and disappeared.

A native of *Eilein Anabuich* (the Unripe Island), a village in North Harris, caught a Mermaid on a rock, and to procure her release, she granted him his three wishes. He became a skilful herb-doctor, who could cure the king's evil and other diseases ordinarily incurable, a prophet, who could foretell, particularly to women, whatever was to befall them, and he obtained a remarkably fine voice. This latter gift he had only in his own estimation ; when he sang, others did not think his voice fine or even tolerable.

CHAPTER V.

THE WATER-HORSE (*Each Uisge*).

THE belief in the existence of the Water-horse is now in the Highlands generally a thing of the past, but in olden times almost every lonely freshwater lake was tenanted by one, sometimes by several, of these animals. In shape and colour it resembled an ordinary horse, and was often mistaken for one. It was seen passing from one lake to another, mixing with the farmers' horses in the adjoining pastures, and waylaid belated travellers who passed near its haunts. It was highly dangerous to touch or mount it. Those whom it decoyed into doing so were taken away to the loch in which it had its haunt, and there devoured. It was said to make its approaches also in other guises—as a young man, a boy, a ring, and even a tuft of wool (*ribeag clòimhe*); and any woman upon whom it set its mark was certain at last to become its victim. The cow-shackle round its neck, or a cap on its head, completely subdued it, and as long as either of these was kept on it, it could be as safely employed in farm labour as any other horse.

In Skye it was said to have a sharp bill (*gob biorach*), or, as others describe it, a narrow brown slippery snout. Accounts are uniform that it had a long flowing tail and mane. In colour it was sometimes grey, sometimes black, and sometimes black with a white spot on its forehead. This variation arose, some say, from the water horse being of any colour like other horses, and others say from its having the power of changing its colour as well as its shape. When it came in the shape of a man, it was detected by its horse-hoofs and by the green water weeds or sand in its hair. It was then very amorous, but the end of those who were unfortunate enough to encounter it was to be taken to the loch and devoured. However much benefit the farmer might at first derive from securing one with the cap or cow-shackle he was ultimately involved by it in ruinous loss.

The following tales will illustrate the character of the superstition better than a lengthened dissertation :

FARMERS AND WATER-HORSES.

Stories to the following effect are common in Mull and the neighbourhood :

A strange horse, which cannot be driven away, is seen all winter among the rest of the farm horses. In olden times horses were little housed during winter; the stable door was left open, and the horses, after eating the little straw allowed them, went out to pick up what they could. When spring work comes on the strange horse is caught like the rest and made to work. Perhaps for greater security the cow-shackle is put round its neck. It proves as docile and easily managed as any horse could be. It is the best horse the farmer has, and is fat and sleek when the rest are lean and ragged. It works thus all spring, and in summer is employed to take home peats from the moor. It is placed foremost in a string of three or seven horses, which have creels on their backs, in ancient fashion, and are tied each to the tail of the horse before it. The farmer rides the foremost of the team. On the way it becomes restive and unmanageable, and sets off at full speed, followed by the rest, towards the loch. Observing that the shackle has slipped off, the man, in passing through a narrow gateway, plants a foot against each pillar and throws himself off its back, or he tumbles on the sands of the shore, and jumping up, cuts the halter of the hindmost horse. Those that remain tied are dragged into the loch, and next day their entrails or livers come ashore.

The most celebrated tale of this class was that of the son of the tenant of Aros, in Mull.

MAC-FIR AROIS.

The heir of Aros, a young man of great personal activity, and, it is said, of dissolute manners, having an opinion of himself that there was no horse he could not ride, was taken by a Water-horse into Loch Frisa, a small lake about a mile in length in the north-west of Mull and devoured. This occurred between his espousal and marriage, and the Lament composed by his intended bride is still and deservedly a popular song in Mull. There seems to be this much truth in the story, that the young man was dragged into Loch Frisa by a mare which he was attempting to subdue and drowned. It would appear from the song that his body was recovered. The popular details of the incident vary considerably, and are of interest as illustrative of the growth of tales of superstition.

One account has it that a remarkably handsome grey mare came among horses belonging to the tenant of Aros pasturing on the rushes at the end of Loch Frisa. One day his son haltered and mounted it. The grey stood quite quietly till it got the young man on its back. It then rushed into the loch.

Another account says the young man found a mare in the hills, which he took to be one of those belonging to his father. He caught it with the intention of riding home, but the mare took out to Loch Frisa, and he was there devoured by Water-horses.

A third account says the Water-horse was kept all winter, with the cow shackle about its neck, and remained so quiet and steady, that at last the shackle was neglected. The son of the tenant rode it one day to the peat-moss, three other horses following behind in usual form, when it suddenly rushed away to the lake, and nothing was ever seen of the youth or the horses but the livers.

A fourth account says, in spring a band of men went to the hill to catch a young horse wanted for harrowing or to send to market. They were unable to catch it, and next day Aros's son himself went with them. He caught what he supposed to be the horse wanted and jumped on its back. The horse rushed at full speed towards the loch, and the young man found he could not throw himself off. The horse's liver came ashore next day, the animal, it is supposed, having been killed by the other Water-horses tenanting the lake, when they felt the smell of a man off it.

There is still another account, that Mac-fir Arois was twice taken away by the Water-horse. The first time, he managed to put a foot on each side of a gate, in passing through, and allowed the horse to pass on. The second time, a cap which hitherto had kept the horse, was forgotten. In the terrible career of the steed to the loch, the young man clasped his arms round its neck, and could not unclasp them. His lungs came ashore next day.

THE TALKING HORSE AT CRU-LOCH.

This is a lonely little lake above Ardachyle (*Aird-a-chaoil*, the height of the sound) in the north-east of

Mull. A person passing it late at night, on his way home, saw a horse with a saddle on, quietly feeding at the loch side. He went towards it with the intention of riding it home, but in time he observed green-water herbs (*liaranaich*) about its feet and refrained from touching it. He walked on and before long was over-taken by a stranger, who said that unless he (the Water-horse, who was also the speaker) had been friendly and a well-wisher, he would have taken him to the loch. Among other supernatural information it told the man the day of his death.

ISLAND OF COLL.

At noontide, while the cattle were standing in the loch, the herdsman near Loch Annla was visited by a person in whose head he observed *rathum*, that is, water weeds. When going away the stranger jumped into the loch and disappeared without doing any harm. People used to hear strange noises about that loch, no doubt caused by the Water-horse, which was the herds-man's visitor.

THE NINE CHILDREN AT SUNART.

A number of children went on a Sunday to amuse themselves in the neighbourhood of the 'Loch of Disaster' (*Loch na Dunach*) in this district. They fell in with a horse, caught it, and in their thoughtless sport mounted it. Its back got longer till they were

all mounted, except one, who had a Bible in his
pocket. He touched the horse with his finger, and had
to cut it off to save himself. The horse rushed into
the lake, and the children, nine in number, were never
more seen. The liver of one of them came ashore
next day.

This tale is widely spread, and is obviously a pious
fraud to keep children from wandering on Sundays to
play in lonely places, and from meddling with any
horse they may find.

KILLING THE RAASAY WATER-HORSE.

'The Woman's Loch' (*Loch na Mna*) near Dùn
Can, the highest hill in this island, derives its name
from having been the scene of the abduction of a
woman by the Water-horse that haunted it. The big
Smith (*An Gobha Mòr*), who lived in the neighbourhood,
resolved to kill the horse, and by his success he earned
himself the title of 'Alastair na Béisde' (Alexander of
the monster). He built a hut close by, with an opening like the syver of a drain, leading towards the loch.
When he got the wind favourable, he killed and roasted
a wether-sheep in the hut. The wind blew the savoury
smell towards the loch, and the Water-horse, attracted
by it, made its way into the hut by the entrance left for
it. The smith had his irons ready in the fire, and
rushing with them at the Water-horse killed it. On
examination the monster proved to be merely grey

o

turves (*pluic ghlas*), or, as others say, a soft mass (*sgling*) like jelly-fish (*Muir-tiachd*).

THE WATER-HORSE AT LOCH CUAICH.

Some thirty years ago, a small islet in this lake, of about an half an acre in extent, was tenanted by a strange specimen of the Highland freebooter, named Macphie. He was a deserter from the army, who at first took refuge in a cave in the neighbourhood. He took away by force a girl of twelve years of age, and, coming next day to her parents, said if it would give any satisfaction he would marry her, but refusing to part with her. A sort of ceremony of marriage was gone through, but Macphie seems for several years to have looked upon the girl merely as his daughter. Her first child was born when she was eighteen years of age, and she had several more of a family. After his marriage Macphie removed to the islet mentioned, and remained there undisturbed for many years. He supported himself by fishing, hunting, and taking now and then a sheep or goat from the lands surrounding the loch. Such was his terror of being surprised by soldiers that he always carried arms about him, and slept with a bayonet and loaded gun beside his bed. The country people were afraid of him and he was commonly reported to be not 'canny.' He was at last evicted by a south country farmer, when he removed with his family to Fort William.

In his time a Water-horse was quite commonly seen in Loch Cuaich, floating on its side, or as it is called, 'making a film' (*deanadh sgleò*) and 'making a salmon of itself' (*deanadh bradain dheth fhein*), disporting itself and then disappearing.   One stormy night Macphie, by his own account, was roused by a loud rattling noise at the door, as if some one were trying to enter.   It stood in the door and Macphie knew it to be the Water-horse in the shape of a man.   He fired twice at it, but it did not move.   He called to his wife to bring a silver coin, and when he put this in the gun and fired, the figure went away and was heard plunging into the loch.   The people round the loch heard three shots from the islet that night, for whatever cause they may have been fired.

THE WATER-HORSE AT TIREE.

A man working in the fields in Caolas, in the east end of the island, saw a Water-horse coming from *Loch an Air*, a small marshy lake, full of reeds.   He ran off in terror, and left his coat behind.   The Water-horse tore the coat into shreds and then made after the man. The dogs came out when it came near the house and drove it away.

A son of one of the chamberlains of the island, last century, found a horse on the moors, and being struck with its excellence mounted it.   The horse tore away at full gallop and could not be stopped.   It galloped all round the country, till at last one side of the reins broke, and the horse rushed out on Loch Basibol, carrying its ill-fated rider with it.

WATER-HORSE AND WOMEN.

A young woman herding cattle drove her charge to a sequestered part of the hill, and while there a young man came her way, and reclining his head on her lap fell asleep. On his stretching himself she observed that he had horse-hoofs, and lulling him gently managed to get his head rested on the ground. She then cut out with her scissors the part of her clothes below his head and made her escape. When the Water-horse awoke and missed her it made a dreadful outcry.

This tale, with unimportant variations, is known over the whole Highlands. Sometimes the young woman is sitting on the turf wall (*tota*) forming the end of the house when the Water-horse, in the shape of a handsome young man, comes her way ; sometimes she is one of a band of women, assembled at the summer shieling—the rest are killed and she makes her escape. She detects the character of the youth by the water weeds or the sand in his hair. Many of the stories add that the young man (or Water-horse) came for her on a subsequent Sunday after dinner, or to church, to which (as in the story of the Water-horse of Loch Assapol in the Ross of Mull) she went for security rather than keep an appointment previously made with him, and took her to the loch. In Sutherlandshire the scene of the incident is laid at *Loch Meudaidh* in Durness, and the descendants of the woman to whom it occurred are still pointed out. She detected the young man by the sand in his hair, and on looking back, after she had got to some distance, she saw him tearing up the earth in his fury.[1]

A Water-horse in man's shape came to a house in which there was a woman alone; at the time she was boiling water in a clay vessel (*croggan*), such as was in use before iron became common. The Water-horse, after looking on for some time, drew himself nearer to her, and said in a snuffling voice, "It is time to begin courting, Sarah, daughter of John, son of Finlay." "It is time, it is time," she replied, "when the little pitcher boils." In a while it repeated the same words and drew itself nearer. She gave the same answer drawing out the time as best she could, till the water was boiling hot. As the snuffling youth was coming too near she threw the scalding water between his legs, and he ran out of the house roaring and yelling with pain.

[1] Such was the terror inspired a few years ago by a report that the Water-horse of Loch Meudaidh had made its re-appearance that the natives would not take home peats that they had cut at the end of the loch by boat (the only way open to them), and the fuel was allowed to go waste.

THE WATER-HORSE AT LOCH BASIBOL, TIREE.

On the north side of this loch, which has been already mentioned as a haunt of the Water-horse, there was a farm, where there are now only blowing sand-banks, called the Town of the Clumsy Ones (*Baile nan Cràganach*) from five men, who resided there, having each six fingers on every hand. They were brothers, and it was said the Water-horse came every night, in the shape of a young man, to see a sister, who staid with them.

With the tendency of popular tales to attach themselves to known persons, this incident is related of Calum Mor Clarke and his family. Calum had three sons, Big Fair John (*Iain Bàn Mòr*), Young Fair John (*Iain Bàn Òg*), and Middle Fair John (*Iain Bàn Mead-honach*). The four conspired to beguile the young man from the loch, who came to see the daughter, into the house, and got him to sit between two of them on the front of the bed. On a given signal these two clasped their hands round him and laid him on his back in the bed. The other two rushed to their assistance; the young man assumed his proper shape of a Water-horse and a fearful struggle ensued. The conspirators cut the horse in pieces with their dirks, and put it out of the house dead.[1]

---

[1] A Water-horse was killed in Skye, where the stream from Eisgeadal falls into Loch Fada, at the foot of Storr, by sticking a knife into it. It had previously killed a man.

Not far from the south end of the same loch there is a place called *Fhaire na h-aon oidhch'*, 'the one night's watch,' said to derive its name from an incident of which the Water-horse was the hero, similar to that told of the Urisk of Glen Màili (see page 197).

THE KELPIE.

The Kelpie that swells torrents and devours women and children has no representative in Gaelic superstition. Some writers speak as if the Water-horse were to be identified with it, but the two animals are distinctly separate. The Water-horse haunts lochs, the Kelpie streams and torrents. The former is never accused of swelling torrents any more than of causing any other natural phenomenon, nor of taking away children, unless perhaps when wanted to silence a refractory child. A Shetland friend writes : " Kelpies, I cannot remember of ever hearing what shape they were of. They generally did their mischief in a quiet way, such as being seen splashing the water about the burns, and taking hold of the water-wheel of mills, and holding them still. I have heard a man declare, that his mill was stopped one night for half an hour and the full power of water on the wheel, and he was frightened himself to go out and see what was wrong. And he not only said but maintained that it was a Kelpie or something of that kind that did it."

THE WATER-BULL (*Tarbh Uirge*).

This animal, unlike the Water-horse, was of harmless character, and did no mischief to those who came near its haunts. It staid in little lonely moorland lochs, whence it issued only at night. It was then heard lowing near the loch, and came among the farmers' cattle, but was seldom seen. Calves having short ears, as if the upper part had been cut off with a knife, or, as it is termed in Gaelic, *Carc-chluasach* (*i.e.* knife-eared), were said to be its offspring. It had no ears itself and hence its calves had only half ears.[1]

In the district of Lorn, a dairy-maid and herd, before leaving in the evening the fold, in which the cows had been gathered to be milked and left for the night, saw a small ugly very black animal, bull-shaped, soft and slippery, coming among the herd. It had an unnatural bellow, something like the crowing of a cock. The man and woman fled in terror, but, on coming back in the morning, found the cattle lying in the fold as though nothing had occurred.

THE KING OTTER.

The Water Dog (*Dobhar-Chù*), called also the King Otter (*Righ nan Dòbhran*), is a formidable animal, seldom seen, having a skin of magic power, worth as

---

[1] *Corc-chluasach* is also applied to calves the ears of which are in any way naturally marked, as if with a knife, slit in the points, serrated in the upper part, or with a piece out of the back.

many guineas as are required to cover it. It goes at
the head of every band of seven, some say nine, otters,
and is never killed without the death of a man, woman,
or dog. It has a white spot below the chin, on which
alone it is vulnerable. A piece of its skin keeps misfortune away from the house in which it is kept, renders
the soldier invulnerable in battle by arrow or sword or
bullet, and placed in the banner makes the enemy turn
and fly. " An inch of it placed on the soldier's eye,"
as a Lochaber informant said, " kept him from harm or
hurt or wound though bullets flew about him like
hailstones, and naked swords clashed at his breast.
When a direct aim was taken, the gun refused fire."

Others say the vulnerable white spot was under the
King Otter's arm, and of no larger size than a sixpence.
When the hunter took aim he required to hit this
precise spot, or he fell a prey to the animal's dreadful
jaws. In Raasa and the opposite mainland the magic
power was said to be in a jewel in its head, which made
its possessor invulnerable and secured him good fortune;
but in other respects the belief regarding the King Otter
is the same as elsewhere.

The word *dobhar* (pronounced dooar, dour), signifying
water, is obsolete in Gaelic except in the name of this
animal.

BIASD NA SROGAIG.

This mythical animal, 'the beast of the lowering
horn,' seems to have been peculiar to Skye. It had

but one horn on its forehead, and, like the Water-bull, staid in lochs. It was a large animal with long legs, of a clumsy and inelegant make, not heavy and thick, but tall and awkward. Its principal use seems to have been to keep children quiet, and it is little to be wondered at if, in the majority of cases, the terrors of childhood became a creed in maturer years. *Scrogag*, from which it derives its name, is a ludicrous name given to a snuff horn and refers to the solitary horn on its forehead.

THE BIG BEAST OF LOCHAWE.

This animal (*Beathach mòr Loch Odha*) had twelve legs and was to be heard in winter time breaking the ice. Some say it was like a horse, others, like a large eel.

CHAPTER VI.

SUPERSTITIONS ABOUT ANIMALS.

Buarach-bhaoi, lamprey.—The *Buarach-bhaoi* (lit. wild or wizard shackle), called also *Buarach na Baoi* (the shackle of the furious one), was believed to be a leech or eel-like animal to be found at certain fords and in dark waters, that twisted itself like a shackle round the feet of passing horses, so that they fell and were drowned. It then sucked their blood. It had nine eyes or holes in its head and back, at which the blood it sucked came out. Hence it was called *Buarach-bhaoi nan sùilean claon* (the furious shackle of the squinting eyes). In Skye, it was believed the animal was to be found in Badenoch. It was said to haunt the dark waters of Loch Tummel (*Tethuil*, hot flood, from the impetuosity of the river), in Perthshire, and was also known on the west coast of Argyllshire. The word is translated 'lamprey' in dictionaries, but the description suggests the tradition of some species of gymnotus or electric eel.

Cirein Cròin, Sea Serpent.—This was the largest animal in the world, as may be inferred from a popular Caithness rhyme :

> " Seven herring are a salmon's fill,
> Seven salmon are a seal's fill,
> Seven seal's are a whale's fill,
> And seven whales the fill of a Cirein Cròin."

To this is sometimes added, "seven Cirein Cròin are the fill of the big devil himself." This immense sea-animal is also called *Mial mhòr a chuain*, the great beast of the ocean, *cuartag mhòr a chuain*, the great whirlpool of the ocean, and *uile-bhéisd a chuain*, the monster of the ocean. It was originally a whirlpool, or the sea-snake of the Edda, that encircled the whole world.

Gigelorum.—The *Giolcam-daoram*, or Gigelorum, is the smallest of all animals. It makes its nest in the mite's ear and that is all that is known about it.

Lavellan.—This animal is peculiar to the north, where it is said to be able to hurt cattle from a distance of forty yards : " Lavellan, animal in Cathanesia frequens, in aquis degit, capite mustelae sylvestri simile, ejusdemque coloris, bestia est. Halitu Bestiis nocet. Remedium autem est, si de aqua bibant in quâ ejus caput coctum est." (Sibbald's *Scot. Ill.*, lib. 3, fol. 11.) Pennant, when at Ausdale, Langwell, Caithness-shire, says : " I inquired here after the Lavellan, which, from description, I suspect to be the water shrew mouse.

The country people have a notion that it is noxious to cattle ; they preserve the skin, and, as a cure for their sick beasts, give them the water in which it has been dipt. I believe it to be the same animal which, in Sutherland, is called the water mole." It is also mentioned by Rob Donn, the Sutherland bard, in his satirical song on " Mac Rorie's Breeches " : " Let him not go away from the houses, to moss or wood, lest the Lavellan come and smite him."

Bernicle Goose, Cadhan.—In the Hebrides, as in England, the Bernicle Goose was believed to grow from the thoracic worm, attaching itself to floating wood that has been some time in the water, often so closely as to hide the surface of the log. *Calum na Cròige*, a native of Croig in Mull, who went about the country some thirty or forty years ago, the delight of youngsters by his extraordinary tales of personal adventures and of wonders he had seen, and the energy with which, sitting astride on a stool, he raised with their assistance the anchor, hoisted sail, and performed other nautical feats, told that in the Indian seas, he and a comrade jumped overboard to swim to land. They swam for a week before reaching shore, but the water was so warm they felt no inconvenience. The loveliest music Calum ever heard was that made by Bernicle Geese as they emerged from barnacles that grew on the soles of his feet !

Eels (Easgunn).—It is still a very common belief in the Highlands that eels grow from horse hairs. In a

village of advanced opinions in Argyllshire, the following story was heard from a person who evidently
believed it :

"In the island of Harris, in a time of scarcity, a
person went out for fish, and succeeded only in getting
eels. These animals are not eaten in the Highlands
and his wife would not taste them. The man himself
ate several. By and by he went mad, and his wife had
to go for succour to a party of Englishmen, who had a
shooting lodge near. On arriving with loaded guns,
the sportsmen found the eel-eater in the fields fighting
a horse. He was so violent that they had to shoot
him. On inquiry it turned out that the cause of his
madness and fighting the horse was that the eels he
had eaten had grown from horse hairs!"

Whale.—The round-headed porpoises, or caaing
whales (*mucun bearraich*, lit. dog-fish pigs), derive their
Gaelic name from being supposed to grow from dog-
fish. An overgrown dog-fish, still retaining its own
shape, is called *Burraghlas.*

Herring.—The food of the Herring is said to consist
of crustacea and small fishes, but there is ordinarily
so little appearance of food in their stomach that an
easier explanation has been found in saying, they live
on the foam they make with their own tails! A door-
keeper at Dowart Castle is said to have successfully
warned a M'Kinnon from Skye of the dangers awaiting
him at the banquet to which he had been invited, by

asking him if they were getting any herring in the north at present, and then praising the herring as a royal fish (*iasg righ*) that never was caught by its mouthful of food or drink (*air a bhalgum no air a ghreim*). On hearing this remark M'Kinnon turned on his heel and made his escape.

Flounder.—According to Sutherland tradition, the wry mouth of the flounders (*Leòbag*, as it is called in the north) arose from its making faces at the rock-cod. A judgment (which children, who make faces, are liable to) came upon it, and its mouth remains as it then twisted it. In Tiree and Iona the distortion is said to have been caused by St. Columba. Colum-Kil met a shoal of flounders and asked :

" Is this a removal, flounder ? "

" Yes it is, Colum-Kil crooked legs," said the flounder.

" If I have crooked legs," said St. Columba, "may you have a crooked mouth," and so the flounder has a wry mouth to this day.

Lobster.—The three animals that dart quickest and farthest in the sea, according to a popular and perhaps truthful rhyme, are the lobster, mackerel, and seal. " The dart of lobster, the dart of mackerel, and the dart of seal ; and though far the lobster's dart, farther is the mackerel's dart, and though far the mackerel's dart, farther is the seal's dart."

Serpents.—A serpent, whenever encountered, ought

to be killed. Otherwise, the encounter will prove an omen of evil. The head should be completely smashed (*air a spleatradh*), and removed to a distance from the rest of the body. Unless this is done, the serpent will again come alive. The tail, unless deprived of animation, will join the body, and the head becomes a *beithis*, the largest and most deadly kind of serpent.[1] A person stung by one should rush to the nearest water. Unless he reaches it before the serpent, which also makes straight for it, he will die from the wound.

Another cure for the sting is water in which the head of another serpent has been put. There was a man in Applecross who cured epilepsy by water in which he kept a living serpent. The patient was not to see the water. Farquhar, the physician, obtained his skill in the healing art from being the first to taste the juice of a white serpent. He was a native of Tongue, in Sutherland-shire, and on one occasion was met by a stranger, who asked him where he got the walking-stick he held in his hand. The stranger further got him to go to the root of the tree from which the stick had been cut, take a white serpent from a hole at its foot and boil it. He was to give the juice without touching it to the

---

[1] The big beast of Scanlastle in Islay was one of this kind. It devoured seven horses on its way to Loch-in-daal. A ship was lying at anchor in the loch at the time, and a line of barrels filled with deadly spikes, and with pieces of flesh laid upon them, was placed from the shore to the ship. Tempted by the flesh, the 'loathly worm' made its way out on the barrels and was killed by the spikes and cannon.

stranger. Farquhar happened to touch the mess with his finger, and it being very hot, he thrust his finger in his mouth. From that moment he acquired his un-rivalled skill as a physician, and the juice lost its virtue.

A week previous to St. Bridget's Day (1st February, O.S.) the serpents are obliged to leave their holes under ground, and if the ground is then covered with snow they perish. In the popular rhyme relating to the subject the serpent in Argyllshire and Perthshire is called the 'daughter of Edward,' but in Skye *an ribhinn*, the damsel. In both cases the name is probably a mere euphemism suggested by the rhyme to avoid giving unnecessary offence to the venomous creature.

Rats and Mice.—When a place is infested to a troublesome extent with rats or mice, and all other means of getting rid of the pests have failed, the object can be accomplished by composing a song, advising them to go away, telling them where to go, and what road to take, the danger awaiting them where they are, and the plenty awaiting them in their new quarters. This song is called the Rat (or Mouse) Satire, and if well composed the vermin forthwith take their de-parture.

When the islet of Calv (*an Calbh*, the inner door), which lies across the mouth of Tobermory harbour, was let in small holdings, the rats at one time became so numerous that the tenants subscribed sixpence a-piece,

and sent for *Iain Pholchrain* to Morven, to come and
satjrize the rats away.   He came and made a long ode,
in which he told the rats to go away peaceably, and
take care not to lose themselves in the wood.   He told
them what houses to call at, and what houses (those of
the bard's own friends) to avoid, and the plenty and
welcome stores—butter and cheese, and meal—to be got
at their destination.   It is said that after this there was
an observable decrease in the number of rats in the
island !

An Ardnamurchan man, pestered with mice, in
strong language tried to get them away, and all who
have had experience of the annoyance, will heartily
join him in his wishes.   The poet, with whips and
switches, gathers the mice in a meadow near a stream,
and sends a number of the drollest characters in the
district to herd them, and 'old men, strong men,
striplings, and honest matronly women, with potato
beetles,' to chase them.   At last he gets them on board
a boat at *Eabar an ròin*, and sends them to sea.

> " The sea roaring boisterously,
>   The ocean heaving and weltering,
>   The tearing sound of sails splitting,
>   The creaking of the keel breaking,
>   The bilge water through the hull splashing
>   Like an old horse neighing."

And leaving them in this evil plight, the song ceases.

Cormorant.—This bird passes through three stages of
existence ; it is "seven years a scart (*pelecanus cristatus*),

seven years a speckled loon (*colymbus arcticus*), and seven years a cormorant (*pelecanus carbo*)" (*Seachd bliadhna na sgarbh, seachd bliadhna na learg, 's seachd bliadhna na bhallaire bodhain*).

Magpie.—The pyet (*piaghaid*) is called 'the messenger of the Campbells' (*Gille ruith nan Caimbeulach*), a name also given (for what reason the writer has not been able to ascertain) to a person who is 'garrulous, lying, interfering with everbody' (*gobach, briagach, 'g obair air na h-uile duine*). It is said of a meddling chatterbox, "What a messenger of the Campbells you have become!" It is 'little happiness' (*beagan sonais*) for any one to kill a magpie.

Beetles.—The *Ceardalan* or dung-beetle is spared by boys when met with, but the *daolag* or clock is mercilessly killed. The reason assigned is, that when the former met those who came to seize the person of our Saviour, and was asked how long since he had passed, it said, "twenty days ago yesterday" (*fhichead latha gus an dé, chaidh Mac Dhé seachad*), but the latter said, " it was only yesterday" (*an dé, an dé chaidh Mac Dhé seachad*). Hence, when boys hammer the life out of a ' clock,' they keep repeating with savage unction, "The day before yesterday, wretch " (*air a bhò 'n dé, bhradag*), or a rhyme :

> " Remember yesterday, yesterday,
> Remember yesterday, wretch,
> Remember yesterday, yesterday,
> That let not the Son of God pass."

Emmet (Caora-Chòsag).—This animal is shaken between the palms of the hand and laid upon the table. It is believed by boys to indicate the weather of the following day, by lighting on its back or belly and the alacrity with which it moves away.

Skip-Jack.—This insect (*Gobhachan, i.e.* little smith or *Buail a Chnag,* give a knock), when laid on its back emits a loud crack in springing to its proper position. It is a favourite amusement of boys when they get hold of one to make it go through this performance. In Skye, when watching it preparing to skip, they say,

> " Strike with your hammer, little smith,
> Or I will strike your head." [1]

---

[1] " Buail an t-òrd, a ghobachain,
No buailidh mi sa cheann thu."

CHAPTER VII.

MISCELLANEOUS SUPERSTITIONS.

Gisvagun, Eapagun, Upagun.—Of the same class with magical charms and incantations, that is, of no avail to produce the results with which they are credited, were various minor observances and practices, to which importance was attached as lucky or unlucky, and ominous of, if not conducive to, future good or ill. In some cases these observances became mere customs, followed without heed to their significance or efficacy; and many were known to, and believed in only by, the very superstitious. So far as causing or leading to the result ascribed to them was concerned, they were, 'like the Sunday plant,' without good or harm, but a mind swayed by trifling erroneous beliefs of the kind is like a room filled with cobwebs. Superstition shuts out the light, makes the mind unhealthy, and fills it with groundless anxieties.

The Right-Hand Turn (Deiseal).—This was the most important of all the observances. The rule is " *Deiseal* (*i.e.* the right-hand turn) for everything," and consists in doing all things with a motion corresponding to the course of the sun, or from left to right. This is the manner in which screw-nails are driven, and is common with many for no reason but its convenience. Old men in the Highlands were very particular about it. The coffin was taken *deiseal* about the grave, when about to be lowered ; boats were turned to sea according to it, and drams are given to the present day to a company. When putting a straw rope on a house or corn-stack, if the assistant went *tuaitheal* (*i.e.* against the course of the sun), the old man was ready to come down and thrash him. On coming to a house the visitor should go round it *deiseal* to secure luck in the object of his visit. After milking a cow the dairy-maid should strike it *deiseal* with the shackle, saying "out and home" (*mach 'us dachaigh*). This secures its safe return. The word is from *deas*, right-hand, and *iul*, direction, and of itself contains no allusion to the sun.

Rising and Dressing.—It is unfortunate to rise out of bed on one's left side. It is a common saying when evil befalls a person, who seems to himself to have rushed to meet it, " I did not rise on my right hand to-day." [1]

Water in which eggs have been boiled or washed should not be used for washing the hands or face. It is also a common saying when mischance befalls a person through his own stupidity, " I believe egg-water was put over me."

[1] " Is mise nach d'éirich air mo làimh dheis an duigh."

When done washing himself a person should spit in the water, otherwise if the same water should be used by another for a like purpose, there will be danger of quarrelling with him before long.

Clothes.—When a person puts on a new suit it is customary to wish him luck of it : "May you enjoy and wear it." A man should be always the first to do this, the tailor, if he has the good sense. It is unlucky if a woman be the first to say it, and prudent women delay their congratulations and good wishes till they are satisfied some male friend has spoken first. It is less unfortunate if the woman has had a male child.

If a person wearing a dress dyed with *crotal*, a species of lichen, be drowned, his body will never be found. This belief prevails in the north, and there the home-made dress indicated, which is of a reddish-brown colour, is frequently seen.

Houses and Lands.—There should be placed below the foundation of every house a cat's claws, a man's nails, and a cow's hoofs, and silver under the door-post. These will prove omens of the luck to attend the house. If an outgoing tenant leaves the two former below the door it is unfortunate for the incoming tenant, as his cattle will die.

An expectant occupier, or claimant, will secure to himself possession of land by burning upon it a little straw. This straw was called 'a possession wisp' (*Sop seilbhe*). If, for instance, there were two claimants to

land and one of them burnt a 'possession wisp' on it,
he might go about his business with his mind easy as
to the result of the lawsuit. Or, if a tenant ran in debt
and had to leave his farm, another, who had a promise
of the holding, came and burnt a 'possession wisp,' no
evil or debt of those formerly attaching to it would
then follow the holding.

Baking.—In baking oatmeal cakes there is a little
meal left on the table after the last cake is sprinkled
previous to being fired.   This remnant should not be
thrown away or returned to the meal chest, but be
kneaded between the palms into a little cake, to be
given to one of the children.   This little bannock was
the *Bonnach Fallaid,* called also *Siantachan a chlàir*
(the charmer of the board), to which in olden times
housewives attached so much importance.   Unless it
was made the meal lost its substance, and the bread of
that baking would not be lasting (*baan*).   On putting
a hole through it with the forefinger, as already
explained, it was given to children, and placed beside
women in childbed, to keep the Fairies away.   It
mightily pleased little children, and was given to them
as a reward for making themselves useful.

> " A little cake to Finlay,
> For going to the well."

Its origin is said to have been as follows :

A man fell in with a skull in a graveyard and took
it to a tailor's house, where bread was being baked.

The tailor gave it a kick, saying, "There was one period of the world when your gabful of dough was not small, and if I had you on a New-Year's day, I would give you your fill." When the New Year came round, a stranger came to the tailor's house asking for a mouthful of dough. The tailor set his wife to bake, and whatever she baked the stranger ate, and then asked for more. The tailor's stock of meal, and that of his neighbours, was devoured, and still the stranger asked for more. An old man of the neighbourhood was consulted, and he advised that the remnants, or dry meal used for sprinkling the cakes, should also be baked for the voracious guest. On this *Fallaid* cake being given the stranger declared himself satisfied and went away.

If bread, when being baked, breaks frequently a hungry stranger will come to eat it. Many cakes breaking are a sign of misfortune, by which the housewife is warned that "something is making for her."

If the cake for breakfast falls backwards, the person for whom it is intended should not be allowed to go on a journey that day; his journey will not be prosperous. The evil can, however, be remedied by giving plenty of butter, ' without asking,' with the cake. To avert this omen, cakes should not be placed to harden at the fire on their points, but on either of the two sides or on their round edge. An old woman in Islay got into a great rage at a wake on seeing the cakes (that is, quarters of a *farl* or large round bannock) placed on their points.

It is not good to count the cakes when done baking. They will not in that case last any time.

Removal Cheese (Mulchag Imrich).—When leaving the summer pastures in the hills, on Lammas day, and returning with the cattle to the strath, a small cheese made of curds was made from that day's milk, to be given to the children and all who were at the *àiridh*, for luck and good-will. The cows were milked early in the morning, curds were made and put in the cheese vat (*fioghan*), and this hastily-prepared cheese was the *mulchag imrich*, and was taken with the rest of the furniture home for the purpose mentioned.

Leg Cake (Bonnach Lurgainn).—This was a cake given to the herd when he came with news that a mare had foaled, or to the dairy-maid when she brought word that a cow had calved.

Giving Fire out of the House.—On the first day of every quarter of the year—New-Year day, St Bride's day, Beltane, and Lammas—no fire should be given out of the house. On the two last days especially it should not be given, even to a neighbour whose fire had gone out. It would give him the means of taking the substance or benefit (*toradh*) from the cows. If given, after the person who had come for it left, a piece of burning peat (*ceann fòid*) should be thrown into a tub of water, to keep him from doing harm. It will also

prevent his coming again.   On New-Year's day fire
should not be given out of the house on any considera-
tion to a doubtful person.   If he is evil-disposed, not a
beast will be alive next New Year.   A suspected witch
came on this day to a neighbour's house for fire, her
own having gone out, and got it.   When she went
away a burning peat was thrown into a tub of water.
She came a second time and the precaution was again
taken.   The mistress of the house came in, and on
looking in the tub found it full of butter.

Thunder.—In a storm of thunder and lightning iron,
for instance the poker and tongs, put in the fire, averts
all danger from the house.   This curious belief seems
to have been widespread at one time throughout the
Western Highlands, though now its memory barely
survives.   Its *rationale* seems to have been in some way
to propitiate the fire, of which lightning is the most
powerful exhibition.   A woman in Cnoydart (a Roman
Catholic district), alarmed by the peals of a thunder-
storm, threw holy water on herself, put the tongs in the
fire, and on being asked the reason, said, " The cross of
Christ be upon us ! the fire will not harm us." Perhaps
the practice had some connection with the belief that the
Beither, or thunder-bolt, was of iron, a sharp-pointed
mass.   It seems one of the most irrational practices
possible, but was probably of remote origin.   In Kent
and Herefordshire, a *cold iron bar* was put on the barrels,
to keep the beer from being soured by thunder.

Theft.—The stealing of salt, seed of plants, and lint make the thief liable to judgment without mercy. He may escape punishment from men but he will never attain to rest, as the rhyme says:

> "The stealer of salt, and the stealer of seeds,
> Two thieves that get no rest;
> Whoever may or may not escape,
> The stealer of grey lint will not." [1]

Another version of the rhyme is :

> "Thief of salt and thief of seeds,
> Two thefts from which the soul gets no repose;
> Till the fish comes on land
> The thief of lint gets never rest."

Salt.—In addition to the testimony this rhyme bears to the value of salt, there was a saying, that a loan of salt should be returned as soon as possible ; if the borrower dies in the meantime and without restitution being made his ghost will revisit the earth. No fish should be given out of the house without being first sprinkled with salt. Meal taken out of the house in the evening was sprinkled with salt to prevent the Fairies getting its benefit.

Combing the Hair.—A person should not comb his hair at night, or if he does, every hair that comes out should be put in the fire. Otherwise they will meet his feet in the dark and make him stumble. No sister

---

[1] " Meirleach salainn 's méirleach frois,
Da mheirleach nach fhaigh fois ;
Ge b'e co thig no nach d'thig a nios,
Cha d'thig meirleach an lìn ghlais."

should comb her hair at night if she have a brother at sea.

If the hair is allowed to go with the wind and it passes over an empty nest, or a bird takes it to its nest, the head from which it came will ache.

No person should cut his own hair, as he will by doing so become an unlucky person to meet.

If the hair, when thrown on the fire, will not burn, it is a sign the person will be drowned.

Bird Nests.—On falling in with a nest for the first time that year, if there be only one egg in it, or if there be an odd egg in it, that egg should be broken.

Any one finding a cuckoo's nest will live to be widowed.

Hen's First Egg.—A young hen's first egg should be tapped on the hearth, saying, "one, two, three," etc., and as many numbers as were repeated before the egg broke, or the youngster, who was persuaded to try the experiment, got tired, so many eggs would that hen lay.

Euphemisms.—By giving diseases and other evils a good name, when speaking of them, the danger of bringing them upon oneself by his words is turned away. It will be remembered that for a similar reason the ancients called the Fairies Eumenides, and the Celt called the Fairies 'good people.' The smallpox was called 'the good woman.' Epilepsy 'the outside disease.'

In telling a tale of any one being taken away by the Fairies, the ill-will of the ' people ' was averted by prefixing the narrative with the words, " A blessing on their journeying and travelling ! this is Friday and they will not hear us."

When a person sneezes it is customary for the bystander to say " Thank you," to which is sometimes added, " We will not take his name in vain." Some say, " God be with you," others, " God and Mary be with you," and others, " St. Columba be with you." By saying, " The hand of your father and grandfather be over you," the Fairies are kept away. Any words would seem to have been deemed availing, and some of the phrases used were not choice. If the bystander should say, " Your brains the next time !" the person sneezing should answer, " The bowl of your head intercept them ! "

When a child yawns, the nurse should say, " Your weariness and heaviness be on yonder grey stone ! "

When the story of a house having taken fire is told, the narrative should be prefixed by saying, " St Mary's well be in the top of every house ! the cross of Christ be upon us !" This averts a similar calamity from the house in which the tale is told.

In some places old people are to be found who, when a person comes in with any tale of misfortune, of the death of one of the cattle, a neighbour's house taking fire, etc., pull threads from their clothes and throw them in the fire, saying, "Out with the evil tale!" or, " To tell it to themselves."

In speaking of the dead, it is proper to speak of them only in commendatory terms—*de mortuis nihil nisi bonum.* Hence *moladh mairbh* (Praise of the Dead) denotes faint praise, not always deserved. In speaking of the dead, old people always added, " His share of paradise be his " (*chuid a fhlaitheanas da*), or " His portion of mercy be his " (*chuid a thròcair da*). If their tale was not to the credit of the deceased or they were obliged to make any statement unfavourable to him, they said, " It is not to send it after him."

Boat Language.—When in a boat at sea, sailing or fishing, it was forbidden to call things by the names by which they were known on land. The boat-hook should not be called *croman*, but *a chliob*; a knife, not *sgian*, but *a ghiar* (the sharp one); the baling dish, not *taoman*, but *spùidseir*; a seal, not *ròn*, but *bèisd mhaol* (the bald beast); a fox, not *sionnach*, but *madadh ruadh* (the red dog); the stone for anchoring the boat was not *clach*, but *cruaidh* (hardness). This practice prevails much more on the east coast than on the west, where it may be said to be generally extinct. It is said to be carefully observed among the fishermen about the Cromarty Firth. It was deemed unlucky by east coast fishermen coming to Tiree (as several boats used to do annually to prosecute the cod and ling fishing), to speak in a boat of a minister or a rat. Everywhere it was deemed unlucky among seafaring men to whistle in case a storm should arise. In Tiree, Heynish Hill (the highest in the island) was known at sea as *a Bhraonach*; *Hogh* Hill (the next highest) as *Bheinn Bhearnach no Sgoillte* (the Notched or Cloven Hill), and a species of whale as *cas na poite* (the leg of a pot). It should not be said " He was drowned" (*bhàthadh e*) but " he journeyed" (*shiubhail e*) ; not "tie a rope" (*ceangail ròp*), but " make it " (*dean e*). In the north it was held that an otter, while in its den, should not be called *béisd du* (the black beast, its common name), but *Carnag*. It would otherwise be impossible for the terriers to drive it from its refuge.

Fresh Meat.—When fresh meat of the year's growth is tasted for the first time, a person should say,

> " A death-shroud on the grey, better grey, old woman,
> Who said she would not taste the fresh meat,
> I will taste the fresh meat,
> And will be alive for it next year."

This ensures another year's lease of life.

Killing those too long alive.—If a person is thought to be too long alive, and it becomes desirable to get rid of him, his death can be ensured by bawling to him thrice through the key-hole of the room in which he is bedrid,

> " Will you come, or will you go ?
> Or will you eat the flesh of cranes ?"

Funerals.—It was customary to place a plate of salt, the smoothing iron, or a clod of green grass on the breast of a corpse, while laid out previous to being coffined. This, it was believed, kept it from swelling. A candle was left burning beside it all night. When it was placed in the coffin and taken away on the day of the funeral, the boards on which it had been lying were left for the night as they were, with a drink of water on them, in case the dead should return and be thirsty. Some put the drink of water or of milk outside the door, and, as in Mull and Tiree, put a sprig of pearlswort above the lintel to prevent the dead from entering the house.

When coffining the corpse every string in the shroud was cut with the scissors; and in defence of the practice there was a story that, after burial, a woman's shade came to her friends, to say that all the strings in her shroud had not been cut. Her grave was opened, and this was found to be the case.

The only instance the writer has heard of Cere-cloth, that is, cloth dipped in wax in which dead bodies were wrapped, being used in the Highlands, is, that the Nicholsons of Scorrybreck, in Skye (a family said to be of Russian descent through *Neacal mòr* who was in Mungastadt), had a wax shirt (*Leine Chéir*) which, from the friendship between themselves and the chief of the Macleods, was sent for from Dunvegan on every occasion of a death.

Q

The Watch of the Graveyard (Faire Chlaidh).—The person last buried had to keep watch over the grave-yard till the next funeral came. This was called *Faire Chlaidh*, the graveyard watch, kept by the spirits of the departed.

At Kiel (*Cill Challum Chille*), in Morvern, the body of the Spanish Princess said to have been on board one of the Armada blown up in Tobermory Bay was buried. Two young men of the district made a paction, that whoever died first the other would watch the church-yard for him. The survivor, when keeping the promised watch, had the sight of his dead friend as well as his own. He saw both the material world and spirits. Each night he saw ghosts leaving the church-yard and returning before morning. He observed that one of the ghosts was always behind the rest when returning. He spoke to it, and ascertained it to be the ghost of the Spanish Princess. Her body had been removed to Spain, but one of her little fingers had been left behind, and she had to come back to where it was.

When two funeral parties met at the churchyard, a fight frequently ensued to determine who should get their friend first buried.

Suicides.—The bodies of suicides were not taken out of the house, for burial, by the doors, but through an opening made between the wall and the thatch. They were buried, along with unbaptized children, outside the common churchyard.

It was believed in the north, as in Skye and about Applecross (*a Chomrach*) in Ross-shire, no herring would be caught in any part of the sea which could be seen from the grave of a suicide.

Murder.—It was believed in Sutherlandshire that a murdered body remained undecayed till 'touched.

The Harvest Old Wife (*a Chailleach*).—In harvest, there was a struggle to escape being the last done with the shearing, and when tillage in common existed, instances were known of a ridge being left unshorn (no person would claim it) because of it being behind the rest. The fear entertained was that of having the ' famine of the farm ' (*'gort a bhaile*), in the shape of an imaginary old woman (*cailleach*), to feed till next harvest. Much emulation and amusement arose from the fear of this old woman ; and from it arose the expression, " Better is a mercy-leap in harvest than a sheaf additional " (*'As fearr leum-iochd a's t' fhogaradh na sguab a bharrachd*). The *cum-iochd*,[1] or mercy-leap, is where a rocky mound or a soft spot, where no corn grows, occurs in a ridge. Its occurrence was a great help to the shearing being done.

The first done made a doll of some blades of corn, which was called the ' old wife,' and sent it to his nearest neighbour. He in turn, when ready, passed it to another still less expeditious, and the person it last

---

[1] *Leagadh-iochd* is the remission of arrears of rent, lit. a merciful letting down.

remained with had the 'old woman' to keep for that year. The old wife was known in Skye as the Cripple Goat (a *Ghobhar Bhacach*).

The fear of the Cailleach in harvest made a man in *Saor-bheinn*, in the Ross of Mull, who farmed his land in common with another, rise and shear his corn by moonlight. In the morning he found it was his neighbour's corn he had cut.

Big Porridge Day (*La u Bhrochain mhòr*).—In the Western Islands, in olden times (for the practice does not now exist anywhere), when there was a winter during which little sea-ware came ashore, and full time for spring work had come without relief, a large dish of porridge, made with butter and other good ingredients, was poured into the sea on every headland where wrack used to come. Next day the harbours were full.

This device was to be resorted to only late in the spring—the Iona people say the Thursday before Easter —and in stormy weather. The meaning of the ceremony seems to have been that, by sending the fruit of the land into the sea, the fruit of the sea would come to land.

Fires on Headlands.—In Skye, fires were lighted on headlands at the beginning of winter to bring in herrings.

Stances.—Particular stances, or sites of buildings, were accounted unlucky, such for instance as the site of a byre in which the death of several cattle had occurred ; and it was recommended, to prevent the recurrence of such misfortunes, that the site should be altered.

Names.—So with regard to names. If the children of a family were dying in infancy, one after the other, it was thought that, by changing the name, the evil would be counteracted. The new name was called a ' Road name ' (*Ainm Rathaid*), being that of the first person encountered on the road when going with the child to be baptized. It was given ' upon the luck ' (*air sealbhaich*) of the person met.

The Mac-Rories, a sept of the Mac-Larens, in Perth-shire, were descendants of one who thus received his name. His parents, having lost a previous child before its baptism, were advised to change the name. They were on their way through the Pass, called *Lairig Isle*, between Loch Erne and Glen-dochart, to have their second child baptized, when they were met by one Rory Mac Pherson. He was an entire stranger to them, but turned back with them, as a stranger ought to do to avoid being unlucky, and the child was called after him. *Clann 'ic-Shimigeir*, a sept of the Mac Neills, have also a road name.

Delivery of Cattle and Horses.—Before delivering a cow to the buyer at a market, the seller should pass the end of the rope, by which she is led, three times round his body. When taking delivery of a horse, from one of whom you are not sure, you should come *deiseal* between him and the horse, and take hold of the halter inside his hand, that is, between him and the horse. Otherwise, the seller's eye will be after the beast.

Trades.—Masons were said to be able to raise the devil, or, as the Gaelic expression more forcibly describes it, "to take the son of cursing from his roots" (*mac-mollachd thoirt as a fhriamhaichean*).

Smiths, being people who work among iron, were deemed of more virtue against the powers of evil than any other tradesmen.

Tailors were looked upon with a feeling akin to that entertained in the south, where "nine tailors made a man." The reason probably was that in olden times every man fit to bear arms thought it beneath him to follow a peaceful occupation, and only the lame and cripple were brought up as tailors.

Tinkers are known as *Luckd-Ceaird*, that is literally 'tradesmen,' and the name is a memory of days when they held the first rank as hand-craftsmen.

Saor, a joiner, means literally 'a free-man,' whence it would appear that from the earliest times the trade was highly esteemed.

Iron.—An oath on *cold iron* was deemed the most binding oath of any ; when people swore on their dirks it was only because it was at the time the cold iron readiest to hand. A man who secreted iron, and died

without telling where, could not rest in his grave.   At
Meigh, in Lochaber, a ghost for a long time met people
who were out late.   An old man, having taken with
him a Bible and made a circle round himself on the
road with a dirk, encountered it, and, in reply to his
inquiries, the ghost confessed to having stolen a plough-
share (*soc a chroinn*), and told where the secreted iron
was to be found.   After this the ghost discontinued its
visits to the earth.

Cold iron, *e.g.* the keys passed round the body of a
cow, after her return from the bull, keeps her from
ath-dàir, that is, seeking to go on the same journey
again.

Empty Shells.—Empty whelk shells (*Faochagun
failmhe*) should not be allowed to remain in the house
for the night.   Something is sure to come after them.

Similarly, water in which feet have been washed (*i.e.*
out of which the use or benefit has been taken) should
not be left in the house for fear the noiseless people
come and plunge about in it all night.

Protection against Evil Spirits.—On every occasion of
danger and anxiety, the Highlander of former days
commended himself to the protection of the Cross.   In
a storm of thunder he blessed himself saying, " the
Cross of Christ be upon us."   When he encountered a
ghost or evil spirit at night, he drew a circle round
himself on the road with the point of his dirk, or a
sapling in the name of Christ, " the Cross of Christ be

upon me," and while he remained in the circle no evil could come near him.

A person was also safe while below high-water mark. Fairies and evil spirits had no power below the roll of sea-weed.

When walking the high road at night, it is recommended to keep to the side paths in case of meeting the wraiths of funerals. The ghostly train may throw a person down, or compel him to carry the bier to the churchyard.

Misnaming a Person.—If a person be accidentally misnamed, as *e.g.* being called John when his name is Donald, he who made the mistake, on observing it, instantly exclaimed, " The Cross of Christ be upon us."

Gaining Straw (Sop Seile).—At certain seasons of the year, principally at Beltane and Lammas, a wisp of straw, called *Sop-seile* (literally a spittle wisp), was taken to sprinkle the door-posts and houses all round sunwise (*deiseal*), to preserve them from harm. When a new cow came home it was also sprinkled to preserve it from the evil eye. The liquid used was menstruum.

In spring the horses, harness, plough, etc., were similarly sprinkled before beginning to plough.

Propitious Times.—A great number of the observances of superstition were regulated by days of the week or year. There were certain days on which alone certain works could be commenced under favourable auspices and with any chance of being successfully done.

Unlucky Actions.—It is unlucky to wind black thread at night. A vicious wish made to one another by women quarrelling, in olden times, was, " The disease of women who wind black thread at night be upon you ! " Some say the reason of the evil omen is, that black thread is apt to disappear at night, or be taken by the Fairies, and be found through the house next morning. Superstition probably assigned some more occult reason.

It is 'little happiness' for anyone to kill a magpie or a bat.

It is unlucky for a person on a journey to return the way he went. This belief had its origin in the instructions given to the 'man of God,' who rebuked the idolatry of Jeroboam. " Eat no bread, nor drink water, nor turn again by the same way that thou camest " (1 Kings xiii. 9).

CHAPTER VIII.

AUGURY.[1]

THE anxiety of men to know the future, the issue of their labours, and the destinies awaiting them, makes them ready listeners to the suggestions of fancy, and an easy prey to deception. The mind eagerly lays hold on anything that professes to throw light on the subject of its anxiety, and men are willing victims to their own hopes and fears. Where all is dark and inscrutable, deception and delusion are easy, and hence augury of all kinds, omens, premonitions, divinations, have ever exercised a noticeable power over the human mind.

The ordinary manner which superstition takes to forecast the future is to look upon chance natural appearances under certain circumstances as indications of the character, favourable or unfavourable, of the event about which the mind is anxious. Any appearance in nature, animate or inanimate, can thus be made an omen of, and an inference be drawn from it of impend-

[1] *Manadaireachd.*

ing good or bad fortune. If it be gloomy, forbidding, awkward, or unpleasant, it is an unlucky omen, and the subsequent event, with which the mind associates it, will be unfavourable, but if pleasant, then it is a good omen, and prognosticates pleasant occurrences.

Omens which proceed upon a similarity of character between the prognostic and its fulfilment are easy of interpretation. There are other omens which have no connection, natural, possible, or conceivable, with the impending event, and of which consequently the meaning is occult, known only to people of skill instructed in their interpretation. These probably had their origin in one or two accidental coincidences. For instance, if the appearance of a fox is to be taken as an omen, it will naturally be taken as a bad sign, the stinking brute can indicate nothing favourable ; but no amount of sagacity will teach a person that an itching in the point of his nose prognosticates the receipt of important news, or the cuckoo calling on the house-top the death of one of the inmates within the year. His utmost acuteness will fail to find in a shoulder-blade any indication of destiny, or any prophetic meaning in the sediment of a cup of tea. The meaning of these is a mystery to the uninitiated, and it is easy to see how they might be reduced to a system and lead to the wildest delusions of fortune-telling.

Everything a Highlander of the old school set about, from the most trifling to the most important, was under

the influence of omens.   When he went to fish, to catch
his horse in the hill, to sell or buy at the market, to ask
a loan from his neighbour, or whatever else he left home
to do, he looked about for a sign of the success of his
undertaking, and, if the omen were unpropitious, returned
home.   He knew his journey would be of no avail.   He
consulted mystagogues as to his fate, and at the proper
seasons looked anxiously for the signs of his luck.
Like the rest of mankind, he was, by means of these,
pleased or depressed in anticipation of events that were
never to occur.   Hence the saying, " Take a good omen
as your omen, and you will be happy."

Probably the Greek μαντεία, prediction by an oracle,
is cognate to the Gaelic *manadh*, a foretoken, anything
from which a prediction can be drawn.   Both among
Greeks and Celts a great number of omens were taken
from birds.

As already mentioned, it is a bad sign of a person's
luck during the day that he should rise from bed on
his left hand, wash himself with water in which eggs
have been boiled, or the cakes for his breakfast should
frequently break in the baking, or fall backwards.   The
coming evil can be averted in the latter case by giving
plenty of ' butter without asking ' (*Im gun iarraidh*)
with the cakes.   Indeed, ' butter unasked for ' is of
sovereign value as an omen of luck.   A cake spread
with it, given to fishermen, secures a good day's fishing.
It is reckoned good in diseases, particularly measles,

and a most excellent omen for people going on a journey. Its not being given to Hugh of the Little Head, on the morning of his last battle, was followed by his losing the battle and his life.

Omens are particularly to be looked for at the outset of a journey. If the first animal seen by the traveller have its back towards him, or he meet a sheep or a pig, or any unclean animal, or hear the shrill cry of the curlew, or see a heron, or he himself fall backward, or his walking-stick fall on the road, or he have to turn back for anything he has forgot, he may as well stay at home that day ; his journey will not prosper. A serpent, a rat, or a mouse is unlucky unless killed, but if killed becomes a good omen. If the face of the animal be towards one, even in the case of unlucky animals, the omen becomes less inauspicious.

It is of great importance what person is first met. Women are unlucky, and some men are the most unfortunate omen that can be encountered. These are called *droch còmhalaichean, i.e.* bad people to meet, and it was told of a man in Skye, that to avoid the mischance of encountering one of them when setting out on a journey, he sent one of his own family to meet him. If he met any other he returned home. In a village in Ayrshire there are three persons noted for being inauspicious to meet, and fishermen (upon whom as a class this superstition has a strong hold) are much dissatisfied at meeting any of them. One of them is not so bad if he puts his hand to his face in a manner peculiar to him. It is inauspicious to meet a person from the same village as oneself, or a man with his head bare, or a man going to pay rent. Old people going to pay rent, therefore, took care to go away unobserved. A plain-soled person is unlucky, but the evil omen in his case is averted by rolling up the tongue against the roof of the mouth. The Stewarts were said to have insteps ; water flowed below their foot; it was, therefore, fortunate to meet any of them. All risk of a stranger proving a bad *còmhalaiche* is avoided by his returning a few steps with the traveller.

A hare crossing one's path is unlucky, and old people, when they saw one before them, made considerable de-tours to avoid such a calamity. The disfavour with which this harmless animal and the pig were regarded no doubt arose from their being unclean under the Levi-tical Law. The hare chews the cud, but divides not the hoof ; the pig divides the hoof, but does not chew the cud.

The fox is unlucky to meet, a superstition that pre-vails also in East Africa. The King of Karague told Captain Speke that " if a fox barked when he was leading an army to battle, he would retire at once, knowing that this prognosticated evil " (*Journal*, p. 241).

It is unlucky to look back after setting out. Old

people, if they had to turn to a person coming after them, covered their face. This superstition probably had its origin in the story of Lot's wife. Fin MacCoul, according to a popular tale, never looked back after setting out on a journey. When he went on the expedition that terminated in his being " in the house of the Yellow Forehead without liberty to sit down or power to stand up," he laid spells on his companions, that no man born in Ireland should follow him. Fergus, who was born in Scotland, followed, and Fin, hearing footsteps behind him, called out without turning his head, in a phrase now obsolete, *Co sid a propadh mo cheaplaich*? *i.e.*, it is supposed, "Who is that following my footsteps?"

To be called after is a sure omen that a person will not get what he is going in search of. This belief gave great powers of annoyance to people of a waggish humour. When everything prognosticated success, and the fishing boat had left the shore, or the old man, staff in hand, had set out on his journey, some onlooker cried out, "There is the fox before you and after you"; or, "Have you got the fish-hooks?" or, "Have you taken the Bait-stone?"[1] Immediately a damp was thrown on the expedition, a return home was made for that day, and the wag might be glad if

---

[1] The Bait-stone (*Clach shuill*) was a stone on which to break shell-fish, potatoes, etc., to be thrown into the water to attract fish. The broken bait was called *soll, faoire.*

the party called after did not make him rue his impertinence.

Of omens referring to other events in the life of man than the success of particular expeditions may be mentioned the following :

A golden plover (*Feadag*, Charadrius pluvialis), heard at night, portends the near approach of death or other evil. The cry of the bird is a melancholy wailing note.

A pied wagtail (*Breac an t-sìl*, motaeilla alba), seen between them and the house, was a sign of being turned out of the house that year and 'losing the site' (*call na làraich*).

The mole burrowing below a house is a sign the tenants will not stay long on that site.

If the cuckoo calls on the house-top, or on the chimney (*luidheir*), death will occur in the house that year.

In spring and early summer the omens of happiness and prosperity, or misery and adversity for the year, are particularly looked for. It is most unfortunate if the first foal or lamb seen that season have its tail toward the beholder, or the first snail (some say stonechat) be seen on the road or on a bare stone, and a most unmistakable sign of misfortune to hear the cuckoo for the first time before tasting food in the morning, 'on the first appetite' (*air a chiad lomaidh*), as it is called. In the latter case, the cuckoo is said 'to soil upon a person' (*chac a chuthag air*), and, to avoid such an indignity, people have been known, at the time of the cuckoo's visit, to put a piece of bread below their pillow to be eaten the first thing in the morning.

Cock-crowing before midnight is an indication of coming news. Old people said the bird had 'a tale' to tell; and, when they heard it, went to see if its legs were cold or not. If cold, the tale will be one of death; if hot, a good tale. The direction in which the bird's head is turned indicates the direction in which the tale is to come.

In visiting the sick, it is a sign of the termination of the illness whether it be the right or the left foot that touches the threshold first.

Women pretended to know when they laid their hand on a sick person whether he would recover.

It is a good sign if the face of the chimney-crook (*aghaidh na slabhraidh*) be toward the visitor, but an evil omen if its back be toward him.

R

CHAPTER IX.

PREMONITIONS AND DIVINATION.

PREMONITIONS.

THESE are bodily sensations by which future events may be foreknown. An itching in the nose foretells that a letter is coming, and this in olden times was a matter of no small consequence. There is an itching of the mouth that indicates a kiss, and another indicating a dram. A singing or tingling in the ears denotes death, a friend at the moment of its occurence has expired and news of his death will be heard before long; an itching of the cheek or eyes, weeping; itching of the left hand, money; of the right, that one is soon to meet a stranger with whom he will shake hands; of the elbow, that he will soon change beds or sleep with a stranger; of the brow, that some person will make you angry before long.

Hot ears denote that some person is speaking about your character. If the heat be in the right ear, he is supporting or praising you; if in the left, he is speaking ill of you (*Chluas dheas gam thoirt a nuas ; 's a chluas chli gam shior-chàineadh*).   In the latter case persons of a vindictive nature repeated the following words :

> " He who speaks of me,
>   If it be not to my advantage,
>   May he be tossed
>   On sharp grey knives,
>   May he sleep in an ant-hill,
>   And may it be no healthy sleep to him,
>   But a furious woman between him and the door,
>   And I between him and his property and sleep." [1]

The evil wish went on, that " an iron harrow might scrape his guts," and something about " a dead old woman " that my informant could not remember.

Trial (Deuchainn).—The *deuchainn* al. *diachuinn,* sometimes called *frìdh,* omen, was a 'cast' or trial made by lots or other appeal to chance to find out the issue of undertakings—whether an absent friend was on his way home or would arrive safe ; whether a sick man will recover ; whether good or bad fortune awaits one during the year ; what the future husband or wife is to be ; the road stolen goods have taken, etc.   This

---

[1] " A neach tha gam iomradh,
      Mar h-ann air mo leas e,
      Esan bhi ga iomluain
      Air sgeanabh geura glasa,
      Cadal an tom seangain da,
      'S na na cadal fallain da;
      Ach baobh eadar e 's an dorus,
      'S mis' eadar e 's a chuid 's a chadal.
      Cliath-chliat iarruinn a sgrlobadh a mhionaich,
      .   .   .   Cailleach nharbh   .   .   .   ."

cast may be either for oneself or for another, "for him and for his luck " (*air a shon 's air a shealbhaich*).   On New-Year day people are more disposed to wonder and speculate as to their fortunes during the year upon which they have entered than to reflect upon the occurrences of the past.   Hence these ' casts ' were most frequently made on that day.   Another favourite time was Hallowmas night.   Most of them might be made at any time of the year, and the difficulty was not in making them but in interpreting them.

In making a ' cast ' for one's future partner, the approved plan is for him to go at night to the top of a cairn or other eminence where no four-footed beast can go, and whatever animal is thence seen or met on the way home is an omen of the future husband or wife. It requires great shrewdness to read the omen aright.

Another way is to shut the eyes, make one's way to the end of the house, and then, and not till then, open the eyes and look around.   Whatever is then seen is an indication of fortune during the year.   It is unlucky to see a woman, particularly an old woman bent with age and hobbling past.   A man is lucky, particularly a young man riding gaily on a mettlesome horse.   A man delving or turning up the earth forebodes death ; he is making your grave, and you may as well prepare. A duck or a hen with its head below its wing is just as bad, and the more that are seen in that attitude the speedier or more certain the death.   A man who had

the second sight once made a 'trial' for a sick person
at the request of an anxious friend. He went out next
morning to the end of the house in the approved
manner. He saw six ducks with their heads under
their wings, and the sick man was dead in less than
two days.

Other seers, who made 'trials' for reward, made the
person who consulted them burn straw in front of a
sieve and then look through to see 'what they should
see.' From the objects seen the seer foretold what was
to befall.

When a trial was made to ascertain whether an
absent friend would return, if on going out to the end
of the house a man is seen coming, or a duck running
towards the seer, his safe arrival will soon be; but if
the object be moving away, the indication is unfavourable. By this trial it may also be known whether the
absent one will return empty-handed or not.

Another mode of *deuchainn*, for the same purpose, is
to take a chance stick and measure it in thumb-breadths,
beginning at its thick or lower end, and saying, when
the thumb is laid on the stick, no or yes as the opinion
of the person consulting the oracle may incline, and
repeating yes, no, alternately till the other end is
reached. According to the position of the last thumb
will the answer be affirmative or negative or doubtful.

When a young woman wants to ascertain whether a
young man in whom she feels an interest loves her,

let her look between her fingers at him and say the following charm.   If his first motion is to raise his right arm she is secure of his affections.

> " I have a trial upon you,
> I have a looking at you,
> Between the five ribs of Christ's body ;
> If it be fated or permitted you
> To make use of me,
> Lift your right hand,
> And let it not quickly down." [1]

In the detection of theft the diviner's utmost skill could only determine the direction the stolen goods had taken.

DIVINATION.

Divination (Fiosachd).—The same causes which in other countries led to oracles, astrology, necromancy, card-reading, and other forms of divination, in the Scottish Highlands led to the reading of shoulder-blades and tea-cups, palmistry, and the artless spinning of tee-totums (*dòduman*).   In a simple state of society mummeries and ceremonies, dark caves, darkened rooms, and other aids to mystification are not required to bring custom to the soothsayer.   The desire of mankind, particularly the young, to have pleasant anticipations

---

[1] " Tha deuchainn agam dhuit,
Tha sealltuinn agam ort,
Eadar còig aisnean cléibh Chriosd ;
Ma tha 'n dàn no 'n ceadachadh dhuit,
Feum dheanadh dhiom,
Tog do làmh dheas a suas,
'S na luaith i nìos."

of the future, supply all deficiencies in his artifices. One or two shrewd guesses establish a reputation, and ordinarily there is no scepticism or inquiry as to the sources of information. It is noticeable that the chief articles from which the Highland soothsayer drew his predictions, supplied him with a luxury.

Shoulder-blade Reading (Slinneineachd).—This mode of divination was practised, like the augury of the ancients, as a profession or trade. It consisted in foretelling important events in the life of the owner of a slaughtered animal from the marks on the shoulder-blade, speal or blade-bone. Professors of this difficult art deemed the right speal-bone of a black sheep or a black pig the best for this purpose. This was to be boiled thoroughly, so that the flesh might be stripped clean from it, untouched by nail or knife or tooth. The slightest scratch destroyed its value. The bone being duly prepared was divided into upper and lower parts, corresponding to the natural features of the district in which the divination was made. Certain marks indicated a crowd of people, met, according to the skill of the diviner, at a funeral, fight, sale, etc. The largest hole or indentation was the grave of the beast's owner (*uaigh an t-sealbhaduir*), and from its position his living or dying that year was prognosticated. When to the side of the bone, it presaged death ; when in its centre, much worldly prosperity (*gum biodh an saoghal aige*).

Mac-a-Chreachaire, a native of Barra, was a celebrated shoulder-blade reader in his day. According
to popular tradition he was present at the festivities
held on the occasion of the castle at *Bàgh Chiòsamul*
(the seat of the MacNeills, then chiefs of the island)
being finished. A shoulder-blade was handed to him,
and he was pressed again and again to divine from it
the fate of the castle. He was very reluctant, but at
last, on being promised that no harm would be done
him, he said the castle would become a cairn for thrushes
(*càrn dhruideachun*), and this would happen when the
Rattle stone (*Clach-a-Ghlagain*) was found, when
people worked at sea-weed in *Baile na Creige* (Rock-
town, a village far from the sea), and when deer swam
across from Uist, and were to be found on every dung-
hill in Barra. All this has happened, and the castle is
now in ruins. Others say the omens were the arrival
of a ship with blue wool, a blind man coming ashore
unaided, and that when a ground officer with big fingers
(*maor na miar mòra*) came, Barra would be measured
with an iron string. A ship laden with blue cloth was
wrecked on the island, and a blind man miraculously
escaped ; every finger of the ground officer proved to
be as big as a bottle (!), and Barra was surveyed and
sold.

When Murdoch the Short (*Murchadh Gearr*), heir to
the Lordship of Lochbuy in the Island of Mull, circ.
A.D. 1400, was sent in his childhood for protection

from the ambitious designs of his uncle, the Laird of Dowart, to Ireland, he remained there till eighteen years of age. In the meantime his sister (or half-sister) became widowed, and, dependant on the charity and hospitality of others, wandered about the Ross of Mull from house to house with her family. It was always "in the prophecy" (*san tairgneachd*) that Murdoch would return. One evening, in a house to which his sister came, a wedder sheep was killed. After the meal was over, her oldest boy asked the farmer for the shoulder-blade. He examined it intently for some time in silence, and then, exclaiming that Murdoch was on the soil of Mull (*air grunnd Mhuile*), rushed out of the house and made for Lochbuy, to find his uncle in possession of his rightful inheritance.

On the night of the massacre of Glencoe, a party of the ill-fated clansmen were poring over the shoulder-blade of an animal slain for the hospitable entertainment of the soldiers. One of them said, " There is a shedding of blood in the glen" (*tha dòrtadh fuil sa ghleann*). Another said there was only the stream at the end of the house between them and it. The whole party rushed to the door, and were among the few that escaped the butchery of that dreadful night.

It is a common story that a shoulder-blade seer once saved the lives of a company, of whom he himself was one, who had 'lifted' a cattle spoil (*creach*), by divining that there was only the stream at the end of the house between them and their pursuers.

A shoulder-blade sage in Tiree sat down to a substantial feast, to which he had been specially invited, that he might divine whether a certain friend was on his way home or not. He examined the shoulder-bone of the wedder killed on the occasion critically, unable to make up his mind. "Perhaps," he said, "he will come, perhaps he will not." A boy, who had hid himself on the top of a bed in the room, that he might see the fun, could not help exclaiming, "They cannot find you untrue." The bed broke, and the diviner and his companions, thinking the voice came from the skies, fled. When the boy recovered he got the dinner all to himself.

Palmistry (Dearnadaireachd).—Of this mode of divination, as practised in the Highlands, nothing seems now to be known beyond the name. Probably from the first the knowledge of it was confined to gipsies and such like stray characters.

Divination by Tea, or Cup-reading (Leughadh chupaichean).—When tea was a luxury, dear and difficult to get, the 'spaeing' of fortunes from tea-cups was in great repute. Even yet young women resort in numbers to fortune-tellers of the class, who for the reward of the tea spell out to them most excellent matches.

After drinking the tea, the person for whom the cup is to be read, turning the cup *deiseal*, or with the right-hand turn, is to make a small drop, left in it, wash its sides all round, and then pour it out. The fortune is then read from the arrangement of the sediments or tea-leaves left in the cup. A large quantity of black tea grounds (*smùrach du*) denotes substance and worldly gear. The person consulting the oracle is a stray leaf standing to the one side of it. If the face of the leaf is towards the grounds, that person is to come to a great fortune ; if very positively its back, then farewell even to the hope " that keeps alive despair." A small speck by itself is a letter, and other specks are envious people struggling to get to the top, followers, etc. Good diviners can even tell to their youthful and confiding friends when the letter is likely to arrive, what trade their admirer follows, the colour of his hair, etc.

CHAPTER X.

DREAMS AND PROPHECIES.

DREAMS (*Bruadar*) have everywhere been laid hold of
by superstition as indications of what is passing at a
distance or of what is to occur, and, considering the
vast numbers of dreams there are, it would be matter
of surprise, if a sufficient number did not prove so like
some remote or subsequent event, interesting to the
dreamer, as to keep the belief alive. On a low calcu-
lation, a fourth of the population dream every night,
and in the course of a year, the number of dreams in a
district must be incredible. They are generally about
things that have been, or are, causes of anxiety, or
otherwise occupied men's waking thoughts. " A dream
cometh through the multitude of business," Solomon
says, and a Gaelic proverb says with equal truth " An
old wife's dream is according to her inclination"
(*Aisling caillich mas a dùrachd*). Its character can
sometimes be traced directly to the health or position
of the body, but in other cases, it seems to depend

on the uncontrolled association of ideas. Out of the numberless phantasies that arise there must surely be many that the imagination can without violence convert into forebodings and premonitions.

To dream of raw meat indicates impending trouble ; eggs mean gossip and scandal ; herring, snow ; meal, earth ; a grey horse, the sea. To dream of women is unlucky ; and of the dead, that they are not at rest. In the Hebrides, a horse is supposed to have reference to the Clan Mac Leod. The surname of horses is Mac Leod, as the Coll bard said to the Skye bard :

> " Often rode I with my bridle,
> The race you and your wife belong to."[1]

In some districts horses meant the Macgnanean, and a white horse, a letter.

Prophecies (Fàisneachd).—In Argyllshire and Perthshire, the celebrated Thomas the Rhymer (*Tòmas Reuvair, T. Réim*) is as well known as in the Lowlands of Scotland. He is commonly called " the son of the dead woman " (*mac na mna mairbh*), but the accounts vary as to the cause of this name. One account says, he was, like Julius Caesar, taken out through his mother's side, immediately after her death ; another, that the cry of the child was heard in the mother's tomb after her burial, and on the grave being opened Thomas was found in the coffin. A third account

[1] " Is tric a mharcaich mi le 'm shréin
An dream gam bheil the fhéin 's do bhean."

says, that a woman, whose husband had been cut in four pieces, engaged a tailor, at the price of the surrender of her person, to sew the pieces together again. He did so in two hours time. Some time after the woman died and was buried. Subsequently, she met the tailor at night, and leading him to her tomb, the child was found there. Both the Highland and Lowland accounts agree that Thomas's gift of prophecy was given him by a Fairy sweetheart, that he is at present among the Fairies, and will yet come back.

The Highland tradition is, that Thomas is in Dunbuck hill (*Dùn buic*) near Dunbarton. The last person that entered that hill found him resting on his elbow, with his hand below his head. He asked, " Is it time ? " and the man fled. In the outer Hebrides he is said to be in Tom-na-heurich hill,[1] near Inverness. Hence MacCodrum, the Uist bard, says :

> " When the hosts of Tomnaheurich come,
> Who should rise first but Thomas ? "[2]

He attends every market on the look-out for suitable

---

[1] *Tom-na-h-iubhraich*, the Boat Mound, probably derives its name from its resemblance to a boat, bottom upwards. Another popular account makes it the abode of the Feinné, or Fin Mac Coul and his men. There is a huge chain suspended from the roof, and if any mortal has the courage to strike it three times with his fist, the heroes will rise again. A person struck it twice, and was so terrified by the howling of the big dogs (*donnal na con mòra*) that he fled. A voice called after him, " Wretched mischief-making man, that worse hast left than found" (*Dhuine dhon a dhòlaich, 's miosa dh'fhàg na fhuair*).

[2] " Dar thigedh sluagh Tom na h-iubhraich,
Co dh' eireadh air tùs ach Tòmas ? "

horses, as the Fairies in the north of Ireland attend to steal linen and other goods, exposed for sale. It is only horses with certain characteristics that he will take. At present he wants but two, some say only one, a yellow foal with a white forehead (*searrach blàr buidhe*). The other is to be a white horse that has got "three March, three May, and three August months of its mother's milk" (*trì Màirt, trì Màigh, agus trì Iuchara 'bhainne mhàthar*); and in Mull they say, one of the horses is to be from the meadow of Kengharair in that island. When his complement is made up he will become visible, and a great battle will be fought on the Clyde.

> "When Thomas comes with his horses,
> The day of spoils will be on the Clyde,
> Nine thousand good men will be slain,
> And a new king will be set on the throne."[1]

You may walk across the Clyde, the prophecy goes on to relate, on men's bodies, and the miller of Partick Mill (*Muilionn Phearaig*), who is to be a man with seven fingers, will grind for two hours with blood instead of water. After that, sixteen ladies will follow after one lame tailor,[2] a prophecy copied from Isaiah iv. 1. A stone in the Clyde was pointed out as one, on which a

---

[1] "Nuair thig Tòmas le chuid each,
Bi latha nan creach air Cluaidh,
Millear naoi mìle fear maith,
'S theid righ òg air a chrùn."

[2] "Bi sia baintighearnun diag as deigh an aon tàilleir chrùbaich."

bird (*bigein*) would perch and drink its full of blood, without bending its head, but the River Trustees have blasted it out of the way that the prophecy may not come true. The same prophecy, with slight variation, has been transferred to Blair Athole in Perthshire. "When the white cows come to Blair, the wheel of Blair Mill will turn round seven times with people's blood."[1] The writer was told that the Duke of Athole brought white cattle to Blair more than fifteen years ago, but nothing extraordinary happened.

Other prophecies, ascribed to the Rhymer, are, "the sheep's skull will make the plough useless," "the south sea will come upon the north sea," and "Scotland will be in white bands, and a lump of gold will be at the bottom of every glen."[2] The former has received its fulfilment in the desolation caused by the extension of sheep farms, the second in the making of the Caledonian canal, and the last in the increase of highroads and houses.

In the North Highlands, prophecies of this kind are ascribed to *Coineach Odhar* (*i.e.* Dun Kenneth), a native of Ross-shire, whose name is hardly known in Argyll-shire. He acquired his prophetic gift from the

[1] "Meair thig an cro bàn do Bhlàr, cuirear seachd cuir de chuibhle mhuilinn Bhlàir le fuil sluaigh."

[2] "Cuiridh claigionn na caorach an crann s fheum, no an crann araidh air an fharadh;

　　Thig a mhuir deas air a mhuir tuath;
　　Bi Albainn na criosun geala,
　　'S meall òir ann am bun gach glinne."

possession of a stone, which he found in a raven's nest. He first found a raven's nest with eggs in it. These he took home and boiled. He then took them back to the nest, with a view to finding out how long the bird would sit before it despaired of hatching them. He found a stone in the nest before him, and its possession was the secret of his oracular gifts. When this became known an attempt was made to take the stone from him, but he threw it out in a loch, where it still lies.

He prophesied that " the raven will drink its fill of men's blood from off the ground, on the top of the High Stone in Uig,"[1] a place in Skye. The High Stone is on a mountain's brow, and it is ominous of the fulfilment of the prophecy, that it has fallen on its side. Of the Well of Ta, at *Cill-a-chrò* in Strath, in the same island, he said :

" Thou well of Ta, and well of Ta,
　Well where battle shall be fought,
　And the bones of growing men,
　　Will strew the white beach of Laoras ;
　And Lachlan of the three Lachlans be slain
　Early, early,
　　At the well of Ta."[2]

[1] "Olaidh am fitheach a shàth, bhar an làir, air mullach clach àrd an Uig."

[2] " Tobar Tàth sin, 's tobar Tàth,
　Tobar aig an cuirear blàr,
　'S bi cnaimhean nam fear fàs
　　Air tràigh bhàn Laorais
　'S marbhar Lachunn nan trì Lachunn
　Gu moch, moch, aig tobar Tàth.
　Al. Torcuil nan trì Torcuil."

S

In Harris a cock will crow on the very day on which it is hatched, and a white calf, without a single black hair, will be born, both which remarkable events have, it is said, occurred. A certain large stone will roll up the hill, turning over three times, and the marks of it having done so, and the proof of the prophecy, are still to be seen. On the top of a high stone in Scaristavor parks,[1] the raven will drink its fill of men's blood, and the tide of battle will be turned back by Norman of the three Normans (*Tormod nan trì Tormoidean*) at the Steps of Tarbert (*Càthaichean an Tairbeart*).[2]

The Lady of Lawers.—Of similar fame for her prophetic gifts was the Lady of Lawers (*Bantighearna Lathuir*), one of the Breadalbane family, married to Campbell of Lawers. Her prophecies relate to the house and lands of Breadalbane, and are written, it is believed, in a book shaped like a barrel, and secured with twelve iron hoops or clasps in the charter room of

---

[1] This stone is about ten ft. high, and is one of the three fragments into which a larger stone, used by an old woman of former days as a hammer to knock limpets off the rocks (*òrd bhàirneach*), was broken. Of the other two, one is in *Uigh an du tuath*, and one in Tarnsa Islet. At a spot from which these three fragments can be seen, there is hidden an urn of silver and an urn of gold (*croggan òir 's cr. airgid*). It is easy to find a place whence one can see two, but when about to see the third, one of the first two disappears. Five or six yards make all the difference. A herdsman once found the spot, but when digging for the treasure he happened to see a heifer that had fallen on its back in a stream. He ran to its rescue, and never could find the place again.

[2] *Càth*, prob. a step path in a rock.

Taymouth Castle. This book is called 'The Red Book of Balloch.'

An old white horse will yet take the lineal heirs of Taymouth (or, according to another version, the last Breadalbane Campbells) across Tyndrum Cairn. When she said this there were thirty sons in the family, but soon after twenty-five of them were slain in the battle at *Sron-a-chlachair* near Killin (*Cill-Fhinn*).

If the top stone were ever put on Lawers Church no word uttered by her would ever come true, and when the red cairn on Ben Lawers fell the church would split. In the same year that the cairn, built by the sappers and miners on Ben Lawers, fell, the Disruption in the Church of Scotland took place.

> "A mill will be on every streamlet,
>   A plough in every boy's hand,
>   The two sides of Loch Tay in kail gardens ;
>   The sheep's skull will make the plough useless,
>   And the goose's feathers drive their memories from men." [1]

This was to happen in the time of " John of the three Johns, the worst John that ever was, and there will be no good till Duncan comes."

A stone called the 'Boar Stone' (*Clach an Tuirc*),

---

[1] " Bi muilionn air gach sruthan,
   Crann an làmh gach giullain,
   Da thaobh Loch Tatha na ghàracha-càil,
   Cuiridh claigionn na caorach an crann o fheum,
   'S cuiridh ite gèoidh an cuimhn' a duine."

a boulder of some two or three hundred tons in a meadow near Loch Tay, will topple over when a strange heir comes to Taymouth, and the house will be at its height of honour when the face of a certain rock is concealed by wood.

CHAPTER XI.

IMPRECATIONS, SPELLS, AND THE BLACK ART.

IMPRECATION (*Guidhe*).

THE imprecations, which form so important a part of the vocabulary of thoughtless and profane swearing, are in Gaelic corruptions of English expressions. Thus, one of the commonest—*diabhul Mac-eadhar* is a corruption of 'devil may care,' and though no language has a monopoly of oaths and curses, and English is not always to blame, it is some satisfaction that needless profanity is not entirely of native growth.

Most Gaelic imprecations are mere exclamations, condemnatory not so much of the person himself as of what he is saying or doing. Of these the following are of common use :

A bad meeting to you ! (*Droch còmh 'l ort !*).
A bad growth to you ! (*Droch fàs ort !*).
Bad understanding to you ! (*Droch ciall ort !*).
Bad accident to you ! (*Droch sgiorram ort !*).
Bad ———? to you ! (*Gum bu droch drùileach !*
           or *drùthalach dhuit !*).

Black water upon you ! (*Bùrn du ort !*).[1]
A down mouth be yours ! (*Beul sìos ort !*).[2]
A wry mouth be yours ! (*Beul seachad ort !*).
Go to your grandfather's house ! (*Tigh do sheamar dhuit !*).
The mischief be in your side ! (*An dunaigh ad chliathaich !*).
The burning of your heart to you ! (*Losgadh do chridhe ort !*).
Little increase to you ! (*Beagan piseach ort !*).
Little prosperity to you ! (*Beagan àidh ort !*).
The spell of your death-stroke be yours ! (*Sian do ghonaidh ort !*).
Death without a priest to you ! (*Bàs gun sagart ort !*).
Wind without rising be yours ! (*Gaoth gun dìreadh ort !*), *i.e.* a
    wind that will throw you on your beam-ends, and not allow
    you to right.
Your black certain death-stroke to you ! (*Sàr du do ghonaidh
    ort !*).
The place of the dead be yours ! (*Marasg, i.e.* marbh-thasg,
    ort !).
The number of Friday be yours ! "The curse of Friday be
    yours !" "The end of the seven Saturdays to you !"
May you be late ! (*Gu ma h-anamoch dhuit !*).
The direction in which you turn the back of your head, may
    you never turn your face ! (*An 'toabh bheir thusa cùl do
    chinn, gar an d' thig an t-aon latha bheir thu t' aghaidh !*),
    etc., etc.

When a curse proceeds from rage or malevolence, it
is at the same time a confession of impotence. The

---

[1] Does this refer to excommunication ? A candle was then extinguished
in water.

[2] Perhaps this means burial with the face downwards. The mother of an
illegitimate child, which died in infancy, and the paternity of which was
denied, declared if she had known that would be the case, she would have
buried the child with its face downward. This was said to be in Tiree,
but all the writer's inquiries failed to find any one who had ever heard of
such a thing being done. It is a saying "a down mouth to women if they
are not to be found everywhere" (*Beul sìos air na mnathan, mar faighear
's gach àit iad*).

party uttering it is unable at the moment to indulge his rancour in any other way. If he had the power he would bring all the woes he threatens or imprecates there and then on his enemy's devoted head. Patience is no element of wrath and rarely enters the house of malevolence, and if the man who curses his enemy had the artillery of heaven at command, he would at that moment devote his enemy to unspeakable misery. This impotence of rage is the reason why curses are so frequently ascribed to angry old women.

Those who have seen old women, of the Madge Wildfire school, cursing and banning, say their manner is well calculated to inspire terror. Some fifteen or twenty years ago, a party of tinkers quarrelled and fought, first among themselves, and then with some Tiree villagers. In the excitement a tinker wife threw off her cap and allowed her hair to fall over her shoulders in wild disorder. She then bared her knees, and falling on them to the ground, in a praying attitude, poured forth a torrent of wishes that struck awe into all who heard her. She imprecated " Drowning by sea and conflagration by land ; may you never see a son to follow your body to the graveyard, or a daughter to mourn your death. I have made my wish before this, and I will make it now, and there was not yet a day I did not see my wish fulfilled," etc., etc. " Once," says one who is now an old man, " when a boy

I roused the anger of an old woman by calling her names. She went on her knees and cursed me, and I thought I was going to die suddenly every day for a week after."

The curse causeless will not come, but a curse deserved is the foreshadowing of the ultimate issue of events. The curse of the oppressed, who have no man to deliver them, is at times but the presage of the retribution which the operation of the laws of the moral world will some day bring about. Hence we find such expressions as, "She cursed him and obtained her wish." The curse came upon the oppressor, not because of the malediction, but because what was asked for was part of the natural sequence of events in the moral government of the world. For this reason, the curse of the poor is undesirable. There is something wrong in the relation between superior and inferior when it is uttered; authority has been misused, and wisdom and patience have been awanting, selfishness has overstepped its due limit, and the just influence of the superior has degenerated into wantonness of power. In the expatriations from the Highlands, there was much in this respect to be reprobated, and it is most creditable to Highlanders, and is greatly to be ascribed to the influence of religion over them, that in the songs made at the time of the Clearances, there are no curses against the oppressor.

A common expression in the imprecations used by

old women was, "May no benefit be in your cheese, and no cheese in your milk."[1]

There is said to be a curse on an estate in Argyllshire, that a lineal descendant will never succeed to it, and on one of the principal castles in Perthshire, that no legitimate heir (*oighre dligheach*) will own it till the third generation (*gus an treasa linn*). This latter curse was caused by the haughtiness of an old woman, a former mistress of the castle, who lived entirely on marrow.

All evil wishes can be counteracted by the bystander saying, after each curse, "The fruit of your wish be on your own body" (*Toradh do ghuidhe far*, etc.). On the occasion above referred to, of the banning by the tinker wife, her frightful tirade became ludicrous from the earnestness with which this was done by one of the native women who was listening.

SPELLS (*Geasan no Geasaibh*).

A person under spells is believed to become powerless over his own volition, is alive and awake, but moves and acts as if asleep. He is like St. John's father, not able or not allowed to speak. He is compelled to go to certain places at certain hours or seasons, is sent wandering or is driven from his kindred and changed to other shapes.

In nursery and winter evening tales (*sgialachdun 'us ur-sgeulun*) the machinery of spells is largely

---

[1] "Nach faicear toradh ad ìm, no ìm ann ad bhainne."

made use of. In the former class of tales they are usually imposed on king's children by an old woman dwelling near the palace, called "Trouble-the-house" (*Eachrais ùrlair*, lit. confusion of the floor). Her house is the favourite place for the king's children to meet their lovers. She has a divining rod (*slacan druidheachd*), by a blow from which she can convert people into rocks, seals, swans, wolves, etc., and this shape they must keep till they are freed by the same rod. Nothing else can deliver them from the spell.

The story usually runs that the king is married a second time. His daughter by the first marriage is very handsome, and has a smooth comb (*cìr mhìn*) which makes her hair, when combed by it, shed gold and precious gems. The daughters by the second marriage are ugly and ill-natured. When they comb their hair there is a shower of fleas and frogs. Their mother bribes Trouble-the-house to lay spells on the daughter of the first marriage. Unless the princess enters the house the old woman is powerless to do this. One day the beautiful princess passes near the house, and is kindly and civilly asked to enter. "Come you in," says the designing hag, "often did I lick the platters and pick the bones in your father's house."[1] Misled by this artful talk, the princess

[1] "Is tric a bha mise 'g imlich na mias agus a' lomadh nan cnàmh an tigh t' athar."

enters, is struck with the magic rod, and converted into a swan.

It is a popular saying that seals and swans are "king's children under enchantments" (*clann sigh fo gheasaibh*). On lonely mountain meres, where the . presence of man is seldom seen, swans have been observed putting off their coverings (*cochull*) and assuming their proper shape of beautiful princesses in their endeavours to free themselves from the spells. This, however, is impossible till the magician, who imposed them, takes them away, and the princesses are obliged to resume their coverings again.

The expressive countenance and great intelligence of the seal, the readiness with which it can be domesticated, and the attachment which, as a pet, it shows to man, have not unnaturally led to stories of its being a form assumed by, or assigned to, some higher intelligence from choice or by compulsion. In Caithness, seals are deemed to be the fallen angels, and the Celtic belief that they are "king's children under spells" is paralleled in the Shetland tales of the Norway Finns. These are persons, a native of these northern islands writes (in a private letter), who come across from Norway to Shetland in the shape of large seals. A Shetlander on his way to the fishing, early in the morning, came across a large seal lying asleep on a rock. Creeping quietly up he managed to stab it with his knife. The animal was only slightly wounded and floundered into the water, taking the knife along with it. Sometime afterwards the fisherman went, with others, to Norway to buy wood. In the first house he entered he saw his own big knife stuck up under a beam. He gave himself up for lost, but the Norwegian took down the knife and gave it back to him, telling him never again to disturb a poor sea-animal taking its rest.

There is a sept in North Uist known as "the MacCodrums of the seals" (*Clann 'ic Codrum nan ròm*), from being said to be descendants of these enchanted seals. The progenitor of the family, being down about the shore, saw the seals putting off their coverings and washing themselves. He fled home with one of the skins and hid it above the lintel of the door, '*arabocan*' as it is called in that part of the country. The owner of the covering followed him. He clad her with human garments, married her, and had a family by her. She managed ultimately to regain possession of her lost covering and disappeared.

West of Uist there is a rock called *Connsmun*, to which the neighbouring islanders are in the habit of going yearly to kill seals. On one of these expeditions a young man, named Egan, son of Egan, killed a large seal in the usual manner by a knock on the head, and put a withe through its paw to secure it, while he himself went to attend to other matters. When he came back, however, the seal was gone. Sometime after he was driven away in a storm, and landed in a district he did not recognize. He made his way to one of the houses, and was very hospitably entertained. His host, who had been surveying him intently, when the meal was over asked his name. He told, and his host said, " Egan, son of Egan, though I have given you meat, and cheese, and eggs, upon your two hands be it, Egan, son of Egan, you put the withe through my fist." [1]

THE BLACK ART.

Nothing was known in the Highlands of the dark science beyond what is conveyed in the name given to it, ' Satan's black school ' (*Sgoil du Shatain*), and a few anecdotes of its more illustrious students. All accounts agree that Michael Scott was an advanced scholar. He, by his skill in it, made a brazen man, whom he compelled to do all his work for him. By means of him he brought the Flanders Moss (*Mhòinteach Fhlans-rach*), in the Carse of Stirling, across from the continent on bearers (*lunnun*). The moss is twenty-three miles long, and lies north of Stirling, where, unfortunately, the bearers broke. The Mull doctor (*an t-ollamh*

---

[1] " Ged thug mi biadh 'us càise 's uibhean duit, air do dhà làimh, Iogain 'ic Iogain, chuir thu 'n gad roi mo dhòrn."

Muileach)[1] and the Islay doctor (*an t-ollamh Ileach*) also attended the school, and adventures are assigned to them as to the other scholars.

Cameron of Locheil (*Mac Dhò'uill dui*, the son of Black Donald, is the Highland patronymic of the chiefs of this house), Macdonald of Keppoch (*Mac-ic-Rao'uill*), and Mackenzie of Brahan were at the school together, and when their education was finished the devil was to get as his fee whoever of them was hindmost. The three young men made a plan to chase each other round and round in a circle so that none of them should be hindmost. At last the devil was for clutching some one, but the young man pointed to his shadow which was behind. The devil in his hurry caught at it, and the young man never had a shadow from that day.

Locheil hired a servant maid to attend to a set of valuable china dishes of which he was the possessor. Her post was onerous, and she had another waiting-maid under her. Her life was to be the forfeit of any of the dishes being broken. One night when ascending the stairs with the dishes on a tray, the under-servant leading the way with a light, she noticed that the sugar bowl was in two and began to weep. A gentleman, whom she had not till then observed, was walking backwards and forwards on the stair-head. He asked her

---

[1] The Mull doctor passed a house from which loud sounds of talking proceeded. He remarked that in that house were either twenty men or three women.

why she wept, and she told. He asked what she would give to have the bowl made whole as it was before? Would she give herself? She thoughtlessly said she would give anything. The bargain was struck, and on drying her tears and looking up the maid found the bowl whole. She told all this to her master, and when the devil came that same night to claim her, Locheil gave his former teacher a hospitable reception. When it waxed late, the devil, afraid of the cock-crowing, was preparing to go away. Cameron coaxed him to remain till the inch still remaining of the candle on the table should burn down. Whenever he gave his consent Cameron blew out the candle and gave it to the servant, telling her her life depended on its safe custody. In this manner the devil was cheated by his own scholar.

A drover bought a flock of goats from Macdonald of Keppoch, who himself accompanied the drove to Locheil-side. Here, in crossing a ford, the goats were taken away by the stream, and went past the drover as red stalks of fern (*nan cuiseagun ruadha rainich*), all except one dun hornless goat (*gobhar mhaol odhar*). The drover returned in search of Macdonald and found him lying on the heather, seemingly asleep. He pulled his hand to awaken him, but the hand came away with him. In the end, however, the hand was put right, and the goats were restored to the astonished drover.

Another time Keppoch and his dairy-maid had a trial of skill in sorcery. While she was milking a cow in the cattle-fold, Macdonald, who was looking on, by his charms prevented the cow from yielding her milk. The dairy-maid removed to the other side of the cow and defeated his conjurations. He then removed the hoop on the milk-pail. This also she counteracted.

Macdonald is said to have put a stop in his own country to the women winding black thread at night, but how or why does not appear.

The mighty magician, Michael Scott, had a narrow escape from becoming the prey of the arch-fiend. On his death-bed he told his friends to place his body on a hillock. Three ravens and three doves would be seen flying towards it ; if the ravens were first the body was to be burned, but if the doves were first it was to receive Christian burial. The ravens were foremost, but in their hurry flew beyond their mark. So the devil, who had long been preparing a bed for Michael, was disappointed.

CHAPTER XII.

THE DEVIL.

SUPERSTITION, in assigning to the devil a bodily shape and presence, endeavoured to make him horrible, and instead made him ridiculous. For this no doubt the monkish ceremonies of the middle ages are, as is commonly alleged, much to blame. The fiend was introduced into shows and dramatic representations with horns, tail, and the hoof of one of the lower animals ; the representation was seized upon by the popular fancy, and exaggerated till it became a carica-ture. The human mind takes pleasure in mixing the ludicrous with the terrible, and in seeing that of which it is afraid made contemptible. There is, as is well known, but one step from the sublime to the ridiculous, and, in being reduced to a bug-bear, the impersonation of evil has only come under the operation of a common law. One bad effect to be traced to the travesty is, that men's attention is diverted from the power of evil as the spirit that now worketh strife, lying,

T

dishonesty, and the countless forms of vice, and the foul fiend is become a sort of goblin, to frighten children and lonely travellers.

In Gaelic the exaggeration is not carried to the same lengths as in English. There is nothing said about the fiend's having horns or tail. He has made his appearance in shape of a he-goat, but his horns have not attracted so much attention, or inspired such terror, as his voice, which bears a horrible resemblance to the bleating of a goat. A native of the Island of Coll is said to have got a good view of him in a hollow, and was positive that he was crop-eared (*corc-chluasach*).[1] He has often a chain clanking after him. In Celtic, as in German superstition, he has usually a *horse's hoof*, but also sometimes a *pig's foot*. This latter peculiarity, which evidently had its origin in the incident of the Gadarean swine, and in the pig being unclean under the ceremonial law, explains the cloven hoof always ascribed to him in English popular tales. In Scripture, the goat, as pointed out by Sir Thomas More, formed the sin offering, and is an emblem of bad men. The reason why a *horse's hoof* has been assigned to him is not so apparent. In the Book of Job, Satan is described as " going to and fro in the earth"; and the red horses, speckled and white, which the prophet Zechariah (i. 8) saw among the

---

[1] This was *Nial na Buaile*, who lived in a house alone several miles from any other house. The hollow is called *Sloc-an-tàilisg*.

myrtle trees, were explained to him to be those whom
" the Lord hath sent to walk to and fro through the
earth." The similarity of description may be casual,
but it is on grounds, equally incidental and slight, that
many of the inferences of superstition are based.

In addition to his Scripture names, the arch-fiend is
known in Gaelic by the following titles :

The worthless one (*am fear naçh fhiach*).
The one whom I will not mention (*am fear nach abair mi*).
Yon one (*am fear ud*).
The one big one (*an aon fhear mòr*).
The one from the abyss (*an t-aibhisteir*) from *aibheis*, an abyss, a
    depth.
The mean mischievous one (*an Rosad*).
The big sorrow (*an dòlas mòr*).
The son of cursing (*Mac-mollachd*).
The big grizzled one (*an Riabhach mòr*).
The bad one (*an donas*).
The bad spirit (*ain-spiorad, droch-spiorad*).
Black Donald (*Dòmhnull Du*).

In the North Highlands he is also known as *Bidein,
Dithean, Bradaidh.* It is said that *Connan* was a name
given to him, and that *aisling connain*, a libidinous
dream, means literally ' a devil's dream.' The name
must have been very local. There is a fable about
Connan and his twelve sons pulling a plant in the peat
moss, in which the name denoted the wren, and there
was a St. Connan, whose memory is preserved in
Cill-Chonnain, a burying-ground in Rannoch, and
Feill-Connain, the autumn market at Dalmally in
Glenorchy.

The occasions on which the devil has appeared in a bodily shape, have been at meetings of witches; at card-playing, which is the reading of his books; when he comes to claim his prey; and when summoned by masons or magicians. He is apt to appear to persons ready to abandon their integrity, and to haunt premises which are soon to be the scene of signal calamities. He sometimes comes in unaccountable shapes and in lonely places for no conceivable purpose but to frighten people.

The following tales will illustrate the character of his appearances and the notions popularly entertained regarding him.

CARD-PLAYING.

A party of young people were playing cards; a stranger joined them and took a hand. A card fell below the table, and the youth, who stooped to lift it, observed the stranger to have a horse's hoof. The devil, on being thus detected, went up the chimney in smoke.

This story is universal over the Highlands. Cards are notoriously known as the devil's books. When boys play them, the fiend has been known to come down the chimney feet foremost, the horse's or pig's foot appearing first. When going away, he disappears in smoke, and neighs horribly in the chimney.

RED BOOK OF APPIN.

This celebrated book contained charms for the cure of cattle, and was so powerful that its owner had to

place an iron hoop about his head every time he opened
it. All accounts agree that it was got from the devil,
but they differ as to how this was done. Very likely
the book was a treatise on the treatment and diseases
of cattle, and the origin of the stories of its magic virtue
lay in the fact that the Stewarts, who owned it, had a
magnificent fold of Highland cattle.

The first, who got the book, rode an entire horse (an
animal that no evil power can touch) to a meeting of
witches. The devil wrote in a red book the names of
the assembled company. The man, instead of letting
the devil write his name, asked to be allowed to do so
himself. On getting the book for that purpose he
made off with it.

By another account (and the person from whom it
was heard was positive as to its being the only correct
account) it was got by a young lad under the following
circumstances. The youth was apprenticed to the
miller at Bearachan on Lochawe-side. His master was
unkind, and made him work more than he was fit for.
One night he was up late finishing a piece of work.
About midnight a gentleman, whom he did not recognize, entered the mill and accosted him kindly. Turning the conversation that ensued on the harsh conduct
of the miller, the stranger promised to better the un-
happy prentice's condition if they met at the Crooked
Pool (*Cama-linn*) in the Middle Mountain (*Monadh
Meadhonach*) on a certain night. An assignation to

that effect was made, but after the strange gentleman went away the lad got frightened, and next day told about the visitor he had. A conclave of sixteen ministers was called, and the matter was deliberated upon. As the youth had given his promise it was deemed necessary he should keep it, but he was advised to take a wand with him and at the place appointed trace a circle with it round himself, out of which he was not to move whatever temptation or terrors the stranger might bring to bear upon him. A committee of the clergy went to watch on a neighbouring eminence the result of the interview. The strange gentleman came at the appointed hour, and before giving the money promised, civilly asked the lad to write his name in a book. For this purpose the book was not handed but thrown to the youth, and he, on getting it into his possession, refused to give it up again. The strange gentleman now showed himself in his true colours. Finding remonstrances and coaxing of no avail to get the book or the lad out of the circle he got wild, and tried the effects of terror. First he became a grizzled greyhound (*mial-chu riabhach*), and came wildly dashing against the circle ; then a roaring bull ; then a flock of crows (*sgaoth ròcais*) sweeping above the youth, so near that the wind caused by their wings would have carried him out of the circle if he had not clung to the heather. When cock-crowing time came the devil abandoned his attempts and disappeared. The book became the Red Book of Appin, and was last in possession of the Stewarts of Invernahyle (*Inbher-na h-aoile*).

COMING FOR THE DYING.

A native of the neighbourhood of Oban, on his way home from Loch Awe-side, after crossing the hills and coming in above Kilmore, was joined by three strangers. He spoke to them, but received no answer. At a small public-house on the roadside he asked them in for a refreshment. They then told him they had business to attend to, and that after entering the house he was not on any account to come out or attempt to go home that night. On parting, the strangers turned off the high road by a private road leading to a neighbouring gentleman's house. The night proved unusually stormy, and the man did not move from the inn till morning. He then heard that the gentleman, towards whose house the three mysterious strangers had gone, had died the previous evening just about the time they would have arrived there. No person in the house or neighbourhood saw anything of them.

It has been already mentioned that the devil, or his emissaries, in the shape of three ravens, waited to catch the soul of Michael Scott as soon as it left the body. A freebooter of former days, who made a house underground for his wife in Loch Con, in Lower Rannoch (*Bun Raineach*), that he and his men might swear he had no wife above ground, and then married another, was at his death carried away by twelve ravens.

MAKING THE DEVIL YOUR SLAVE.

Those who had the courage to perform the awful *taghairm*,[1] called up the devil to grant any worldly wish they might prefer ; the disciples of the black art made him their obedient servant.　Michael Scott, whose reputation as a magician is as great in the Highlands as in the Lowlands, made him his slave.　He could call him up at any time.

In Michael's time the people of Scotland were much confused as to the day on which Shrovetide was to be kept.　One year it was early and another it was late, and they had to send every year to Rome to ascertain the time (*dh' fhaotainn fios na h-Inid*).　It was determined to send Michael Scott to get "word without a second telling" (*fios gun ath-fhios*).　Michael called up the devil, converted him into a black ambling horse (*fàlaire dhu*), and rode away on the journey.　The devil was reluctant to go on such an expedition, and was tired by the long distance.　He asked Michael what the women in Scotland said when they put their children to sleep or 'raked' the fire (*smàladh an teine*) for the night.　He wanted the other to mention the name of the Deity, when the charm that made himself an unwilling horse would be broken.　Michael told him

[1] See page 304.

to ride on—"Ride you before you, you worthless wretch (*marcaich thusa, bhiasd, romhad*), and never mind what the women said." They went at such a height that there was snow on Michael's hat when he disturbed the Pope in the early morning. In the hurry the Pope came in with a lady's slipper on his left foot. "You rode high last night, Michael," said the Pope. Michael's reply called attention to the Pope's left foot. "Conceal my secret and I will conceal yours,"[1] said the Pope, and to avoid the chance of being again caught in a similar intrigue he gave Michael "the knowledge of Shrovetide," viz., that it is always "the first Tuesday of the spring light," *i.e.*, of the new moon in spring.

In Skye this adventure is ascribed to 'Parson Sir Andro of Ruig' in that island. He is said to have started on his terrible journey from the top of the Storr Rock, a scene the wildness of which is singularly appropriate to the legend. The Storr is a hill upwards of 2000 feet high, and on its eastern side, from which the parson must have set out for Rome, is precipitous, as if the hill were half eaten away, and the weird appearance of the scene is much increased by the isolated and lofty pillars from which the hill derives its name,[2] standing in front. Not unfrequently banks of

---

[1] 'S àrd mharcaich thu 'n raoir a Mhìcheil. Seall air do chois chlì. Ceil orm 's ceilidh mi ort.

[2] *Fiacaill storàch* means a buck tooth.

mist come rolling up against the face of the cliffs, concealing the lower grounds, and giving a person standing at the top of the precipices one of the most magnificent views it is possible to conceive. He seems to look down into bottomless space, and where the mist in its motions becomes thin and the ground appears dark through it, there is the appearance of a profounder depth, a more awful abyss. The scene gives a wildly poetical character to the legend of the redoubtable parson and his unearthly steed.

COMING MISFORTUNE.

A part of the parish of the Ross of Mull is known ecclesiastically as Kilviceuen (*Cill-mhic-Eòghain*, the burying-place of the son of Hugh). Its ancient church was of unhewn stone, and its last minister, previous to its being united to Kilfinichen, was named Kennedy, a native of Cantyre, an Episcopalian, in the reign of Charles II. Tradition records that he came to his death in the following manner.

His parishioners, about the end of spring, were taking a new millstone from *Port Bheathain* on Squrraside to the mill, by means of a pole run through its eye. The parson threw off his cassock, and assisted them. The cassock was left where it was thrown off. In the evening his wife sent a servant-maid for it. The maid found, lying on the cassock, a large black dog, which would not allow her to touch the garment. She came home without it, and refused to return. The wife herself and another servant then went, were bitten by the dog, and ultimately twelve persons, including the minister, died of hydrophobia.

So shocking an event could not take place without superstition busying itself about it. On Beltane night shortly before the event, the minister's servant-man had gone early to bed, while it was yet day. There was "a large blazing fire of green oak" (*beòlach mhòr dhearg de glas darach*) on the floor of the room, and he closed and locked the door before going to bed. Through the night he heard a noise as of some one feeling for the lock and trying to open the door. He remained quiet, thinking the noise was made by young men, who came courting and had mistaken the door. Soon, however, the door opened, and a person whom he did not recognize entered. The stranger, without saying a word, went and stood at the fire. When he turned his back the servant observed that his feet were horse's feet (*spògun eich*). In a short time the apparition went away, locking the door after it. The man rose and went to an old man in great estimation for his piety, who lived alone at *Creag nan Con* (the Dog Rock). The old man's hut was a poor one, its door being made of wicker work and of the form called *sgiathalan*. No remonstrances could induce him to stay another night in the minister's house, and it was arranged that he should sleep at the hut, and in the day time go to his work at the manse. He told the sight he had seen, and the good man inferred from the time of night at which the devil had been seen that evil was near the house. It was shortly after this that the dog went mad, and the frightened servant was the only one of the minister's household that escaped.

THE GAÏCK CATASTROPHE (*Mort Ghàthaig*).

On the last night of last century[1] a disastrous casualty, in which six persons lost their lives, occurred in the deer forest of Gaïck in Badenoch. The wild tract of mountain land, to which the name is given, was not formally made into a deer forest till 1814, but its loneliness made it a favourite haunt of wild game at all times. There was not a house in the large extent of near thirty square miles beyond a hut for the shelter of hunters. Captain MacPherson of Ballychroän, an officer in the army, with some friends and gillies were passing the night of the 31st December, 1800, in this hut, when an avalanche, or whirlwind, or some unusual and destructive agency came upon them, and swept before it the building and all its inmates. When people came to look for the missing hunters they found the hut levelled to the ground, and its fragments scattered far and wide. The men's bodies were

---

[1] " A nollaig mu dheire de'n cheud
Cha chuir mi e'n aireamh na mias."

scattered over distances of half a mile from the hut ; the barrels of their guns were twisted, and over all there was a deep covering of snow, with here and three a man's hand protruding through it. The whole Highlands rang with the catastrophe, and it is still to be heard of in the Hebrides as well as in the district in which it occurred. Popular superstition constructed upon it a wild tale of diabolical agency.

Captain MacPherson was popularly known as "The Black Officer of Ballychroän" (*Ofhichier du Baile-chrodhain*). He is accused of being a "dark savage" man (*dorcha doirbh*), who had forsaken his wife and children, and had rooms below his house, whence the cries of people being tortured were heard by those who passed the neighbourhood at night. About the end of 1800 he was out among the Gaïck hills with a party of hunters, and passed the night in the hut mentioned. Late at night strange noises were heard about the house, and the roof was like to be knocked in about the ears of the inmates. First came an unearthly slashing sound, and then a noise as if the roof were being violently struck with a fishing rod. The dogs cowered in terror about the men's feet. The captain rose and went out, and one of his attendants overheard him speaking to something, or some one, that answered with the voice of a he-goat. This being reproached him with the fewness of the men he had brought with him, and the Black

Officer promised to come next time with a greater number.

Of the party who went on the next hunting expedition not one returned alive. The servant who said he had heard his master speaking to the devil refused positively to be one of the party, neither threats nor promises moved him, and others followed his example. Only one of the previous party, a Macfarlane from Rannoch, a good and pious man it is said, went. It was observed that this day the officer left his watch and keys at home, a thing he had never been known to do before. Macfarlane's body was not found on the same day with the rest. It was carried further from the hut than the searchers thought of looking, and a person who had found before the body of one lost among the hills, was got to look for his remains. There is a saying that if a person finds a body once he is more apt to find another. When the melancholy procession with the dead bodies was on the way from the forest, even the elements were not at peace, but indicated the agency that had been at work. The day became exceedingly boisterous with wind and rain, so much so, when the Black Officer's body was foremost, that the party was unable to move on, and the order had to be changed.

Two songs at least were composed on the occasion. One, strong in its praises of Captain MacPherson, will be found in *Duanaire*, p. 13 ; the other, among other things, says of him—

> " The Black Officer of Ballychroän it was,
> He turned his back on wife and children ;
> Had he fallen in the wars in France,
> The loss was not so lamentable." [1]

THE BUNDLE OF FERN.

A shepherd in Benderloch saw a large bundle of ferns rolling down the hillside, and, in addition to the downward motion given by the incline, it seemed to have a motion of its own. It disappeared down a waterfall. Of course this was Black Donald ; what else could it be?

THE PIG IN THE INDIGO POT.

A former tenant of the farm of Holm, in Skye, and his wife had gone to bed, leaving a large pot full of indigo dye on the floor. The pig came in and fell into the pot. The wife got up to see what the noise was, and on looking into the pot saw the green snout of a pig jerking out of the troubled water. She roared out that the devil was in the pot. Her husband shouted in return to put on the lid, and jumping in great excitement out of bed, he threw

---

[1] " Ofhichier du Bhaile-chrodhain a bh'ann,
  Thréig e a bhean 's a chlann
  Nan do thuit e'n cath na Fraing,
  Cha bhiodh an call co farranach."

his weight on the lid to keep it down till the devil was drowned. His wife was remarkable for always commending what her husband did, and kept repeating, " Many a person you will confer a favour on this night, Murdoch " (*Is iomadh duine d'an dean thusa feum a nochd, a Mhurchiadh*). At last the noise in the pot subsided, and Murdoch nearly called up the party he had sought to drown on finding it was his own pig he had been so zealously destroying.

AMONG THE TAILORS.

It is a saying that the only trade that the devil has been unable to learn is that of tailoring. The reason is that when he went to try, every tailor left the room, and having no one to instruct him, he omitted to put a knot on the thread he began to sew with. In consequence the thread always came away with him, and he gave up the trade in despair. It is presumed that he wanted to learn the trade to make clothes for himself, as no one would undertake the making of them.

TAGHAIRM, OR " GIVING HIS SUPPER TO THE DEVIL."

The awful ceremony to which this name was given was also known among old men as " giving his supper to the devil." It consisted in roasting cats alive on spits till the arch-fiend himself appeared in bodily shape.

He was compelled then to grant whatever wish the persons who had the courage to perform the ceremony preferred, or, if that was the object of the magic rite, to explain and answer whatever question was put to him.

Tradition in the West Highlands makes mention of three instances of its performance, and it is a sort of tribute to the fearless character of the actors that such a rite should be ascribed to them. It was performed by Allan the Cattle-lifter (*Ailein nan creach*)[1] at *Dail-a-chait* (the Cats' Field), as it has since been called, in Lochaber, and by Dun Lachlan (*Lachunn odhar*) in the big barn at Pennygown (*sabhal mòr Peighinn-a-ghobhann*), in Mull. The details of these two ceremonies are so exactly the same that there is reason to think they must both be versions of an older legend. Nothing appears to create a suspicion that the one account was borrowed from the other. The third instance of its performance was by some of the " children of Quithen " (*Clann 'ic Cuithen*), a small sept in Skye, now absorbed, as so many minor septs have been, into the great family of the Macdonalds. The scene was a natural cavity called the " Make-believe Cave " (*an Eaglais Bhréige*), on East Side, Skye. There is the appearance of an altar beside this church, and the locality accords well with the alleged rite. The following is the Mull legend.

---

[1] Allan was a native of Lochaber, the most notorious district in the High-lands for cattle-lifters, and derived his name from having lifted a creach "for every year of his life, and one for every quarter he was in his mother's womb." He died at the age of 34.

Lachlan Oär and a companion, Allan, the son of Hector (*Ailein Mac Eachuinn*)—some say he had two companions—shut themselves up in the barn at Penny-gown, on the Sound of Mull, and putting cats on spits roasted them alive at a blazing fire. By-and-bye other cats came in and joined in the horrible howling of those being roasted, till at last the beams (*sparrun an tighe*) were crowded with cats, and a concert of caterwauling filled the house. The infernal noise almost daunted Lachlan Oär, especially when the biggest of the cats said, " When my brother the Ear of Melting comes—" Allan the son of Hector did not allow the sentence to be finished. " Away cat," he cried, and then added to his companion, in an expression which has become proverbial in the Highlands when telling a person to attend to the work he has in hand, and never mind what discouragements or temptations may come in his way, " Whatever you see or hear, keep the cat turning" (*De sam bith a chì no chluinneas tu, cum an cat mun cuairt*). Dun Lachlan, recovering courage, said, " I will wait for him yet, and his son too." At last the Ear of Melting came among the other cats on the beams, and said, while all the other cats kept silence, " Dun Lachlan, son of Donald, son of Neil, that is bad treatment of a cat " (*Lachuinn uidhir 'ic Dhò'uill ic Néill, 's olc an càramh cait sin*). Allan to this called out as before, " Whatever you see or hear, keep the cat turning," and the fearful rite was proceeded with. At last the Ear

of Melting sprang to the floor and said, " Whomsoever
the Ear of Melting makes water upon will not see the
face of the Trinity" (*Ge b'e co air a mùin Cluas a
Leoghaidh cha 'n fhaic e gnùis na Trianaid*). " The
cross of the sword in your head, wretch ; your water is
sweat" (*Crois a chlaidheamh a'd cheann, a bhiasd; 's
tu mùn fallais*), answered Dun Lachlan, and he struck
the cat on the head with the hilt of his two-handed
sword. Immediately the devil, under the potent spell,
assumed his proper shape, and asked his wild sum-
moners what they wanted with him ? One asked
Conach 'us clann (" Prosperity and children "), and Dun
Lachlan asked " Property and prosperity, and a long
life to enjoy it " (*Cuid 'us conach, 'us saoghal fada na
cheann*). The devil rushed out through the door crying,
" Prosperity ! Prosperity ! Prosperity ! " (*Conach !
Conach ! Conach !*)

The two men obtained their desires, but were
obliged (some say) to repeat the *taghairm* every year
to keep the devil to the mark.

When Dun Lachlan was on his deathbed his nephew
came to see him, and in the hope of frightening the old
fellow into repentance, went through a stream near the
house and came in with his shoes full of water. " My
sister's son," said Lachlan, " why is there water in your
shoe ? " (*a mhic mo pheathar, c' arson tha bogan a'a
bhróig ?*) The nephew then told that the *two* companions who had been along with Lachlan in the

performance of the *taghairm*, and who were both by this time long dead, had met him near the house, and to escape from them he had several times to cross the running stream ; that they told him their position was now in the bad place, and that they were waiting for his uncle, who, if he did not repent, would have to go along with them. The old man, on hearing this melancholy message, said, " If I and my two companions were there, and we had three short swords that would neither bend nor break, there is not a devil in the place but we would make a prisoner of."[1]   After this the nephew gave up all hopes of leading him to repentance.

A native of the island of Coll and his wife came to see him.   Lachlan asked them what brought them ? " To ask," said the Coll man, " a yoke of horses you yourself got from the devil " (*dh ' iarraidh seirreach each fhuair thu fhein o'n douus*).   Lachlan refused this and sent the man away, but he sent a person to overhear what remarks the man and his wife might make after leaving.   The wife said, " What a wild eye the man had ? "   (*Nach b' fhiadhaich an t-sùil bh'aig an duin 'ud?*) Her husband replied, " Do you suppose it would be an eye of softness and not a soldier's eye, as should be ? " (*Saoil am bi suil an t-slauchdain, ach sùil an t-saighdeir mar bu chòir?*)   On this being reported to Lachlan, he called the Coll man back and gave him what he wanted.

---

[1] Nam bithinn fhìn 's mo dhà chompanach ann, 's trì groilleinean againn nach lùbadh's nach briseadh, cha bhiodh deamhan a stigh nach cuireamaidan làimh.

Martin, in his *Description of the Western Islands*, p. 110, quoted by Scott (*Lady of the Lake*, note 2 T), after describing a mode of *Taghairm* by taking a man by the feet and arms to a boundary stream and bumping him against the bank till little creatures came from the sea to answer the question of which the solution was sought, says :—" I had an account from the most intelligent and judicious men in the Isle of Skie, that about sixty-two years ago the oracle was thus consulted only once, and that was in the parish of Kilmartin, on the east side, by a wicked and mischievous set of people, who are now extinguished, both root and branch." The *Taghairm* here referred to seems to be that above-mentioned as having been performed by the M'Quithens in the Make-believe or False Cave on East Side, Skye. The race have not borne a good reputation, if any value is to be attached to a rhyme concerning them and other minor septs in Skye :—

> " The M'Cuthan, expert in lies,
> The M'Quithens, expert in base flattery,
> The M'Vannins, expert as thieves,
> Though no bigger than a dagger handle." [1]

---

[1] There is a venom and an emphasis in the original impossible to convey in a translation.

> " Clann 'ic Cuthain chuir nam briag,
> Clann 'ic Cuithein chur an t-sodail,
> Clann 'ic Mhannain chuir na braide
> Ged nach b'fhaid aid na cas biodaig."

Another method of *Taghairm*, described by Martin, was by wrapping a person in a cow-hide, all but his head, and leaving him all night in a remote and lonely spot. Before morning his "invisible friends" gave him a proper answer to the question in hand, or, as Scott explains it, "whatever was impressed upon him by his exalted imagination, passed for the inspiration of the disembodied spirits who haunt the desolate recesses." This method of divination cannot have been common ; at least the writer has been able to find no trace of it.

As a third mode of *Taghairm*, Martin briefly describes that above detailed, viz., the roasting of a live cat on a spit till at last a very large cat, attended by a number of lesser cats, comes and answers the question put to him.

Both Martin and Scott fall into the error of supposing that the object of the *Taghairm* was solely divination, to ascertain the future, the issue of battles, the fate of families, etc. The mode by roasting live cats was too fearful a ceremony to be resorted to except for adequate reasons, and the obtaining of worldly prosperity, which was the object of the Mull *Taghairm*, is a more likely reason than curiosity or anxiety as to a future event.

The naming of the word *Taghairm* is not at first sight obvious. There is no doubt about the last syllable being *gairm*, a call. *Ta* is probably the same root that appears in so many words, as *tannasg*, *taibhse*, etc., denoting spectres, spirits, wraiths, etc., and *Taghairm* means nothing else than the 'spirit-call,' in fact, " the calling of spirits from the vasty deep."

GLAS GHAIRM—POWER OF OPENING LOCKS.

This was a rhyme or incantation by which the person possessing the knowledge of it could shut the mouths of dogs and open locks. It was reckoned a very useful gift for young men who went a-wooing. Archibald, son of Murdoch, or, as he was also popularly known, Archibald the Light-headed (*Gileasbuig Mhurchaidh*, *G. Eutrom*), who was about twenty years ago a well-known character in Skye and its neighbourhood, knew the charm, but when he repeated it he spoke so fast that no one was able to learn it from him, and as to his teaching of it to any one, that was out of the question. Poor Archibald was mad, and when roused was furiously so. He went about the country attending markets and wherever there was a gathering of people, and found everywhere open quarters throughout that hospitable island. Indeed, it was not wise to contradict him. He had a keen and ready wit, as numerous sayings ascribed to him testify, and composed several songs of considerable merit. The fear which dogs had of him, and which made them crouch into corners on seeing him, was commonly ascribed to his having the *Glas Ghairm*, but no doubt was owing to the latent madness which his eyes betrayed, and of which dogs have an instinctive and quicker perception than men. On their offering the slightest sign of hostility, Archibald would knock out their brains without as much as looking at their masters.

The *Glas Ghairm* was supposed to be in some way connected with the safety of Israel on the night before the Exodus, " against any of the children of Israel shall not a dog move his tongue, against man or beast " (Ex. xi. 7).

INDEX.

(The figures refer to the page.)

Lightning Source UK Ltd.
Milton Keynes UK
UKHW011140130721
387098UK00002B/662